No Time for Dreams

ASIAN VOICES
A Subseries of Asian/Pacific/Perspectives
Series Editor: Mark Selden

For more books in this series, go to www.rowman.com/series

No Time for Dreams

Living in Burma under Military Rule

Carolyn Wakeman and San San Tin

Introduction by Emma Larkin

ROWMAN & LITTLEFIELD PUBLISHERS, INC.
Lanham • Boulder • New York • Toronto • Plymouth, UK

ROWMAN & LITTLEFIELD PUBLISHERS, INC.

Published in the United States of America
by Rowman & Littlefield Publishers, Inc.
A wholly owned subsidary of The Rowman & Littlefield Publishing Group, Inc.
4501 Forbes Boulevard, Suite 200, Lanham, Maryland 20706
www.rowmanlittlefield.com

Estover Road
Plymouth PL6 7PY
United Kingdom

British Library Cataloguing in Publication Information Available

Library of Congress Cataloging-in-Publication Data

Wakeman, Carolyn.
 No time for dreams : living in Burma under military rule / Carolyn Wakeman and
San San Tin ; introduction by Emma Larkin.
  p. cm. — (Asian voices)
 Includes bibliographical references and index.
 ISBN-13: 978-0-7425-5703-1 (cloth : alk. paper)
 ISBN-10: 0-7425-5703-0 (cloth : alk. paper)
 ISBN-13: 978-0-7425-5719-2 (electronic)
 ISBN-10: 0-7425-5719-7 (electronic)
 1. Tin, San San, 1950– 2. Burma—Politics and government—1948– 3. Women
journalists—Burma—Biography. I. Tin, San San, 1950– II. Title.
 DS530.53.T56W34 2009
 959.105'3092—dc22
 [B]
                                                                    2008040850

Printed in the United States of America

⊚™ The paper used in this publication meets the minimum requirements of
American National Standard for Information Sciences—Permanence of Paper
for Printed Library Materials, ANSI/NISO Z39.48-1992.

To those who live always in fear, always in silence,
surviving in darkness, waiting for change

Contents

~

Preface

I never intended to write a book about Burma. But as I guided the studies of poet and journalist San San Tin at U.C. Berkeley nearly a decade ago, I also listened to her stories, startled by the vividness of her memories. The idea that became *No Time for Dreams* took root when she made the courageous decision to revisit her past and recall Burma's bitter transformation. Western scholars had documented its ongoing military rule and accelerating economic decline, but no one had broken through the isolation, repression, and fear to unfold its lived history. I wanted to reach across the language barrier, capture this sensitive yet defiant woman's voice, and chronicle the painful odyssey of her still inaccessible country.

Over the years as we exchanged drafts, shared research, and assembled a manuscript, I retraced San San Tin's footsteps. Born in Rangoon in 1950, she came of age under military rule. Inspired by her father Ba Tin's leading role in Burma's struggle for independence in the 1930s, she followed an idiosyncratic path. As a university student, she published articles on the virtues of the socialist government's literacy campaigns in the countryside. As a researcher in a government office, she scribbled poems about vitality eroded by military discipline and bureaucratic routine. As a freelance writer, she gathered scarce information to write the first book in Burmese on environmental pollution. Meanwhile she roamed restlessly through the streets of her native city, traveled to Buddhist pilgrimage sites, studied art and law, then discovered an unlikely sense of purpose writing film reviews, translating foreign news, and pushing the boundaries of censorship at the regime's mouthpiece newspaper, *New Light of Burma*.

When mass demonstrations for democracy in 1988 briefly freed the press and government journalists joined a nationwide strike, she rushed to cover those chaotic events for her newly liberated newsroom and for a start-up news magazine. The inevitable military retaliation left at least three thousand dead with untold numbers arrested or in hiding, and she anguished over assignments to prepare propaganda pamphlets for the government press. Seeing no hope for a return of independent journalism, she resigned her post and, as the junta prospered and the country's poverty deepened, wrote freelance short stories, poems, and art reviews for private magazines. She also worked as an external consultant for UNICEF, translating basic health care manuals to be distributed in remote villages. The opportunity to work for a French medical equipment company briefly offered the prospect of improving the country's dismal delivery of health care while earning a steady salary, but her foray into the private sector resulted only in an unhappy encounter with cronyism and corruption. Unable to find a path of integrity that would not lead to jail, she decided at age 49 to accept an invitation to join a journalism training program abroad.

Walking the streets of Rangoon long after her departure, I followed her familiar routes. Aside from the shopping malls, commercial buildings, and gated residences that service the military elite, the city languishes, drained of resources, no longer the national capital, its urban fabric deteriorating. Open-air shops display meager wares for ordinary Burmese who earn perhaps $1 a day—plastic buckets, cotton *longyis*, used auto parts—while aging taxis rattle along rutted streets and overloaded buses ferry gaunt workers from outlying townships. On Ma Kyee Kyee Road dreary apartments and a trash-littered lot replace San San Tin's childhood home. Paint peels from St. Philo's School where strict Catholic nuns tried in vain to curb her rebellious nature. Rangoon University where she studied remains gated and locked, its once gracious grounds untended, the stucco façade of Judson Church cracked and blackened. The turreted expanse of the Secretariat Building, where her father met General Aung San just minutes before his assassination, stands empty and abandoned. Yet amid the despondency and decay one catches glimpses of resilience and revival—a growing independent art scene, an orphanage caring for AIDS victims, a private school teaching English alongside traditional Burmese culture. So while *No Time for Dreams* captures Burma's decline, it also testifies to the determination of its people and the perdurance of its collective spirit. Someday hope may return.

As this book took shape, San San Tin resumed her journalistic career in the United States, able to report the news in Burma only from afar. Someday she will write her story in her own language and her own style. For now, I try to preserve the immediacy of her voice while locating her experiences in the larger context of a changing Burma over the last half century. San San Tin's insights, her passions, and her writer's sensibility infuse these pages, but any errors, misrepresentations, or mistranslations are solely my responsibility.

Carolyn Wakeman
Berkeley, California

Acknowledgments

Many people generously assisted this project. Our greatest debt is to Burmese friends inside the country and abroad who shared information, analysis, and personal experience, sometimes at considerable risk, but who must here remain nameless. Our most sincere thanks go first to Mark Selden and to Donald M. Seekins, who encouraged and guided the manuscript at crucial stages. Nadine Tang, Hal Nathan, Orville Schell, Eric Stover, Sarah McLean, Jeff Rutherford, Christina Fink, Penny Edwards, Sean Turnell, Ingrid Jordt, Janet Bode, Libby Liu, and Dan Southerland helped in ways they may not know. Many colleagues, students, and visiting scholars at the Graduate School of Journalism aided this effort over the years, especially Neil Henry, Lydia Chavez, Ken Light, Mimi Chakarova, Marcia Parker, Adam Hochschild, and the Covering Burma class. Deepest gratitude goes to San San Tin's fellow staff members at the News and Periodicals Corporation who joined the 8-8-88 strike; to her teachers, among them English tutor U Tint Swe; to veteran journalist Ludu Sein Win who urged her to read Western literature; to her fellow writers and poets, most notably Kyi Aye and Kyi Tin Oo, who led the way; and always to Moe Moe (Inya) and so many others, who left too soon. Susan McEachern offered her wise counsel and critical judgment from the beginning, and Jessica Gribble, Jehanne Schweitzer, and Carrie Broadwell-Tkach expertly managed the many details of publication. A special note of gratitude to Matthew Wakeman, who created the cover; Sarah Wakeman, who shared the journey; Robert Tierney, who understood the challenge; and above all to San San Tin's close family members, both supporters and critics, who shaped her pathway. Final appreciation, beyond words, goes to Daw Kyi Kyi and Bo Ba Tin, who gave so much.

~

Introduction

Not long before this book went to press, Burma captured international news headlines when a catastrophic cyclone made landfall on May 2, 2008, in the low-lying mud flats of Burma's Irrawaddy Delta. The cyclone churned up a powerful sea surge that forced a wall of water some forty kilometers inland, obliterating entire villages and killing an estimated 130,000 people. It was a natural disaster of epic proportions.

The ruling military regime in Burma, however, astounded and confounded the international community by initially refusing to allow foreign aid into the country. In the first few bewildering days, the UN was prevented from flying emergency relief supplies into Burma. Aid agencies based inside the country were given only limited access to the affected Delta areas. Aid workers and disaster relief specialists outside the country were denied entry visas. Despite the enormity of the disaster, the ruling generals seemed determined to close the country off to the outside world.

It is not out of character for Burma's rulers to act in this way. Seven months before the cyclone, another event captured the world's attention. In September 2007, Burma's Buddhist monks began marching in protest against the ruling military junta. Eyewitnesses said as many as 100,000 people appeared on the streets of the former capital, Rangoon, each day for nearly a week. The notoriously brutal regime did not respond immediately but maintained an ominous silence, during which courageous Burmese writers, journalists, and bloggers found ways to disseminate up-to-the-minute news and images via the Internet. For the first time in the history of this locked-off nation, immediate events happening in Burma were being relayed to a worldwide audience as they occurred.

But, then, inevitably, the crackdown began. Those of us watching from outside the country (San San Tin among them) saw photographs and film footage of people cheering on the peaceful marchers suddenly being replaced by images of riot police and soldiers beating monks and herding protesters into trucks. It took about three days for the military to quash the demonstrators. Crowds kept assembling and did not fully dissipate until soldiers started shooting directly at unarmed monks and civilians. Meanwhile soldiers raided monasteries by night and locked up thousands of monks and lay people in makeshift detention centers. To prevent any more international news coverage, the authorities turned off the country's Internet servers. The flow of information coming out of Burma halted abruptly, and events that had made global headlines slipped back out of view.

The Burmese regime has been in power for almost half a century, since the despotic General Ne Win established military rule in 1962 with a fiercely xenophobic regime that expelled foreigners and sealed Burma off from the outside world. Industry and agriculture in the resource-rich country once known as the "rice bowl of Asia" deteriorated severely, and by the end of 1987 the United Nations had listed Burma as one of the world's Least Developed Countries along with ten other desperately poor nations, most of them in sub-Saharan Africa. In 1988, a population made destitute rose up against the regime in a nationwide popular movement, which came to a gruesome end when government soldiers killed an estimated three thousand protesters.

Though Ne Win resigned, the military government remained in power under a new name: the State Law and Order Restoration Council (SLORC). General elections were held in 1990 and the hugely popular National League for Democracy (NLD), led by Aung San Suu Kyi, who was later awarded the Nobel Peace Prize, won the popular vote in a landslide victory. The regime, however, chose to ignore the results. Over the following decade, hundreds of NLD delegates were imprisoned and Aung San Suu Kyi was placed under house arrest, where she has remained for most of the intervening years.

Like much of Burma's recent history, the full details of what really happened in September 2007 and the tense and terrifying weeks that followed are still hazy. With security and surveillance heightened throughout the country, and the people involved either arrested or systematically tracked down and intimidated, concrete information has been hard to come by. The junta blamed the "unrest" on an alleged rebel group of bogus monks and reported that only ten people had died in the resulting skirmishes. A United Nations report, based on the official visit of its human rights special rapporteur in November 2007, found evidence of thirty-one deaths and seventy-four "disappearances." Burmese dissidents and activists outside the country list even higher figures, but it is unlikely we will ever know the real toll. This, to my mind, is one of the most insidious effects of the military's ongoing rule. The regime is able to distort the truth and rewrite history in its favor. Somewhere along the way, the true facts disappear and the real stories are lost.

This is why *No Time for Dreams*, a memoir of Burmese writer and poet San San Tin' life under military rule, is so very important. Born in 1950, during the early dawn of Burma's independence from British colonial rule, her story unfolds the hidden reality of a woman's life when Ne Win's socialist government held sway, during the chaotic events of 1988, and in the difficult aftermath of that nationwide uprising.

Big-picture historical events—such as Ne Win's nationalization of private businesses and expulsion of foreign residents—are seen here through the prism of personal perspective. As a teenage pupil at St. Philomena's Convent Girls' School in Rangoon, San San Tin's English-language textbooks are discarded for Burmese-language texts that extol Ne Win's socialist ideals. Her school tunic is exchanged for a green Burmese *longyi*, or sarong, and traditional white blouse—still the standard uniform of Burmese schoolgirls today. The Irish nuns who run the convent school are forced to leave the country, replaced by ill-prepared Burmese teachers. Even the name Cynthia, given to her by the nuns, is revoked in favor of her Burmese name, San San Tin.

From her early days at school, San San Tin dreams of being a writer, but Ne Win's Burma allows no time or space for dreams, as one of her poems conveys. Her personal story details the difficult, and sometimes absurd, twists and turns of a woman's path as she tries to realize literary ambitions in an isolated country where censorship and propaganda exert tight control over the written word. At university, she chooses to study mathematics rather than literature because even the Burmese junta cannot subvert the logical certainty of mathematical theory ($2 + 2$ will always equal 4).

Jobs are hard to come by for university graduates and she eventually ends up working for the state newspaper, the *New Light of Burma*. Often the lone woman on its editorial staff, San San Tin's description of the newsroom provides a backstage view of how news was controlled and subverted during the Ne Win years—using methods that remain in place today. Like all government workers at the time, she is forced to attend one of the regime's political re-education camps (where she is given the Orwellian label of "Trainee 62"). All the while, though, she keeps writing. She writes articles on environmental issues for a friend's magazine and biographies of artists ranging from Picasso to Henry Moore. She also writes poetry, and her translated poems are scattered throughout this book like beautifully composed postcards from different chapters of Burma's history.

In short, San San Tin's memoir is an enlightening chronicle of what it is like to live under military rule. Her father was a colleague of the country's independence hero Aung San and joined the movement against British colonial rule. Later, his political affiliations landed him on the wrong side of the Burmese regime and he spent various stints in prison. As a result, San San Tin's childhood was intimately linked to the vicissitudes of the country's harsh political climate. When she writes about her time as a young woman in Burma, her experiences shed light on the unspoken realities of ordinary life during the upheavals and hardships of the country's modern history. It is a story that could be echoed by many voices in Burma—voices that remain silent.

Published memoirs of life in contemporary Burma like this one are rare. Though Burmese have fled the country since the early years of Ne Win's disastrous reign and the Burmese diaspora is widespread across the globe, few have dared to write their stories in detail, knowing family and friends could be jeopardized or endangered by their words. San San Tin left Burma in the late 1990s, and she recounts her story today with some bravery, aware that much must be left unsaid to protect those still living under the scrutiny of the regime.

The Burmese junta uses several methods to curtail the truth. One involves a meticulous censorship process to check every word that is independently published in Burma—from magazine articles and textbooks to song lyrics and movie scripts. During the Ne Win years, when San San Tin began writing, the censorship board was crude in its ministrations: pages of published books and magazines disapproved of by the censors were simply torn out or inked over. After the country partially opened its doors to the outside world in the 1990s, the censors became more sophisticated. Publishers are now required to submit completed copies of their texts to the censors before a manuscript is delivered to the printer. Anything that does not fit with the regime's idea of reality must be cut and replaced with new and approved text. This method is especially insidious; writers end up self-censoring their own work and publications no longer look blatantly censored, thereby creating an alternative reality sanctioned by the regime.

While independent writing is strictly monitored, state-run newspapers and television spout an undiluted rhetoric of propaganda. The billboards are there for all to see, summing up the regime's message in no uncertain terms. "TATMADAW [the Burmese army] AND THE PEOPLE COOPERATE AND CRUSH ALL THOSE HARMING THE UNION," declares one blood-red billboard hung on the wall of the former palace in the old royal capital of Mandalay.

Perhaps the most powerful mechanism of reality control in Burma is the regime's cadre of government spies, their effectiveness boosted by a vast network of civilian informers (bribed or bullied) who pass on information about neighbors, colleagues, friends, and even families—anyone who criticizes or defies the regime. This all-encompassing system of surveillance ensures there is no public space in Burma where it can be considered safe to openly voice any political or social opinions that contradict those of the ruling State Peace and Development Council (or SPDC, as the regime is now known). Though illicit conversations in the country's ubiquitous teashops can often be obscured amid the rabble of gossip and thick clouds of cheroot smoke, there is always the danger that someone may be listening.

In such an environment, truth only surfaces in secretive ways. Books and clandestine documents circulate among trusted friends. Conversations take place in the relative safety of private homes. Information is sent out of the country through limited and carefully monitored Internet access. Because of this, hard fact becomes enmeshed in rumor and the truth is a dangerous and elusive commodity.

The iron-fisted crackdown on information after the protests of September 2007 and the way in which the authorities blocked access to the hard-hit Irrawaddy Delta after the cyclone in May 2008 demonstrate that the regime's reality control machine is still frighteningly efficient and that reality remains firmly under the regime's command.

This machine ensures that recollections such as San San Tin's memoir of personal life during half a century of military rule cannot be read or heard in Burma. That you are now holding *No Time For Dreams* in your hands is a triumph in itself—I like to think that published stories such as this one stick a wrench in the well-oiled machine; they scupper its inner workings by reclaiming the truth, and telling it.

Emma Larkin
Bangkok

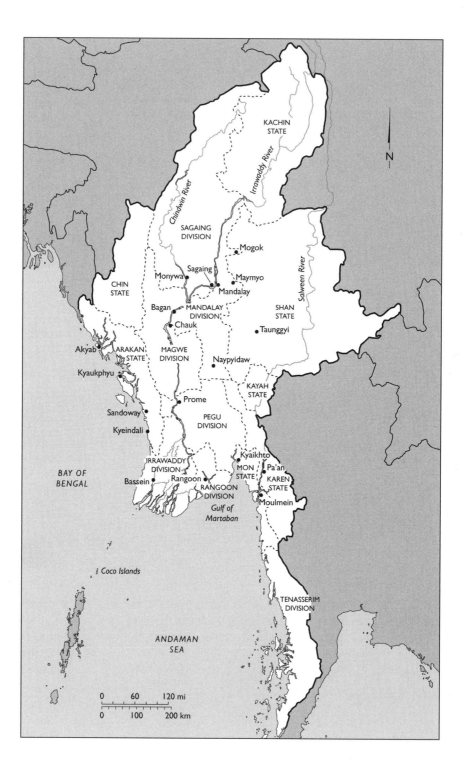

KACHIN
STATE

N

Chindwin River

Irrawaddy River

Salween River

SAGAING
DIVISION

• Mogok

Sagaing
Monywa •   • Maymyo
• Mandalay

Bagan   MANDALAY
DIVISION
• Chauk

SHAN
STATE

CHIN
STATE

MAGWE
DIVISION

• Taunggyi

Akyab •   ARAKAN
STATE

Kyaukphyu •

• Naypyidaw

KAYAH
STATE

Prome •

Sandoway •

PEGU
DIVISION

Kyeindali •

• Kyaikhto

BAY OF
BENGAL

IRRAWADDY
DIVISION
Bassein •   Rangoon •
RANGOON
DIVISION

MON
STATE

Pa'an
•
KAREN
STATE

• Moulmein

_Gulf of
Martaban_

Coco Islands

TENASSERIM
DIVISION

ANDAMAN
SEA

0   60   120 mi
0   100   200 km

~

CHAPTER ONE

Strangers in the Night

Sometime in the early hours of December 3, 1958, loud voices startled me awake. From the doorway of my parents' bedroom I saw two strangers in black jackets searching through a clutter of books, papers, and clothing strewn about the floor. Across the hall in our sitting room, my father, Ba Tin, seemed calm as he reclined in his favorite rattan chair, resting his legs on a cane stool. When he saw me, he called, "*Bokeson*, come," using the nickname "chubby" reserved for his younger daughter. I climbed into his lap as usual, wondering why my father was fully dressed in the middle of the night. Educated in English under British colonial rule, he preferred Western clothing and rarely left the house without his gray slacks freshly pressed and his leather shoes shined. That night he wore traditional Burmese dress, an ankle-length sarong, or *longyi*, and velvet-thonged sandals.

Funeral ceremonies for my mother's aunt had ended just that afternoon with alms offerings of rice and curries at a nearby monastery, concluding the seven-day Buddhist mourning period. Our house in Rangoon had emptied of relatives, and I felt lost without my grandaunt, who lived with us and always slept with me. "This daughter is the favorite of the late aunt," my father explained. The stranger asked only if he was ready yet, and I felt confused when Pe Pe, as we called my father, said his wife was searching for a sweater. Each year brings three seasons in tropical Burma, with the summer heat lasting from March to May, followed by the monsoon season from June to October, then winter from November to February. Evenings sometimes grow cool in December, but I rarely saw Pe Pe wear a sweater.

Soon my mother gathered all seven of us children to pay respect to our father, and I glimpsed the shadow of fear on her face. We knelt beside her, placing our palms together, raising our hands to our foreheads, touching our
heads three times to the floor as we did whenever he left on a journey. Before dawn, carrying a suitcase and a bedroll, he was gone. "They have arrested
your father," our nanny told us in the morning. She came from Mon State in
the southern part of the country and had a flat face, broad lips, a dark com-
plexion, and strong, calloused hands. Her smile reflected her kindness, but
when I asked who the strangers were, she turned away.

When Pe Pe's picture appeared on the front page of *The Mirror* newspaper
alongside several others arrested, we knew he wasn't alone. The army had
seized power a month earlier, ending a decade of parliamentary rule with its
declaration that a military "caretaker" government would safeguard the
country from anarchy and civil war. *The Mirror* article said that for security
reasons the Public Order Preservation Act had been invoked to detain
eleven persons temporarily. Later we read that the junta swept up at least four
hundred potential critics and adversaries, mostly politicians and journalists
suspected as Communist sympathizers, pledging to stabilize unrest across the
country and promising future elections. Despite the arrest of respected politicians like my father, the army still enjoyed respect, especially among the
country's Burman ethnic majority, because of its role in achieving independence from British rule in 1948. No one could anticipate the long-term consequences of the military's accession to power.

In those carefree days of childhood, I knew little about my country's history
or my father's past. I grew up admiring General Aung San, whom we honor as
the father of Burmese independence, but I associated him mainly with the gold
coin necklace I wore on special occasions, like wedding receptions or Buddhist
novitiations. My mother, whom we called May May, often told me, "General
Aung San gave this," and repeated the story of how Aung San had offered my
father a handful of gold coins when he left the army in 1945, soon after the
Japanese defeat in World War II. She was pregnant then with my eldest brother
and money was scarce, but Pe Pe would accept only a single coin. When Aung
San insisted on giving two, my father sold one of the gold pieces and made the
other into a necklace that came to me. My sister, one year older, wore a delicate
heart-shaped gold locket, so my brothers taunted me, saying "a city girl wears a
locket, only a country girl wears a coin." I never liked to wear that necklace but
the family elders were proud of the gold piece and always reminded me that this
was a gift from General Aung San.

Three years before I was born, Aung San, then thirty-two, fell to assassins'
bullets along with six members of the Executive Council on July 19, 1947,

changing the course of Burma's modern history. For more than a decade he had led a defiant crusade against British colonial rule and just months before his death forged a precarious alliance among the country's historically hostile ethnic groups. Despite that foundation for national unity, bitter antagonisms over power and policy festered among competing political factions, and Aung San did not live to lead an independent nation. Every year we honor his sacrifice on July 19, Martyrs' Day.

Once as a child I overheard my father recall that fateful morning. A scheduled cabinet meeting upstairs in the red brick Secretariat Building had interrupted his conversation with Aung San, and Pe Pe waited on the ground floor to resume their discussion. A veteran journalist later told me that my father approached Aung San to ask for the release of an arrested comrade with whom he worked as a political organizer before the war. My uncle gave a different explanation, saying that my father was trying to negotiate a compromise to heal the growing split between the Anti-Fascist People's Freedom League (AFPFL), Aung San's wartime coalition, and the Communist Party of Burma (CPB) to which many of Burma's political leaders had ties. I never knew if my father saw the two jeeps that pulled up under the portico or the uniformed men with Bren guns who ran to the upper floor. What I remember clearly is his description of someone waving a white handkerchief from an upper window just minutes before shots rang out. He felt certain the handkerchief had been a signal.

The web of responsibility for the assassination plot was never fully revealed, but police evidence implicated U Saw, Aung San's chief rival to lead a postcolonial government. Before the Japanese occupation, U Saw had briefly served as Burma's British-appointed prime minister, and police investigators discovered crates of British-issued weapons submerged in Inya Lake near his house. The gunmen were quickly apprehended and testified against U Saw, which led a jury to find him guilty of planning and directing the killings. In May 1948, U Saw was hanged together with eight subordinates accused of carrying out his orders, but suspicions lingered that members of Aung San's own coalition played some role in denying the country its charismatic leader. Following the assassinations, while the nation grieved, U Nu, the most senior of the surviving cabinet members and Aung San's trusted ally, became the first prime minister of a strife-torn but soon to be independent Burma.

Over the years I tried to piece together my father's role in Burma's independence struggle. Born in 1916 in Sandoway, a city in coastal Arakan State, Pe Pe was the eldest son in a prosperous commercial household. "Your grandmother owns four legs of an elephant," he once told us. "Sometimes she has three, sometimes two, sometimes one." When she owned a whole elephant, she had four legs, but if she shared it with a business partner she had two, or sometimes her share shrank to a quarter, which meant one leg. She also owned a large tract of land, some of it planted in orchids, as well as cattle, a sampan, and a timber company that used the elephant to haul warehoused logs.

Soon after my father graduated from the British-administered secondary school in Sandoway in 1934, he traveled in the family sampan to Rangoon carrying merchandise to trade. A promising future managing land, cattle, and timber interests lay ahead, but the nationalist movement spreading opposition to British rule roused his passion. In the colonial capital he joined the radical group *Dobama Asayione* (We Burmese Association) whose members called themselves *thakin*, meaning "master." By appropriating a term of respect reserved for colonial officials, they declared they were masters of their own country.

My father's decision brought swift consequences. The British district governor warned my grandfather, a senior inspector in the Agriculture Department, that he would be fired from the colonial bureaucracy if his son continued to associate with the nationalist movement. Submitting his resignation, my grandfather gave up both salary and status to work as a bookkeeper in his wife's business. Meanwhile my father, then eighteen, followed the dangerous path of political opposition.

Britain had annexed my father's native Arakan district in 1826, which brought control of the Bay of Bengal's important trade routes. Two more Anglo-Burmese wars consolidated all of Upper and Lower Burma in 1886 as a province of British India. Half a century later, as opposition to colonial authority gathered strength, Pe Pe began organizing workers, recruiting sympathizers and spreading the spirit of resistance. My family elders would sometimes mention his fiery speeches urging Burmese dockworkers to join a strike that paralyzed the British-owned oil fields in 1938. My father had also served as general secretary of the All Burma Trade Union, appointed by Aung San, and perhaps even more daring, had translated into Burmese a tract by the Irish radical group Sinn Fein that called for subversion against British rule. I grew up with a strong sense of pride in my father's courage and dedication.

Sometimes as a child I traced with my finger the scar still prominent on his back. The elders said he had been set upon by bandits, but once my mother acknowledged that he had survived an assassination attempt while on a recruiting trip to Pyinmana in the middle of the country. With war sweeping through Asia in 1940 and Japanese troops poised on the Indochina border seeking a land route to India, British authorities tried to crush Burma's political opposition. Targeting activists like my father for attack, they issued a formal arrest warrant for Aung San. The nationalists' leader managed to escape in disguise aboard a Norwegian freighter heading for Japanese-occupied Amoy, intending to seek support from the Chinese Communists. But Japan's intelligence agents approached him first, pledging military assistance for the ongoing struggle against British rule in Burma.

Japanese agents, urging participation in the Greater East Asian Co-Prosperity Sphere's effort to expel Western colonial powers from Asia, soon spirited Aung San to Tokyo. Over the next year twenty-nine other *thakins*, later celebrated as the Thirty Comrades, joined him secretly for training, first in Japan, then in occupied Hainan Island. Meanwhile my father continued organizing at home, traveling mostly between Rangoon and his native Arakan region. After Japan attacked Pearl Harbor in December 1941, British authorities rounded up Burma's resistance leaders, and Pe Pe was seized in Sandoway. Closely guarded, he was taken across the rugged Arakan Mountains on foot, then by boat to Rangoon. When Japan unleashed its first air attacks on the city on December 23, he was confined in the central jail.

By then Japan had occupied the crown colony of Malaya, Hong Kong was poised to surrender, and British troops in Burma could not hope for reinforcements. Implementing a plan for withdrawal to India, colonial authorities urged Rangoon's residents to evacuate. They also emptied the city jail, launching a chaotic period of looting and arson, but freeing my father. By then Aung San and his comrades in exile waited in Japanese-controlled Siam. Pledging to liberate their homeland from foreign rule, they swore a blood oath and established the Burmese Independence Army (BIA) on December 28, 1941, then marched to Rangoon as part of Japan's main occupying force. Pe Pe immediately joined his returned *thakin* comrades and received a military commission by Aung San, who appointed him secretary for BIA headquarters.

My maternal grandmother told many stories about the months of wartime suffering. She described the wail of sirens that sent residents scrambling to makeshift bomb shelters and the streams of frightened refugees who fled the city. She told of homes and shops burned and looted, of desperate food shortages, and of people wearing only rough sacks instead of clothing. Always she complained bitterly about the Japanese, saying they had pressed ordinary citizens into harsh labor, molested Burmese women, and tortured anyone who resisted their commands. The British had treated their subjects decently, she said, because they followed a code of law.

Within months, Burma's nationalists saw that collaboration with Japan offered no prospect of independence from foreign rule. The BIA had not only been subordinated to Japanese command but also renamed the Burmese

Defense Army, and as Japan's occupying force grew to nearly three hundred thousand, Burmese officers were denied a leading role. Contacted by British agents left behind, they agreed to provide covert support for Allied forces fighting to defeat Japan. That decision brought my father's second arrest.

Suspecting BIA involvement in acts of subversion, Japanese military intelligence agents sent my father on a ruse to Mandalay in September 1942, then jailed him in the ancient capital of Amarapura and tortured him to force a confession. He described that experience in a harrowing article I discovered after I reached university. "I was tied by two wires," he wrote,

> one at my left toe and the other at my right thumb. When the electric current flowed, my whole body shook but I denied any knowledge of who had ordered the cutting of a telegraph line installed by the Japanese. It took two to four minutes each time. They used different methods, slow and quick, both difficult. Alternately five Japanese tortured me but I gave no answer. Sometimes blood ran from my nose.

In fact, my father knew many details about secret meetings planning the Burmese army's resistance but managed to withhold that information. He also refused to sign a confession stating that his commanding officer, Bo Let Ya, had ordered him to engage in sabotage. After forty-two days, U Nu and other *thakins* negotiated his release. "Finally after about two months or so Ba Tin was released," Aung San said in a speech after the war. "He was tortured for some days, and when he came out he was still nervous, but he remained alive. Later he was not tortured, perhaps because he belonged to BIA and because of our repeated inquiries about him." Recovering from that ordeal, my father decided to find a wife.

During the British evacuation my mother had fled with her grandmother to spend most of a year taking refuge in a monastery in Bassein, where her relatives donated daily alms. She returned to Rangoon late in 1942 to find areas of the city bombed into ruins and young Burmese women subject to Japanese fancy. Concerned for her safety, her grandmother decided she should marry. The wealthy cousin who served as matchmaker invited several suitors to call, but chose my father because of his high military position and his family's financial standing. As was customary, my mother, then eighteen, had no voice in her betrothal. After a simple gathering with tea and snacks to celebrate my parents' union in November 1943, she moved into the house on Prome Road reserved for BIA officers.

Over the next year, as British and American allies developed clandestine plans for an uprising against Japan's occupying forces, my father was given a field assignment as deputy commander of Military Zone 4. Those coordinated attacks in March 1945 contributed to the final defeat of Japanese troops by the British Indian Army five months later. With the military task accomplished and my mother pregnant, Pe Pe resigned his commission, accepting the gift of two gold coins from Aung San when he returned to civilian life.

When British rule resumed, my father remained politically active for another year, organizing bus drivers and transportation workers into a trade union and giving a speech at Rangoon's magnificent Shwedagon Pagoda during the first National Congress of the AFPFL in 1946. He also tried to mediate between different political factions, but policy conflicts and personal animosities were already unraveling the wartime coalition of nationalist and Communist groups. Distancing himself from political affairs, my father turned to business.

First he became a partner in the Burma Metal and Trade Company that produced cooking pots and other hardware for the postwar recovery. My mother said his cash accumulated so quickly that he stuffed stacks of notes under their mattress, and she always thanked my second eldest brother, born in September 1947, for bringing good fortune to our family. My sister came two years later in 1949, and by the time I arrived on September 19, 1950, two years after Burma's independence, my father had built a comfortable house for his growing family in a quiet residential neighborhood.

Another business opportunity arose when his former commanding officer Bo Let Ya and other shareholders started the country's first seafood enterprise, called the Martaban Company, named after the Gulf of Martaban on Burma's southwest coast. Another *thakin* leader, Thein Pe Myint, who had studied Communist theory with Bo Let Ya in India before the war, wrote the company's slogan, "Every modern person eats seafood," and soon a new industry was born. As general manager, Pe Pe provided jobs to former political comrades, and twice when I was young he visited Tokyo to arrange the purchase of a trawler and the transfer of cold storage technology for a new seafood facility in Rangoon. Even though my grandmother spoke harshly about the military occupation, my father treated Japanese business associates cordially in our home. I grew up admiring the pair of delicately embroidered Japanese landscape scrolls that hung above a table in our sitting room.

That house on upper Ma Kyee Kyee Road defined my childhood. Oil dregs stained the hardwood planks a dark brown to protect against insects and weather, and flowerbeds bordered the lawn leading to our front gate. Jasmine vines clambered over the concrete water tank near the side door, while mango, jackfruit, and drumstick trees provided shade in the tropical heat.

Our neighbors were either successful merchants like my father or government officials, but the lower part of the street was different. There the rough pavement was always dusty in the dry season and muddy during the monsoons. Clerks, hawkers, and peddlers from a nearby rice noodle mill shared shabby houses packed tightly together, sometimes just flimsy sheds without water or sanitation. The elders sheltered me from those conditions so I took privilege for granted, but I also absorbed my father's principles.

Pe Pe's success in business never altered his leftist sentiments. He insisted that our servants gather for meals with the family members and share the same food, and he also installed a manual flush toilet in our thatch-roofed servants' quarters where former political comrades stayed while searching for jobs in Rangoon. When I was seven, he opened an evening school for workers in the annex behind our house, dividing that space into three classrooms and hiring several teachers who lodged in our servants' quarters. One was the wife of a friend in the underground Communist movement, dismissed for political reasons from her job as lecturer at Rangoon University, who became headmistress. For nearly a year, some fifty adults arrived every evening from 5:30 to 9:30 p.m. to attend grades nine and ten, and for a few months a dozen children whose parents had political problems came for daytime study. I returned from my private school eager to greet those new playmates, but the classes stopped immediately when the military caretaker government took my father away.

Our lifestyle changed abruptly after Pe Pe was arrested in 1958. My mother had to cut back on household expenses and sent our driver back to the Martaban Company. My father's houseboy and another helper also disappeared, leaving only the cook, the gardener, and the nanny. I didn't know where our car had gone, a comfortable Vauxhall sedan, but we started hiring a taxi when we needed transportation. My father's friends offered their cars for our use, but my mother rarely accepted. Contact with our family was a risk, she said. After our closest neighbors locked the small gate that connected our two compounds, I learned at a young age how politics drives a wedge between friends.

Those neighbors had moved to Rangoon from the small town of Shwegyin near the Pegu Mountains where the CPB maintained its headquarters. They were rich owners of a vast rice paddy field until the spreading insurgency in 1950 made their native town unsafe. Our relations quickly became like those of an extended family, and we children always used the side gate in our fence rather than the main gate onto the street when we played. We loved flying kites, spinning tops, kicking a soccer ball, and tossing rubber rings onto a stake, and all of us could roll on the lawn to make somersaults. Sometimes our playground turned into a battlefield, but once when we used flower buds from our garden as bullets, Pe Pe spanked me because I was the leader. Urging me to be more ladylike and copy my sister, my mother sometimes pinched my ear painfully for playing with boys. But after Pe Pe's arrest, my friends' father, who accepted a post as an army officer after moving to Rangoon, instructed his sons to stay away.

Deprived of my playmates during the long weeks of school holiday in 1959, I rummaged in Pe Pe's desk for something to relieve the boredom. I discovered a stack of magazines and leafed through back issues of *Life* and *Reader's Digest*, looking for pictures. My father considered English his first language, but we spoke only Burmese at home. When I found a Burmese edition of *The Adventures of Tom Sawyer*, I wondered who or what is Tom, reading the first line, then one page after another, growing interested. Who is Aunt Polly, where is this family, what will happen next, I thought, and within a day finished the whole book. That started me reading, and when nothing on my father's shelves caught my interest, I searched through my mother's Burmese novels. Disapproving of my new pastime, my grandmother worried that I would take an interest in love affairs, saying I was too young for romantic plots. Usually I managed to find a corner at the rear of the house where I could read undisturbed.

Support for our large family rested heavily on my mother's shoulders at age thirty-three. Knowing nothing about contraception or birth spacing, she bore seven children in ten years. Busy with the task of raising five sons and two daughters, she managed the household according to her husband's instructions and accepted whatever money he provided. After Pe Pe's arrest, she never discussed financial affairs with us, but clearly we needed additional income. Probably she received a portion of my father's Martaban salary, but she also began ordering silk and cotton from up-country to sell.

One of Pe Pe's BIA comrades in Amarapura was my mother's source, and she chose my second eldest brother Ko Lay (*ko* is a form of address for an elder brother and *lay* means "little") to be her carrier and keep her company in the daily search for news, contacts, and money. I never knew where she went to peddle her wares, but my brother would return after dark with a heavy bag and head straight to the kitchen to eat. In the past we children were choosy about food and sometimes refused to eat when the meal wasn't to our liking. After my brother started his trips as a carrier for May May, I never heard him complain about a meal or even mention how it tasted.

That summer we found only three curries on the table instead of five or six. There would still be meat or fish along with soup and a vegetable, but the curries were stretched with potatoes. Beans, sardines, dried fish, and fish paste, our customary side dishes, sometimes became the main fare. Most Burmese say the pungent aroma of fish paste, a condiment made from small freshwater fish simmered with chili powder, garlic, and onion, then pounded with dried shrimp, stirs their appetite, but I thought it had a rank smell. When Ko Lay started eating fish paste alone without other dishes, I noticed his change. He knew better than any of us how May May was struggling.

With Pe Pe gone, my eldest brother Ko Gyi (*gyi* means "big") assumed a new role in the household, but when he made all of us children repeat in unison, "The eldest brother replaces the father," I resented his air of authority. After dinner he would instruct us to gather around the table for three hours of schoolwork while he stayed in his bedroom across the hall and watched our reflections in the skylight. My father had installed that pane of glass overhead to let more light into the dining room, but after dark it became a mirror. If my younger brothers started talking or I drew a picture, Ko Gyi called out a warning. It seemed as if we were always being watched by someone.

For two weeks we heard no news about my father, but then May May received word from sympathetic journalists, who found ways to cover the movement of political prisoners, that he was held in Thayet Prison, built by the British in Central Burma. She made that difficult journey only once, carrying packages of food, cheroots, and other items for barter or bribe, then learned in mid-January that Pe Pe would be moved to Insein Prison outside Rangoon. We felt huge relief that he was nearby, held in the annex where political prisoners received more lenient treatment than criminals housed in the main hub-shaped British-built compound that for years was the largest prison in Asia.

Our relief was shortlived. Pe Pe's photograph appeared again in *The Mirror* on January 31, 1959, waiting with several other prisoners at Rangoon's naval base. His jacket looked worn, his mustache unshaved, but most distressing was the news that he would be transported to a newly opened penal colony on the remote Co Co Islands. *The Mirror* also carried a photograph of the ferry boat waiting to transport prisoners to a cargo ship moored near the mouth of the river. We knew the penal colony, far offshore in the Indian Ocean, was a desolate place, and after that, May May worried constantly. My father had diabetes, and she knew his health would fail without proper food.

My mother started spending long periods in front of the small Buddhist shrine inside our front door where we placed flowers, candles, incense, and fresh drinking water, and she also sought the advice of fortunetellers. Superstition runs deep in Burmese culture, and at times of difficulty people commonly rely on supernatural powers. They consult soothsayers and astrologers who explain how to ward off harmful influences, remedy problems, and assure a peaceful life. But even as May May looked for supernatural help, she never stopped trying to find the right contact to arrange Pe Pe's transfer back from the penal colony.

One evening she asked us to put on our finest clothes. Ko Gyi looked like a grown man dressed in a starched white shirt with pointed collar, a Burmese jacket, and a silk *longyi* from my father's wardrobe. My other brothers wore neatly pressed long pants and white shirts, while my sister and I put on special outfits. May May had hired a car from the Martaban Company to take us all to the residence of Brig. Gen. Aung Gyi, second in command of the caretaker government. His acquaintance with my mother was not close, so the help of an intermediary was necessary, and another ex-army officer's wife accompanied us. We waited several hours in that silent house, directed to the sitting room used for unimportant guests, receiving not even a glass of water, a clear breach of Burmese etiquette. When Aung Gyi finally arrived, we moved to the formal sitting room where May May presented all of her children, quite openly appealing for compassion. Her effort proved successful, and Pe Pe spent only forty-five days on the Co Co Islands.

Later he told us how he had been herded onto the lower deck of a rusty merchant ship with other political prisoners and watched helplessly as another *thakin*, suffering from a broken back, was hoisted onboard in a loading crane. Locked in suffocating quarters below decks, the prisoners were ordered at gunpoint to remain silent during that difficult voyage. Then hunger set in quickly. Prisoners received one meager ration a day of coarse rice, watery bean soup, and crude fish paste. They waited desperately for relatives to send food, and Pe Pe described how twenty-six persons had once shared a single green chili, dividing the thirteen seeds in half so that everyone received an equal part. My mother sent provisions and letters, not knowing how much he would receive, but later we saw a photograph of us children covered with many stamps from the prison authorities, who scrutinized every item.

Once Pe Pe returned to the Insein Prison annex, I could visit him regularly. The Catholic girls' school that I started attending in 1959 closed every Thursday while the nuns attended to religious duties, and that was also visiting day at Insein Prison. On Wednesdays my family was busy. Our cook prepared dried foods like fried meat, shrimp, and fish paste spiced with chili while my mother purchased clothing, medicine, and cigars. At eleven we set out, each carrying as much as we could, to wait for a bus at the top of our street on Prome Road. An hour's ride took us to the center of Insein, a busy workers' town with a whuge brick works, a railway factory, and several ceramics workshops. Fresh fish, meat, and vegetables were available at a cheap price in the Insein markets, so the railway station looked like a bazaar as trains from the middle of the country stopped and passengers bought local products.

From the bus terminal we continued by trishaw to the outskirts of town, then followed a red dirt track alongside the prison wall. I never forgot that route. When the wall ended, we turned right to reach the heavy wooden gate where a warden with a big copper key unlocked a small door studded with iron bars set waist-high in the main prison entry. We had to stoop low to enter, a gesture of submission, then heard the gate clang shut behind us.

Ordinary prisoners met their families behind bars, but as a Section 5, Class B prisoner, Pe Pe didn't have to wear the uniform white *longyi*, nor was he chained or handcuffed like other inmates. Instead he waited for us in the visitors' room. Sometimes I wandered out to watch the wardens rummage through our carrying bags and cane baskets, helping themselves to cigarettes and cheroots. Pe Pe smoked strong, bitter cigars, but any form of tobacco was a valuable commodity in prison and could be exchanged for privileges or other goods. My mother spent hundreds of *kyats* before each visit, whereas she paid Mali, our gardener, only sixty *kyats* in monthly wages, and even then he sent cash back to his family in India.

When a general election was called in February 1960, my father had been jailed for more than a year. I knew he would only come home if U Nu's Clean Party defeated the military-backed Stable Party so I avidly supported the Cleans. One afternoon when I managed to join the neighbors' children despite the locked gate, we marched around their garden shouting, "Clean, Clean, win, win; Stable, Stable, lose, lose." As the eldest, I was the leader until their mother called her sons inside and scolded them. Their father was a military officer and supported the Stable Party, with its claims of restoring law and order.

My family rejoiced when U Nu's decisive election victory returned parliamentary democracy to Burma. On March 31, the final day of the caretaker government, I was at the Venus Beauty Parlor on Sule Road for my regular haircut when May May received a telephone message with news of an amnesty. She left immediately, asking a relative to accompany me home. Just at the top of our street I saw a black Humber sedan making the turn. It stopped, and someone called to me. I ran to the car and climbed into Pe Pe's lap, seeing my mother crowded in with several strangers. They all wore Burmese clothing, and everyone was smiling.

CHAPTER TWO

~

No Turning Back

Religious ceremonies serve as important social occasions in Burma. In my childhood wealthy families in Rangoon used horses or cars to carry sons being inducted into the monkhood, while prosperous parents in the countryside hired elephants for the ceremonial procession. Had the novitiation for my two eldest brothers been held in 1959 as my father planned, we would have traveled to Sandoway, invited many guests, hired a Burmese orchestra, and served special foods while my father made three days of offerings. My sister and I would have taken part in an ear-piercing ceremony, seated on velvet cushions, dressed in brocade skirts and gold tiaras, as a gold needle arrived on a gilded plate. Buddhist parents and grandparents all want to see their sons become monks and their daughters wear earrings. That is the tradition.

By the time my father was released from prison in 1960, my two eldest brothers had passed the customary age when young men become monks, and their novitiation was my family's first concern. No longer financially able to host a lavish gathering, my parents invited simply friends to a nearby monastery to commemorate my brothers' passage into manhood and also my father's return. Because ordination into the monkhood confers purification and renewal, it is not uncommon for someone released from arrest to take the vows and thereby cleanse the taint of prison. My father decided to take part along with my brothers, and with May May's consent, asked permission from an elder monk to wear a robe, then shaved his head and practiced the recitations in Pali, the language of the Buddhist scriptures.

When the important day arrived, I searched the line of cinnamon-robed figures to find my father. Walking slowly and looking at the ground, he held a monk's rice bowl and carried a palm leaf fan. Beside him, his younger brother held a round basket to receive offerings of money and small gifts like towels and pens. After the procession my brothers looked triumphant in their monks' robes when I knelt before them, touched my head to the ground, and paid them respect alongside my mother. That day I couldn't avoid honoring their manhood, but at least the ear-piercing ceremony had been forgotten. Burmese women, including my sister, are proud of their diamond earrings, but I never shared that taste.

Slipping away to walk around the monastery grounds and listen to the bamboo leaves rustling in the hot April breeze, I gave thanks that our long months of hardship had ended. For some reason, I remembered the ceremony on my sixth birthday when Pe Pe invited many of the same relatives and friends to celebrate at our home. That day the elders insisted I wear all my jewelry, including a pair of gold anklets, but at my brothers' novitiation four years later no one cared what I wore. By then the pawnbroker had custody of much of the family jewelry, and May May used my gold coin necklace as a deposit whenever she needed money. While Pe Pe was in jail, it went in and out many times.

My father did not return to the Martaban Company after his release, perhaps to distance himself from former political comrades. To supplement his income at the metal company, he set up an import-export business trading in timber, and within months our house grew busy again. Savory curries reappeared on the dinner table, and a stream of visitors passed through. May May welcomed the renewed prosperity, but she also grew more protective, giving my sister and me careful instructions as we approached adolescence. We should not be too friendly with male guests because we were growing up, she cautioned. She also changed our sleeping arrangements and moved us to the room across from her bedroom. My brothers complained that we girls received special favor by being switched to the front of the house, not realizing that May May just wanted to watch us more closely. Her supervision at home gave me few chances to overhear discussions among my father's visitors.

Preoccupied with launching his new business venture, Pe Pe saw little of us during that school year and insisted we join him during our weeks of vacation for morning exercise. We complained about having to wake up before dawn to accompany him on his daily walks, but he valued that chance to chat and joke with us. It took nearly an hour to walk downtown to Bogyoke Market, the sprawling arcade formerly called Scott Market, established by the British in 1925. Beneath its distinctive clock tower, goods of every description spilled from tables and baskets. On schooldays at home we ate a simple breakfast of bread or leftover rice fried with peas, but Pe Pe rewarded us for getting up early and let us sample whatever we liked at the market stalls. Usually we chose *mohinga*, a favorite fish broth and rice noodle soup, but sometimes we tried savory dumplings or noodles simmered in coconut milk. Later our driver met us at a teashop with my younger brother, weakened from pneumonia, and drove us all home.

During that vacation in 1960 when I was almost ten, my mother started training me for my future responsibilities as a wife. Unlike my sister, I resisted helping with housework and kitchen tasks. I preferred to read. The only duties I fulfilled without protest were to change the flowers and drinking water at the altar inside our front door on alternate days with my sister, and to ask Pe Pe each morning what he wished to wear. On days that he chose loose-fitting Burmese attire in the sultry heat, I ironed his *longyi*.

We had two irons, and I knew to use the one my mother reserved for men's clothing, never stopping to think about the various ways she kept her own *longyis* from contact with my father's and brothers' clothing. Not only were hers washed separately from the rest of the laundry, but we had two wires strung behind the house for drying. The men's and children's clothing hung from the top wire alongside my mother's blouses and jackets, but her *longyis* always dried on the lower strand. My sister and I found ours similarly segregated as soon as we reached adolescence.

May May often scolded me for not helping with the housework, and sometimes I quarreled with my elder brothers, who called me lazy. Feeling like an outcast in the family, I took refuge in the shady garden and poured out my complaints silently to the shrubs and trees. In the evenings, the bench under our pine tree became my usual place to read and dream as the sun went down slowly and a gradual coolness replaced the heat of the day.

Perhaps because boys are favored in Burma or because Buddhism teaches us at an early age to accept our destiny, few young girls think about their own path to success and happiness. Groomed to be quiet and docile, they defer to their brothers' aspirations and submit to the expectations of the elders. My friend Daphne and I were different. Encouraging each other, we couldn't just wait for reincarnation to bring a bright future, or trust in some future life we couldn't see. Sometime in fourth grade we decided to become poets. I even chose a pen name and wrote it in chalk under my desk cover. Our most understanding friends called us dreamers, but other classmates said we were crazy. Still, everyone agreed we were the only two who never made mistakes in arithmetic.

After my father's return, I paid little attention to politics or the troubles facing Burma's parliamentary democracy until I returned from school on March 2, 1962, and learned that the army, led by General Ne Win, had seized power. The elders in my family shared rumors of troops and tanks in the streets, but there seemed no great alarm about the sudden return to military rule. Newspaper reports the next day said that Prime Minister U Nu along with his cabinet members and over thirty ethnic leaders had been jailed, and that the son of Burma's first president, an ethnic Shan, age seventeen, had been killed, allegedly for resisting arrest. Still, the army justified its coup with claims that parliamentary rule had failed to unite Burma's political factions or quell the ethnic insurgency. It also invoked the legacy of General Aung San, and vowed to prevent the country's disintegration and preserve the union. Civil war and insurgency had spread during the fourteen years of Burma's independence, so people yearned for stability and peace. At age eleven I felt somehow reassured to have the military in charge.

During the school holiday that year, I only glanced at newspaper articles announcing the improvements soon to be achieved with a socialist economy. I ignored the new Revolutionary Council's declarations that Burma would follow its own path to a socialist society and not take sides in the Sino-Soviet split, and even the strict regulations called the Core of Burma's Socialist Program Party seemed remote from my childhood interests. Having spent almost the entire period of the military's caretaker government in jail, Pe Pe remained cautious. He provided a routine statement of support from the Burma Metal and Trading Company, but he also made clear his doubts. One evening he returned from a meeting called by Brig. Gen. Aung Gyi that informed businessmen about new economic policies to say, "They sing a good tune." As the weeks passed, I sometimes heard family elders remark that Burma's political disputes may have lessened, but only because so many people were in jail.

Students entering the fifth grade class at St. Philo's Convent School always looked forward to new opportunities and freedoms. Our English skills would improve, as the Irish nuns would teach us all subjects except Burmese. We could regularly use the school library and also choose among extracurricular activities, some that gave us a chance to meet boys. In 1962, those dreams never came true. Instead we found all our classes except English taught in Burmese and several school activities cancelled. We no longer sang hymns or recited the prayer "Hail Mary, full of grace" in the morning. And with the library closed to borrowers, I could only gaze at the books inside locked cases. As a primary student, I had occasionally borrowed illustrated children's books or adventures by the popular British writer Enid Blyton, but those happy moments soon faded from memory. Our British textbooks disappeared, and the teachers no longer mentioned Lord Horatio Nelson or Guy Fawkes' Day. Instead we used outdated readers with traditional Burmese stories or tales from the Buddha's life until new socialist textbooks appeared the following year.

The dress code also changed, and we discarded our dark blue tunics, white blouses, blue neckerchiefs, white socks, and sturdy shoes. May May ordered from a tailor our required new uniforms, a gray *longyi* and pink blouse, to wear with velvet-thonged sandals. When she took us for a fitting, concerned as always about our modesty, she made sure the blouses were loosely cut. Later my sister took the seams in herself to make hers fit snugly, but I never bothered.

Changes at my convent school were only one reflection of the military government's tightening control over education. Students returning to classes at Rangoon University found new regulations setting fixed study hours, requiring the locking of dormitories at 8:00 p.m., and prohibiting unauthorized gatherings. Heirs to Burma's proud history of university protest, student leaders showed their opposition cautiously with a one-hour strike on July 7. Everyone could recall the events of 1936, when British authorities expelled U Nu, who led Rangoon University's student union during the independence movement, and Aung San, who edited the campus magazine, for criticizing the university's colonial administration. Their expulsion triggered angry demonstrations across the country, but after one student was killed, the decision was reversed. U Nu and Aung San were then allowed to resume classes.

Four months after the army seized power in 1962, its response to mild protest at Rangoon University was uncompromising. Police entered the campus firing tear gas and swinging clubs to arrest student leaders, then withdrew when demonstrators dispersed. Breaking an uneasy calm, two trucks returned with additional troops who opened fire indiscriminately at close range. Ma Kyee Kyee Road was only ten minutes away, and we heard about the army's brutal suppression from my father's cousin, a lecturer at the university, who described military guards at the campus gates that evening. He spent the night with us, and I heard him talking with Pe Pe until very late.

A huge noise jolted us awake, and we all thought an earthquake had struck until news traveled in the morning that the army had dynamited the student union building. The regime claimed no one died in that blast, but others said a hundred students had been killed along with several workers. Later that day Ne Win spoke threateningly on the radio. "We will fight sword against sword, spear against spear, and there is no turning back," he said. That was when my elders started to fear.

Happy to learn that my parents would soon take us on two trips to Buddhist pilgrimage sites, I had no hint of looming difficulties. First we traveled by train to Mon State to see the famous Kyaikhtiyo Pagoda, built on a flat gold-plated rock that projects precariously over the edge of a cliff. Awed by this natural wonder, we believed the rock maintained its balance because of the Buddha's hair preserved inside the shrine. When we returned to Mon State a month later, we traveled to the railway stop beyond Kyaikhto station, and oxcarts transported us to a small village at the foot of Wayponla mountain, near the site of an ancient city wall. In the mornings we children walked with Pe Pe from our resthouse to a distant pagoda and listened to the chief monk's hour-long *Dhamma* talk in Pali, never understanding a word. After that we could play. I had a favorite rock where I sat and dreamed, gazing out at the distant villages, rice fields, and pagodas dotting nearby hilltops. I also wandered happily on the mountainside with my brothers, climbing trees and sometimes searching for spirits.

According to folk tradition, every tree has a guardian spirit, but not all are benign. The elders warned us especially to beware of the *Ot-sa-sauk* who lived on the mountainside, believed to be shades of humans who died young but were allowed to return to the world for a specified time to guard a pagoda's treasure. The *Ot-sa-sauk* might appear as rich and beautiful women, so when we told Pe Pe we wanted to find an *Ot-sa-sauk* to see her beauty, he joked that he would rather ask her for gold. Without his indulgence, we could never have mentioned our search, as others warned us repeatedly not to trifle with the *Ot-sa-sauk* or treat them lightheartedly. Even the monks' assistants were said to communicate with the spirits, and one afternoon my father's boy helper cried out in terror, certain he had seen his dead grandmother's shade return.

Back at home, accustomed to daily checks of my father's diabetes, I paid little attention when he was hospitalized and never noticed that he was admitted to a pulmonary unit. Caught up with weekly meetings for the Girl Guides, I also practiced daily laps in the school's swimming pool, surprised when I made the team and excited about this new hobby. Then I learned my mother was expecting again after a miscarriage the year before and noticed that my sister was taking special care of May May. Usually she managed the affairs of our kitchen herself, but during this pregnancy she needed frequent rests. That left our cook, Ma Shwe, to oversee the household tasks and prepare the meals alone.

Soon after my father's release from prison, Ma Shwe had come with her brother to take over the housework, recommended by Pe Pe's former driver at Martaban. Among the many maids who passed in and out, she was my favorite. Like other ethnic Karen, she was humble and friendly, and at fourteen she knotted her long hair like an older woman's, while her fair skin and sparkling eyes conveyed her youthful innocence. I felt she should be my schoolmate, but like her brother she had started to work after fourth grade.

Ma Shwe liked chatting with me when she bathed behind our house, and I listened eagerly to her experiences. Sometimes I described the plots of my favorite books in return, as she had no time to read. Busy during the week with household tasks, she spent every Saturday night with her mother in Rangoon's large Karen community. On Sunday nights, she would tell me about the morning sermon at her Baptist church, and often she sang a Burmese version of "Silent Night, Holy Night" in the kitchen. That surprised me because at my convent school, we used to sing hymns in English.

That year May May imposed new restrictions on my sister and me to re-inforce our sense of modesty, telling us to take Ma Shwe as our model. We should watch how she wrapped her *longyi* above her breast like an adult woman when she bathed, and we should cover ourselves in the same way when we came out of the bathroom. I had to wear a blouse with a chemise underneath when I walked around the house, and I could no longer run out-side to shower in the rain. When May May learned that our driver had taken me out alone for a driving lesson, she strictly prohibited any such activity. She believed men could not be trusted with young girls.

I was devastated when I learned from May May that a frequent visitor to our house, a tall, good-looking man named Sein Oke who was a prisoner with my father at Insein, had bothered Ma Shwe in the kitchen. She never men-tioned that encounter, nor did my mother dare complain to my father that his friend had molested our servant. Instead she asked me to inform Pe Pe about Ma Shwe's trouble. Feeling upset, I told my father bluntly that his friend was a womanizer and could never be trusted, but Pe Pe said it was not my concern. A few days later Ma Shwe disappeared with no warning, and I wept to lose my companion without ever saying goodbye. The new cook my mother hired was over forty.

By then I could see that something was wrong again. Pe Pe was busy and distracted, and May May started going out despite her pregnancy, never ex-plaining her business. I knew she was pulling gems from some jewelry and selling the gold, and I could see that the cash in Pe Pe's bureau jumped out again and again. As usual, my gold coin became someone else's treasure. My grandmother came to take care of us before the baby arrived in November, and while I was disappointed not to have a new sister, I rushed home every day to hold this tiny brother. Visitors lavished attention on him, and he quickly grew spoiled.

When the Revolutionary Council announced the nationalization of the Burmah Oil Company in January 1963, I paid little attention to the publicity surrounding the socialist transformation of our economy. But just days later, two strangers wearing black jackets appeared again in our visiting room. I heard them tell my father to follow them, and knew instantly he had been arrested again. My first thought was for my little brother still in his cradle, who had no idea that another catastrophe had befallen his family.

The newspaper reported that Pe Pe was being investigated for a crime connected to Sein Oke, but thanks to the editor's restraint the item appeared only as a filler without a photo. Still I knew my friends would learn what had happened and assume my father was a criminal. My world felt shattered, and I couldn't bear to think of Pe Pe in jail again. I cursed Sein Oke wildly, but all I grasped was that my father had invested in Sein Oke's timber business to pursue a profit. Years later, searching for more information, I read that Sein Oke had diverted state-owned timber and my father was involved. I admired Pe Pe so much, but whatever financial deal he engaged in with Sein Oke left an ache in my heart that never healed.

Again my father was held in Rangoon's central jail where the British had detained him on the eve of the Japanese invasion. Notorious during the war as a Japanese prisoner of war compound, the city jail was close to downtown, and political prisoners and common criminals were confined together. I visited my father only once, passing through the heavy wooden gates, seeing many people crowded behind bars wearing white *longyis*. He met us in a small room close to the head warden's office. However grateful I was for that special favor, I still broke down sobbing. Pe Pe comforted me, telling me not to cry. Soon he learned that he would stand trial. By then his financial resources were exhausted, and with no other option, he instructed May May to sell our family home.

At the start of the school holiday in March 1963, we had to move in with my grandmother's sister. Her house was in a crowded neighborhood, though not quite as shabby as lower Ma Kyee Kyee Road. Rows of low wooden barracks with concrete floors built by the British as railway workers' quarters stood just behind, and across the street was a compound for municipal vehicles. Like many others, my grandaunt rented out space at the front of her house, and stacks of lumber belonging to an Indian timber merchant filled the tiny front yard. The houses stood so close together, we couldn't open the wooden shutters on one side, and the small rooms trapped the summer heat. Well into the evenings we stayed outside to find cooler air, sitting on a cot under an almond tree, waiting for the temperature to drop slightly. In that dim light I couldn't even read. Almond branches blocked the street lamp.

May May was busy consulting a lawyer, attending the trial, searching for good contacts, maybe trying to give a bribe or gain some favor, so my grandmother came to care for the baby. Nearly three months had passed after Pe Pe's arrest when we heard a radio announcement on April 1, 1963, that the Revolutionary Council would issue an amnesty for insurgents at the start of a peace initiative. My uncle said Pe Pe certainly wouldn't be released since his trial was in session, but I kept some hope.

The night of April 5 was especially sultry, with no breeze, no fresh air, and no scent of flowers like on Ma Kyee Kyee Road. We sat on the cot as usual, and I gazed out at the stream of people passing in the street. I had no idea how they earned a living, but they were returning late, and I could tell their work was hard. As I watched and thought about the misfortune of people I didn't know, I saw a stout man step down from a trishaw. It looked like Pe Pe. Without anyone noticing, I ran and called to him. He put his hand on my shoulder as we walked toward the house.

My father told us that General Ne Win had personally made a speech announcing the unconditional release of prisoners, so I asked if Ne Win had noticed him among that group, wondering about their relationship. Pe Pe just shook his head. I didn't dare ask my other question about what had happened to Sein Oke. Later I found a newspaper report that said the Revolutionary Council had freed twenty-three politicians in the April 5 amnesty, as well as five journalists, thirteen students, five Karen insurgents, and three other nonpolitical prisoners besides my father. Sein Oke was among them, but we never saw him again.

The peace negotiations in Rangoon were promoted as a solution to many years of civil war and a further step toward the uniting of the country for the building of Burmese socialism. The official Burmese Broadcasting Service (BBS) roused support by playing songs about peace and popularizing slogans about unity. Members of underground organizations, guaranteed safe passage, came to Rangoon for discussions with military officials, and any opposition members who accepted the terms of surrender received jobs and financial incentives as rewards. But many ethnic leaders and CPB members claimed their demands were never treated seriously. Unable to achieve their goals, they went back underground, and the armed struggle resumed amid rumors that the military was inciting disturbances to justify a campaign of ruthless suppression. Next Ne Win made a gesture to the above-ground opposition.

The Revolutionary Council had begun closing privately owned businesses in order to limit the private sector to retail trade. State agencies and enterprises assumed responsibility for the production, distribution, import, and export of all commodities, so the Trade Ministry assumed many new tasks. In the past, ex-Communists were considered a potential source of opposition, but that year a number received high posts, and Pe Pe was offered a position as the Trade Ministry's general manager. I wondered how he could receive such an offer so soon after his release from jail, but people said the Revolutionary Council gave favor in exchange for support and dispensed benefits as a way of reducing opposition and stifling criticism.

One former military officer later told me that people like my father were simply used to take advantage of their skills and experience, but Pe Pe tried to influence the implementation of the new economic policies. He may also have thought a position inside the bureaucracy would allow him to find jobs for his former comrades. Right after his release from jail he had considered moving our family to Sandoway for a fresh start, but my sister and I cried bitterly at the prospect of leaving Rangoon. I wondered if our distress had affected his decision to accept a civil service position, but he must also have known that rejecting the regime's overtures could bring reprisals. His former commanding officer and business partner, Bo Let Ya, refused to accept any position in the military government and was jailed the following November.

The changing economic policies particularly affected Indian and Chinese residents, many of whom owned flourishing businesses. During the colonial period the British had encouraged immigration to develop the country's commerce and agriculture. As the cultivation of paddy land increased, Burma became the largest rice exporter in the world before World War II, known as the "breadbasket of India." Indians passed freely into Burma and found jobs in the rice fields or as tradesmen, stevedores, railway workers, and nightsoil haulers. They also filled the ranks of the civil service, the police force, the prison system, and the colonial army, and my mother learned enough Hindi as a child to communicate with rickshaw drivers and shopkeepers. Chinese immigrants also found economic opportunity in Burma, opening shops, buying paddy land, and building warehouses to store grain and other commodities. Yet even as immigrants contributed to the country's economic success, they triggered resentment and racial tension.

According to the 1930 census, Rangoon's population numbered 300,000, of whom 212,000 were Indian. Four years later, racial tensions flared during a dockyard strike over wages, and rumors alleged that a Burmese woman had been killed and mutilated by Indian workers. Brawls broke out, and riots spread through the neighborhoods in central Rangoon heavily populated by Indians, some of them migrant laborers from Madras who planted and harvested the rice fields in the Irrawaddy River Delta. Before police restored order, that outburst of racial violence left two hundred Indians dead, many of them killed with swords and spears.

Three decades later, Indians and Chinese who had spent years in Burma and taken Burmese names were forced to leave when the state took over their businesses in 1963. Squatters sometimes took up residence on the recently vacated land, and soon the Indian merchant stopped selling sold lumber from my grandaunt's house. But after my father accepted the Trade Ministry job, we left those crowded conditions behind and moved to the home of a grandaunt on York Road, considered one of Rangoon's best neighborhoods, centrally located near the railway station, the Shwedagon Pagoda and Scott Market. Once again we had a garden and many bedrooms.

My grandaunt's husband was a businessman who ran a printing press in their attached annex. He made a comfortable income printing invitation cards, paper napkins, and labels for clothing, and his business had not yet been affected by the new regulations, but I wondered how she could live with him. We all knew he was unfaithful and spent much time with another woman. One afternoon as I carried my baby brother, Ko Tue, around the courtyard, I became the target of his flirtation. Everyone loved to tickle and stroke the smiling baby, even my grandaunt's husband. But that day when he patted the baby, he whispered that I should start using *thanakha*, a cosmetic made from ground tree bark mixed with water on a slate stone. Burmese women use that pale yellow paste as a sunscreen, cosmetic, and hair oil, and he seemed to suggest that at thirteen I was now a young woman. I nodded politely but then his fingers shifted from the baby's hand to my own. Frightened, I pulled back quickly and ran away.

In that impressionable stage of early adolescence, I could already see how a married woman's life was often miserable. Like many Burmese wives, my grandaunt on York Road could not accept the stigma of divorce and lived with her husband's infidelity until he passed away when she was sixty-two. Some women facing similar circumstances took a different path, and my favorite grandaunt, who moved in with us on Ma Kyee Kyee Road soon after I was born, had refused to tolerate her husband's love affair. When she suffered a sudden heart attack at age thirty-eight, we all assumed that the emotional strain and public disapproval brought her early death.

A new system of quota books was announced after our move to York Road, requiring us to shop at community cooperative stores where inferior quality staple goods were sold at government-subsidized prices. Housewives and children lined up for hours to purchase the daily quota of kerosene, our staple cooking fuel, but everyone could see that state control of production and distribution did not live up to its promise. Not only was the quality of rice at the cooperative shops inferior to that sold by private merchants, but the supply was limited because shipments of grain often started to rot in storage. In our country of bountiful rice harvests, people faced shortages.

Government media denounced those who used the black market to circumvent the state system, and newspapers and magazines carried many articles about the evils of capitalist exploitation. That didn't stop my family from relying on street stalls. May May quickly became fed up with the inefficiency and low quality at the state stores and instead bought goods at more expensive street prices. Even while my father tried to manage the Trade Ministry, his family purchased high quality rice on the black market, contributing to the growth of illegal transactions.

After the Burma Metal and Trading Company was nationalized in 1964, Pe Pe launched several short-lived retail ventures as sideline investments to supplement his salary. Our years of reduced income had taught my mother to manage the household efficiently, but still my father's government pay did not cover our expenses. One small business exported bamboo shoots to Japan while another collected remnant sackcloth to produce vegetable sacks for onions and potatoes. However meager those earnings, it seemed that Pe Pe had inherited his family's instinct for business. Occasionally my mother still pawned her diamond earrings.

Twice in 1964 my father took me to his Trade Ministry office. Awed by its size, I tried out the swivel chair facing his desk, then the side chair and settee. At home we heard his increasing complaints. The minister's goals were impractical and overly ambitious, Pe Pe said, and top ministry officials refused his advice not to extend their responsibility beyond their experience. Concerned about the failings of the new economic policies, he warned us children that even if an inexperienced man could successfully serve a four-person meal, that didn't mean forty inexperienced men could successfully serve a meal to 160. Doing something effectively, he told us, mattered far more than taking on grand tasks. My father knew discontent was spreading. Along with resentment at the nationalization of private businesses came concern about the black market, worry about food shortages, and growing fear of the military's power.

CHAPTER THREE

~

Spreading Socialism

To promote the military government's socialist themes, radio programs in 1964 featured songs celebrating the daily life of farmers and workers. Short stories unfolded sentimental plots about people impoverished by capitalist exploitation, and critics praised the new works of socialist realism. Clear-cut accounts of good struggling against evil captured my sympathies when I was fourteen, and I liked to memorize stirring lines from movies about kind-hearted peasants suffering at the hands of cruel landlords.

Ideological initiatives carried socialist values into the schools, familiarizing Burma's youth with notions of class difference and class struggle, boosting enthusiasm for the new socialist path. Some of my classmates in seventh grade criticized the government because their families' businesses had been taken away, but the celebration of rural culture fed my adolescent idealism. I felt pity for the weak and admired the regime's efforts to improve peasants' lives. Borrowing details from a magazine story, I wrote an enthusiastic essay called "Country Customs" that my teacher praised and read in front of the class.

Politics increasingly reached into the classroom, and I had worn my Girl Guide uniform for less than a year when the Revolutionary Council closed down private organizations, including political parties, with the exception of the official BSPP. After the Girl Guide meetings were cancelled, I joined Paddy Birds, a youth program sponsored by the BBC's Burmese-language radio station. Sometime in the middle of seventh grade our teacher told us to turn in our Paddy Bird membership cards, presumably because of the link to a foreign country.

As the quota system extended, we needed ration coupons to buy paper supplies, which meant purchasing our exercise notebooks at school rather than in retail shops. The inferior grade of paper made the ink from our fountain pens leak through to the next page, so the teachers made us practice with ballpoints rather than fountain pens, then complained because our handwriting grew sloppy. And because the school's quota didn't meet the demand, children also started relying on the black market.

For five years, the nuns at St. Philo's had called me Cynthia, but in 1964 the Revolutionary Council made us give up our English names. Burmese follow no consistent pattern of family and given names, and children often receive names according to the day of the week they are born. After the new instruction, I officially became San San Tin, the name my family picked based on the position of the planets at the time of my birth. But no one at my convent school enforced the regulation, and my friends continued calling each other Amy, Baby, Daisy, Dolly, and Daphne.

The junta took its most drastic step to control education in April 1965, just after the start of the annual summer holiday, by nationalizing Burma's private and missionary schools. Hearing the new regulations announced on the radio, I cried out in disbelief, forgetting how inspired I had been by earlier government directives, like the manifesto pledging improved conditions for the proletarian class. Nationalization of the schools would bring an end to our rigorous instruction, our experienced teachers, even to my swimming team that had won most of its meets. Devastated at the thought of becoming a state schoolgirl, I felt like one of the withered leaves swirling outside in the hot breeze.

When I entered eighth grade, St. Philomena's Convent Girls' High School had disappeared, renamed State High School No. 2, Sanchaung Township, Rangoon. Like every student around the country, I wore a green *longyi* and white blouse, the uniform of the state schools. Until then, missionary educators had set their academic requirements independently, but starting in 1965, St. Philo's followed the state schools' unified curriculum with significantly lower standards. Some of the nonforeign convent teachers remained, but most of our kind Irish Catholic mothers were gone for good. Like other foreigners, the nuns applied for visa extensions, but when the government denied those requests, they had to leave. Unfamiliar faces appeared in our classrooms along with unmotivated teachers transferred from the state system. After a biology teacher was assigned to my physics class and a Burmese teacher started instructing me in math, I lost interest in studying.

With intelligence and experience systematically ignored, a steady brain drain joined the mounting problems created by Burma's special path to socialism. Military personnel took over senior positions in the government bureaucracy and state-controlled enterprises once the private sector was abolished, and the army officers who assumed civilian posts mandated foolish policies with blunt authority. My father knew that military superiors with no expertise were forcing people with professional training to meet pointless demands. He told us that he argued with the Trade Minister again and again, but in 1965 his health was failing, and he needed repeated hospitalizations. By then even I could not deny his illness.

Often he took me with him to the Shwedagon Pagoda, where visitors pay respect at one of the special pillars designated for those born on specific days of the week. At the entrance he bought strings of delicate jasmine blossoms or sprays of glistening eugenia leaves from small vendors for me to place beside the lion-topped pillar for the Tuesday-born. He could no longer kneel beside me to pay respect but remained seated on a step nearby. At home if I was lazy when he asked me to massage his legs, he warned me jokingly not to act in a way I would regret when he was gone. He always had a quick sense of humor so I took those as lighthearted remarks. I didn't realize how quickly his health was failing.

My father passed away at age forty-nine in October 1965. For several years he had suffered from lung cancer and received treatment at the Defense Hospital reserved for the military elite. As a last resort he agreed to an operation performed by the top surgeon at Rangoon General Hospital, but two days later he was gone. I had lost him twice before when he was jailed, but those separations had been temporary. The finality of his absence seemed beyond my grasp. That night I tried to pour out my admiration and love in a poem but couldn't resolve my thoughts, and my verse still has no ending.

> when someone
> calls their father's
> name I long
> to honor
> mine
> but always
> my tongue
> is tied

At Pe Pe's funeral many former BIA officers, political comrades, and business associates came to pay their respects. Some bowed their heads as they passed the casket while others raised their hands in a military salute and one read a long eulogy. Meanwhile intelligence officers stood outside in their dark glasses, scrutinizing the mourners. That outpouring of recognition gave me a new sense of my father's stature, but what kept returning to my thoughts was a Burmese saying, "In the branches of a strong tree, many birds will perch."

With Pe Pe gone, my mother couldn't continue living on York Road where she constantly saw his footprints, so we moved when I was in eighth grade to my grandmother's house on the main street in Tamwe township, a twenty-minute drive from downtown Rangoon. Worried about how to support her eight children, May May relied on a policy offering favor to families of those who had served the country. She had no idea how to run a business but decided to open a shop and after much effort was allocated a large two-room storefront in the heart of the city. Special favor from the Trade Ministry allowed her to buy imported paper and sell it for a profit and also to purchase biscuits produced by a state-run factory at the official price but sell them at the street price.

A year passed as I tried to absorb my father's loss, and at the end of ninth grade I prepared for six days of standardized government tests in Burmese, English, physics, chemistry, and math that would determine my future. Over those months, my teachers had increasingly lost incentive, with school salaries reduced, students no longer motivated, and frustrations multiplying. Instruction grew so lax that my English teacher whiled away class time chatting about her husband or her search for a suitable daughter-in-law. Some girls smiled at her anecdotes, but others of us didn't appreciate the banter. We knew we were falling behind and were ill-prepared for the exams in late March that would decide who had a chance at university placement.

While I waited for the exam results, May May decided I should visit Sandoway after the annual Water Festival to keep in touch with my father's family. On the eve of the Theravada Buddhist New Year, Burmese delight in pouring water on each other to indicate the cleansing of dirt from the past and the welcoming of a fresh new year. That tradition dates from the twelfth century, when people sprinkled each other with sprigs of eugenia leaves dipped in a silver bowl filled with water. Later, people poured water from buckets or sprayed each other with hoses, and children loved to squirt their friends with water pistols. Like every Burmese child, I waited eagerly for those festivities when I was young, but in 1967 I had no wish to take part. Men used the dancing and singing as a chance to make rude jokes, and while many of my friends enjoyed the lively atmosphere and the time for merrymaking and flirtation, I found the crude jesting offensive. I looked ahead to my visit to Sandoway.

The relative I knew best was Pe Pe's brother Oo Lay Kyaw, our favorite uncle, who visited us often while attending the Institute of Education in Rangoon. Knowing that he was friendly and never impatient with our childish mischief, we sometimes hid his bottle of liquor and asked for a ransom, including once when Pe Pe's BIA commander Bo Let Ya visited. My youngest brother would always reveal our hiding place, but our uncle never scolded us. Still, I didn't know what to expect from the rest of my father's family far from the capital city. My first impression was relief that they did not keep a shrine to the *nat* spirits in their home.

Burmese are deeply influenced by the belief in *nats*, but my father had no patience for such practices. At home we followed only the Buddha's teaching, based on the gentle concept of *metta* that embraces kindness, compassion, and forgiveness. My grandmother believed strongly in the power of those capricious and sometimes aggressive spirits, and she said it was because we didn't have a coconut hanging in our house as a shrine to the *nat* spirits that we encountered so many troubles.

In first grade we learned the legend from which Burma's traditional spirit worship is derived. An ambitious king in the year 1044, worried that a blacksmith known for his strength and handsome features would overthrow him, married the blacksmith's sister. Jealous and cruel, the king lured the blacksmith to his palace with the offer of an honorable title, only to throw him into the fire. To his horror, his wife jumped into the flames alongside her brother and both perished, but their spirits lived on in a tree. Because of their hatred for the king, the two spirits killed anyone who came near, so the king cut down the tree and threw it into a river. The trunk floated down to the region of another king, who built a shrine for the brother and sister, and from then on people believed that the two spirits could give many forms of assistance. As a child I hated that cruel king and felt great pity for the ill-fated brother and sister.

Folk superstition in Burma entwines with Buddhist belief, and people say that while Buddhism takes care of the future life, *nat* spirits can help with problems on earth. Thought to live in rivers and trees, villages and cities, kitchens and doorways, celestial *nat* spirits guard and protect, but other *nat* spirits punish if angered. Care must be taken not to displease them, and Burmese often hang a coconut tied with a red band in their homes to commemorate the brother and sister *nat* spirits, splashing it frequently with water and ground *thanakha* bark and drawing a curtain across it after dark so that no light, suggesting the fire in which the blacksmith and his sister perished, will touch the coconut. Even U Nu, a devout Buddhist, was said to offer food to the *nats*, but my aunts in Sandoway seemed to live peacefully without placating those unpredictable spirits.

My grandparents and two aunts, one unmarried and one widowed, lived in a large two-story house on the main street of Kyeindali, a coastal village just south of Sandoway where they sold betel nuts and pursued other business interests. Behind their house was a betel nut orchard so large I couldn't walk to the far end, and I wandered happily among the rows of tall green trunks, watching the betel leaves tossing overhead in the wind. My father's sisters, both in their sixties, helped my grandparents run the local grocery store, and the whole family seemed comfortably rich.

My cousins in Sandoway expected a city girl to shrink from rugged play, but I followed them happily to climb trees and swim in the creek. The water was clear but salty, and my cousins said it filled to a muddy torrent in the monsoon season when it rushed down to the sea from the Arakan Mountains. They told stories about a dead elephant floating by and also taught me about coral reefs, seashells, and the hard life of the fishermen. The one pastime I couldn't share was their interest in hunting. When one cousin showed me a string of dead birds hanging from the muzzle of his air rifle, he felt like a successful warrior, but I had pity for the birds and turned my eyes away.

After a week my uncle Oo Lay Kyaw took me on a half-hour flight from Sandoway to Kyauk Phyu Island to visit his wife, the headmistress at a regional teacher training high school. He was headmaster at the high school on a different island and once a month traveled by ferry to see her. I never knew if it was because of their separation, but they had no children. Kyauk Phyu Island was a beautiful place with a busy fishing harbor and the fresh catch available in market stalls near the docks. From there we visited an even smaller village where I watched Muslim fishermen, who lived in houses made of reeds and thatch, drying their nets in a strengthening wind. May was the start of the monsoon season, so the fishermen listened carefully to the weather forecasts and assured us the front would pass by to sweep into Bangladesh. By the time the wind shifted direction that evening, we were already safely back at my aunt's house. Around midnight the storm unleashed its fury.

The vocational school across the road was constructed of cement slabs, but my aunt lived in a timber house built by the British a hundred years earlier, most likely as a residence for the district officer. Listening to its teak beams creak and tremble, I wondered if they could withstand the gale. At the height of the storm, we could barely hear each other speak above the noise of roofs ripping loose and houses collapsing, but around four a.m. calm returned. In the morning, debris littered the town, and I saw wood beams and corrugated metal sheets tangled with thatch and reeds that just hours earlier had sheltered residents in their homes. People said it was the worst storm to hit Kyauk Phyu Island in sixty years. When I returned to Rangoon, I told my family I had met a cyclone.

In early June 1967, finding my name listed among the 20 percent of my class who passed the qualifying exams for university acceptance, I looked ahead excitedly to continuing my education. Hopefully I could pass the next year's exams, determining college placement, but meanwhile more unfamiliar teachers appeared in our classrooms, clearly favoring the transfer students rather than those of us educated at St. Philo's. Our deteriorating facilities showed new signs of neglect, no one bothered to fill the swimming pool, and Teacher Gwen, our Burmese instructor and swimming coach, had been sent away for a training course. Until then I worried about the erosion of academic standards, but I decided to stop caring. Then suddenly the schools closed throughout Rangoon.

The mismanagement Pe Pe criticized at the Trade Ministry had combined with government quotas and unequal distribution policies to create a crisis. Despite lofty pronouncements about land reform, Burma's peasants continued to suffer, forced to sell their paddy to the government at the junta's regulated price. As rice shortages worsened, newspapers and radio broadcasts claimed that profiteers were benefiting from rising prices. With all basic commodities stored in warehouses owned by Chinese merchants, people responded to the government's cues. Racial prejudice stirred, and many blamed local Chinese for hoarding rice to sell at higher profit.

But the spark that ignited popular anger spread from China, where the Cultural Revolution raged. For more than a year, youthful rebels inspired by Chairman Mao Zedong's appeals had attacked "bourgeois revisionists" like Foreign Minister Chen Yi, who were accused of obstructing China's revolutionary path. To assert political fervor and opposition to revisionism, the staff at China's foreign embassies distributed pamphlets and Mao badges, and I liked wearing the shiny red button given me by a classmate who was half Chinese. Soon the Revolutionary Council prohibited the wearing of foreign badges, which prompted angry Sino-Burmese students at the two high schools where instruction until 1965 had been available in Chinese to pull down the Burmese flag. After that, popular anger focused aggressively on local Chinese, and rioting spread.

Rumors of a government order to open all Chinese warehouses and distribute the stockpiled rice led mobs of Burmese and some Indians to attack not just the warehouses but also Chinese shops and homes, then the Chinese embassy. As the unrest continued, we heard in August that more than one hundred Chinese were dead. Mounting casualties justified the junta's declaration of a curfew in Rangoon from seven p.m. until five a.m. So intense was the anger that a group even surrounded our house, shouting that we were Chinese until we showed them our quota book and proved we had Burmese names. After someone broke into our yard and stole our rooster, again assuming we were Chinese, May May worried that her children might be mistaken on the street, and for days allowed only my younger brother, who had the darkest skin, to go out and buy food.

When May May's shop finally reopened after the violence ended, she needed my help after school selling lottery tickets, a recent venture that supplemented her business in bulk paper and cookies. Lottery sales increased around the city when drawings approached every two months, so I sat at the desk beside stacks of unsold brown paper keeping a frown on my face to ward off insulting comments from male lottery ticket buyers. Sometimes they scribbled notes when they handed me their ticket receipts, saying, "I love you" or "When I win the lottery, I want to marry you." I hated having to endure such comments, and my defense was to tear up the receipts, which ensured those offensive men would win nothing.

After another pilgrimage visit to the pagoda at Wayponla with my family in 1967, I thought how insignificant were my lottery shop complaints. We had learned nothing in school about the struggle for independence in Karen State that raged for decades or about the abuse inflicted by BIA troops on the Karen people during World War II. I knew only that they had been fighting for autonomy since before I was born, and while I read newspaper reports about Karen rebel attacks, I had no direct experience of Burma's continuing civil war until that trip.

Bumping along in an oxcart to reach the train station, we passed a village in ruins. Every thatched hut had been burned to the ground, the two-story wooden houses were badly charred, and even the tallest coconut trees were blackened by fire. With no evidence of refugees or survivors, no sign of a relief camp, we assumed the village had been burned deliberately. Our ox cart driver said Karen rebels were responsible, but people did not dare tell the truth so I was not sure. If a village hosted government troops, rebels sometimes burned those houses, but if even one family sheltered a rebel, perhaps a son or brother, the Burmese army torched the whole village. The image of those charred huts never left my memory.

Notification in July 1968 that I had passed the next level of exams and qualified to attend university fulfilled a dream. I was the fourth child of my parents but only the second to have this opportunity, as my second elder brother Ko Lay and my sister both had bad luck on the tests. Everyone who passed the tenth grade exams could fill out forms for university placement, but by then access to higher education was determined by a complicated new system, called the Intelligence Level Aggregate (ILA). New admissions criteria, vague and confusing, had been issued on July 7, 1963, exactly one year after the dynamiting of Rangoon University's student union. In advance of that anniversary, pamphlets had circulated on campuses to commemorate those who died in the blast. The government responded by closing all colleges except for medical and engineering institutes, which meant that in 1963 the academic year lasted only three months.

It took a year for the Education Ministry to abolish the existing system for university placement, but after 1964 students could no longer apply directly to the college of their choice. The new regulations never stated clearly what factors besides examination results contributed to an applicant's aggregate ILA score, so parents spent much time trying to secure university placement for their children. Decisions scattering the most talented students around the country appeared unpredictable and arbitrary, driven not by educational goals but by an effort to prevent campus protests.

My eldest brother Ko Gyi passed the placement exams in 1965 and was assigned to Moulmein College in Mon State, a day's travel from Rangoon. Even though my mother met with a director from the Education Ministry to appeal for a transfer, Ko Gyi had to attend Moulmein College for a year before his request to attend Rangoon University was approved. Three years later, one of my classmates with exceptionally high grades was assigned to a two-year intermediate college in Shan State, but allowed a transfer to Rangoon University if she declared psychology as her major, an academic subject with low status and few job options that was undersubscribed.

After submitting our ILA forms in April 1968, everyone awaiting college placement was expected to find a volunteer job until instruction began in November. In an office of the Port Department where my father had a friend, I was supposed to gain practical experience, but I just wasted time. Grateful to learn I was admitted to Rangoon University, I next pondered the choice of a major in liberal arts or science. For years I had wanted to study Burmese literature and I still dreamed of becoming a poet, but students taking literature, history, and philosophy classes had to memorize texts and provide rote answers. I resigned myself to the sciences. If I could not think freely about literature, I preferred to stick with mathematics. At least logical thinking and step-by-step procedures would result in a theoretical solution.

CHAPTER FOUR

~

Student Affairs

Burma's premier university, considered the most prestigious in Southeast Asia in the 1940s and 1950s, had been steeped in national politics for at least three decades. Founded as Baptist College, it was renamed Judson College in the mid-nineteenth century, after the British scholar who compiled the first Burmese-English dictionary in 1816, and became Rangoon University, a branch of the University of Calcutta, in 1920. After the Revolutionary Council adopted its new plan for higher education, the name changed in 1964 to Rangoon Arts and Sciences University (RASU), an effort to distance the campus from its British heritage. Colonial buildings like Convocation Hall, the University Library, and Judson Church with its square steeple and arched windows stood out among more recent additions, lending an air of academic dignity and tradition.

Beyond Convocation Hall lay the calm expanse of Inya Lake, where generations of students had strolled along the banks or rented rowboats in search of a breeze. My favorite campus landmark was the stately *thit-poke-pin* tree in front of the science building, its gnarled trunk more than a hundred years old. Poets and writers described its elegance in full leaf and the tracery of its bare branches in summer's heat, but I never found words to capture its beauty. My other favorite spot was the grove of tropical *gant gaw* trees surrounding the library, where sunlight rarely filtered through the dense foliage and summer brought a profusion of fragrant white blossoms. Tree-lined Chancellor Road led to a different kind of landmark, a vacant plot on the east side of the campus, the site of the demolished student union.

On Freshman Day in November 1968, more than two thousand new students gathered in Convocation Hall to hear the rector and several leading professors offer words of introduction that launched our privileged four years of university education. Searching for my high school classmates as we filed out, I could not avoid a cordon of older boys waiting to survey the new female students. Some girls smiled at the male attention, but I kept my eyes fixed on the ground, trying to absorb the news that all lectures for first-year students would be held at the Workers' College, a utilitarian evening degree school close to my home but half an hour's drive from the main campus.

The shift in venue for incoming freshmen was clearly another precaution to limit the number of students gathered in one place, even though no one had dared mount a campus protest since 1963. With the student union abolished and the student magazine suspended, there were no outlets for opposition. The only campus organizations permitted were departmental associations guided by professors or clubs for art, music, hiking, and soccer.

My four closest friends at RASU were all missionary school graduates who shared an independent spirit. Irene was an Anglo-Burmese from St. Philo's whose British father worked at the Royal Thai embassy. Rowena's father had been a representative of Steele Brothers, a British shipping firm that exported rice before nationalization, and Joyce had spent a year in England when her father worked at a government bank in the 1950s. My fourth friend, the only male in our group, had graduated from St. John Diocesan, the missionary boys' school my brothers attended. An accomplished musician, he was the vocalist for a band often featured on the government radio station's English talent show, and he could sing Elvis's songs and any lyrics by the Beatles. We called him Po Shoke (*po* means "boy" and *shoke* means "rascal") because he refused an English name, even though he wore bell bottoms and imitated John Lennon's hairstyle. Among our more traditional classmates, we five stood out. Some called us *bo ru*, meaning "crazy for Western style."

The flat roof of the three-story Workers' College offered a view across the city, but except for an occasional courting couple, few students climbed up. One day we four girls discovered how to pass through a window at the top of the stairs and jump down to a narrow ledge to reach the open roof. From one direction, we could see the streets of Rangoon, a vista dominated by the shimmering beauty of the Shwedagon Pagoda surrounded by its dense grove of trees. From another side we looked toward the Rangoon River flowing to its mouth in the Gulf of Martaban, which made me think about my father making speeches in the small town of Dala on the opposite bank in 1938. Beyond Dala stretched paddy fields, with only a five-minute ferry ride across the river dividing the comfortable life of the city from the rural poor.

Lost in thought, I didn't consider how our wandering on the rooftop might look to students below until we noticed a cluster of boys staring up at us. Male college students seized any excuse for noisy outbursts, perhaps because they lived with so many constraints, and that day we drew their attention. A chorus of taunts greeted us when we climbed down from the roof, and the boys shouted names from the film group Tamada Lu Gyan (*lu gyan* means "tough guy"), which produced Burma's popular action films, to mock our adventurous and unladylike behavior. Those stylized movies centered on the exploits of a hero, played by actor Shwe Ba, who stood resolutely by the side of the common people, and since I was the first to climb down, they called me "Shwe Ba."

The founder of Tamada Films as well as its director and producer, Shwe Ba had also directed a historical film that showed General Aung San and his comrades convening the first AFPFL National Congress at the Shwedagon Pagoda in January 1946. My father took us children to watch that documentary, and when we saw him giving a speech on the screen, we called out, "Pe Pe, Pe Pe." Everyone in the cinema heard us, and afterward several people greeted him. We felt proud, but I wished I could have heard what Pe Pe said on that historic occasion.

University students could no longer look ahead to interesting or challenging work after graduation, and most had to rely on civil service jobs after the private sector disappeared. Regardless of effort or ability, everyone took the same exam administered by the Selection Board for Public Services to qualify for a government post. The exam tested general knowledge, politics, and English, but a passing grade did not guarantee employment. Only a "socialist friend" assured success, and usually a good contact meant you could find a job even if you failed the written test.

I gave little thought to the future but kept busy with required math courses and also attended liberal arts lectures with my friends. In one history class we learned about Burma's warrior kings who engaged in constant fighting and killing to gain power and territory. I could never have succeeded as a history major, as we were expected to take pride in this record of plunder and conquest. I also began to frequent the university library. Never had I seen so many books in one place, and I started borrowing simplified novels in English, starting with *The Adventures of Tom Sawyer*. To my surprise, I could read the first line easily and then, because I knew the story, move ahead steadily page by page. Few students shared my passion for reading, and some never entered the library. Burma's educational system, once among the best in Asia, had deteriorated so seriously that some college students could not even use an English dictionary.

My friends and I sometimes skipped classes to spend time at Po Shoke's house and listen to his newest albums. Usually his parents were not at home, as his mother was a high school teacher and his father an executive engineer in the Myanmar Oil Corporation, called the Burmah Oil Company before it was nationalized in 1963. I knew that workers from those oil fields had joined a nationwide boycott in 1938 after British company authorities fired a labor leader, Thakin Khin. Aung San and other Rangoon University student leaders had traveled around the country making speeches, raising funds and mobilizing workers to march to Rangoon, where my father was one of the strike's main organizers. In 1964, the year before he died, Ne Win invited Pe Pe with other oil field protesters and *thakins* to a May Day ceremony in Chauk, one of the richest oil fields in central Burma, to acknowledge their contribution.

The oil company provided Po Shoke's family with a brick cottage in Rangoon, formerly the residence of a British company official. Only once did I meet his father, a tall man in Western dress and a Baptist, but their house became our haven. Most of the furnishings were foreign, and we thought the four bedrooms and large living room luxurious. Unlike our kitchens with their kerosene burners, Po Shoke's had an electric stove with an oven, considered very special after the junta blocked foreign imports in 1963.

Away from the supervision of our elders, we felt free and relaxed, but I sensed something wrong when I noticed Po Shoke's ashtray. Drugs were a problem for Burmese youth, and unlike other students, he smoked cigarettes without a filter. I could see that almost the entire paper was burnt to ash. Po Shoke said he had used marijuana first, available from roadside vendors, but then wanted something more adventurous, confident that his strong spirit could resist addiction. I watched him deftly remove a cigarette filter, pull out the tobacco, blend it with white powder, and roll the mixture in a fresh paper. He licked his thumb and index finger to seal the side, then caressed the cigarette with his lips like a gambler kissing cards. We knew we couldn't stop our friend, but we made frequent appeals. He listened and sometimes he cried. Drug addicts were often polite, gentle, and emotional, making easy promises they would never keep.

Rangoon's heroin came from the poppy fields in the northeast that supplied a string of refineries in Shan State along the Thai border. Narcotics statutes prohibited planting, possession, trade, or use of the drug, but the laws were flagrantly ignored. Po Shoke never worried about arrest, certain that a bribe could change the results of a urine test. Nor did he care whether the cup, bowl, or bottlecap in which he stirred his heroin was clean. He would watch the candle flame melt the powder until it was ready to inject, then plunge the needle into his vein. Addicts could register to receive treatment, and he consented several times to start the process of recovery, but his condition grew steadily worse. When I told him the needle marks on his arms were a death sentence, he agreed.

Po Shoke's hooded eyes made me sad, but I felt sorry also for his parents who had three children, all talented and all in different ways considered lost. Po Shoke was the youngest. His brother was an artist and the leader of the Little Thunderbirds drama troupe, whose members all were known to be gay. They started performing at the annual Festival of Lights celebration at St. John Diocesan, where students offered a music and dance program on the eve of the November full moon day, after which the families gathered for bowls of *mohinga*. Those school events brought the young performers recognition, and several of them later established reputations as professional actors.

Po Shoke's sister, praised as a "good daughter of socialism" in one issue of the government's *Forward* magazine, was a talented engineer. For a few years after her university graduation she tolerated her assigned work at an electric power plant in Kayah State in the eastern part of the country. Then she quit to go abroad for good, lost to her family and an early example of Burma's brain drain. During my high school years we became familiar with the often-used term "for good," and in 1968 one of my aunts left with her family forever. Gradually my acquaintances began leaving, and some of the most talented doctors, nurses, and engineers found employment abroad until passports stopped being issued in 1975. Often the émigrés knew nothing about America or other Western countries when they filled out their visa applications. They just wanted to leave Burma behind. Sometimes I joked that in the future only soldiers and ex-soldiers, monks and ex-monks, prostitutes, drug addicts, and police would be left inside the country.

In 1969 the Burmese government hosted the Southeast Asian Peninsular Games in Rangoon, and publicity built excitement among university students. Visiting athletes were housed in dormitories at a new RASU compound, called the Thamaing campus, on the far side of Inya Lake where a computer center was under construction. Some of the most attractive women students were selected to carry opening-day banners and present medals at the final awards ceremony, and everyone wanted to attend the international sporting events. What became known as the Peninsular Games affair started when students learned that tickets for the boxing match were available only on the black market. They shouted their objections at the Thamaing compound, and a crowd formed.

When baton-wielding police arrived, students ran to the nearest dormitory, but police barged inside to beat and arrest many young people, including several of my friends. As in 1962 and 1963, the government blamed the protests on the Communists. One of my arrested friends later told me that he had covered his face with a scarf when he joined the demonstration but still a classmate reported him, and he spent three years in jail. He also said the boxing tickets had served as a trigger for growing frustration and dissatisfaction with the government. The student who identified my friend to the police had strong ambition but came from a poor family, which perhaps explained his willingness to provide information. Government incentives and rewards were difficult to turn down.

Students were quick to identify informers, and I was warned to be careful with a classmate named Yan Aung, an avid bodybuilder who arrived before lectures each day in a Japanese Mazda, the car provided to government officers. We sat at the same lab table, and clearly he wanted to befriend me. Once he even called at my house saying he was collecting donations for a classmate, but I had never told him my address and learned that he visited no one else. Another weightlifter, named Myo Chun, also aroused suspicion, but my friends just assumed there were informers in every class, some of them pretending to be students, others actual students who provided information for pay. I could only guess the surveillance was intended as a warning because I often acted independently.

The next year brought another outburst of campus protest. For the celebration of Rangoon University's fiftieth anniversary in December 1970, bamboo booths lined Chancellor Road and a stage was erected on the lawn in front of the Student Affairs Office. The authorities extended the celebration after heavy rains cancelled several of the planned events, which allowed time for a group of students at Moulmein College to leave by train for Rangoon carrying leaflets, ignoring the government's warning not to turn the anniversary into a political event. Our Golden Jubilee ended abruptly when authorities learned about the pamphlets, halted the Moulmein train, and cancelled all remaining events. Aware that discontent was waiting to burst forth, they closed universities around the country for several weeks, trying to extinguish any sparks of protest.

Uninspired by my studies, I started reading articles about the 75 percent of Burma's population who lived in the countryside, praised as the purest embodiment of our cultural heritage. That made me regret spending my entire life in the city. Attending a missionary school and mixing mostly with middle or upper class families, I had only caught glimpses of the world beyond Rangoon during pilgrimage trips to Mon State. Most of my information came from books. When the student volunteer literacy campaign, then in its third year, was announced in 1971, I decided to sign up. I explained first to my grandmother, then to May May, my wish to help my people while gaining experience of village life. When my mother gave permission, I wondered if she ever regretted having no chance for independence as a young woman. She saw me off at the railway station and offered me pocket money, never telling me she had sold another gold bracelet.

In April I left eagerly with other students heading up-country in a special train reserved for volunteers. At night the noise of the rails mingled with our singing, and at every large station townspeople greeted us with welcoming dances accompanied by traditional instruments. Later I learned that township authorities collected cash from local residents to pay for our entertainment, but at the time I felt moved by what seemed genuine appreciation. Only seven cars continued beyond Mandalay, and I got off at Chaung Oo wstation in Central Burma, almost the last stop. Away from the watchful eyes of my family at age twenty, I felt useful and free.

Central Burma unfolds a landscape of dry plains, powerful rivers, ancient cities, and mountainsides dotted with pagodas. The powerful Irrawaddy River carves a path through this region from its source in the Himalayas to the broad rice-growing delta where it flows into the Andaman Sea, nourishing the country's agricultural economy and providing a vital transportation route that links the historic capitals of Mandalay, Amarapura, and Bagan. First we visited the bustling commercial center of Monywa, a large town in Sagaing District on the Chindwin River, where we watched merchants engaged in a lively but illegal trade exchanging Indian and Burmese goods. Six miles away in the village of Khin Mon, I joined twelve other volunteers to begin a two-month literacy assignment among its eight hundred households.

A primary school, a small post office, and several privately owned cottage industries, like an oil press and cotton mill, announced Khin Mon's relative prosperity. But what interested me most that first day was the abandoned temple with faded wall paintings in the middle of the village and also the local legend explaining its name. An ancient king touring the area noticed a beautiful young girl called Khin Mon, we were told, and immediately took her as his wife. The villagers seemed proud of the story, but I felt pity for Khin Mon and wondered how many other wives the king had claimed.

CHAPTER FIVE

~

Lessons in Literacy

Land reform programs in Burma in the 1960s set forth the goal of collectivized agriculture, but traditional landholding patterns proved resistant to change. Tenant farmers still tilled the soil, and the largest landlords retained private ownership of substantial holdings. In Khin Mon the landlords and successful merchants, the richest residents, lived in two-story brick homes or hardwood houses rising on stilts beside the creek with cement cisterns to store rainwater for drinking. Other villagers lived in simple thatched huts vulnerable to seasonal flooding and carried drinking water from a lake, boiling it to make the green tea that accompanied their staple diet of beans, lentils, and coarse rice.

The male literacy volunteers in our group lived in the centrally located house of a village elder, but we women were assigned to two houses in a compound owned by an extended family on the western edge of the village. We didn't know that our hosts were all village council members with comparatively higher living standards who were required to accept us. Before our arrival, the village council arranged where we would be fed each day, and designated families guided us to their homes, offering the best food available, sometimes even a fish curry. Always they apologized for the inferior meals, and I felt sorry that elderly village women had to spend many hours cooking for us. I also couldn't help noticing that the rice was crude, the curries oily, the vegetables overcooked, not knowing that someone had traveled to Monywa by bus or bicycle to purchase those expensive foods. Later, when I reconsidered my experiences in the literacy campaign, I would have liked to apologize to the Khin Mon villagers who provided us with two meals every day.

Instructed to make friends with the local people, we visited villagers in the fields where they worked long hours pulling peanut plants from the soft earth and uncovering handfuls of nuts clustered among the roots. Thinking we could solve their problems, they asked us to bring electricity to their village and a regular supply of water. We could only meet our literacy classes at night, thinking we were making an important contribution.

According to a notice board in the village, more than 30 percent of Khin Mon's residents were classified as illiterate, and with literacy classes mandated by state policy, everyone designated as illiterate had to attend. Many of the adult men had learned to read and write as children at the local monastery, so perhaps 75 percent in my group were women. In a makeshift classroom beneath the raised house of a village administrator, a clerk in the Agriculture Department, my students gathered by the dim light of a storm lamp to sit on the ground on woven mats. I stood beside a small blackboard with a box of chalk and a duster. The Education Department had distributed copies of the Adult Learners' Textbook during our two-day preparation course in Rangoon, and we used a teaching method that started from the easiest letter, *wa*, shaped like an "o," the basis of the Burmese alphabet.

Those weeks of university holiday passed quickly, but before we returned to Rangoon, the township authority arranged a two-day study tour for literacy volunteers. We visited famous pagodas and the Sagaing Nationalities Development School on the bank of the Irrawaddy River where ethnic students prepared for future assignment as teachers and cadres in their native villages. More memorable was our trip to Twintaung Lake high in the mountains, surrounded by coconut and betel trees. The green algae-covered water gave off a strong odor, but another volunteer and I climbed into one of the small boats along the bank made from hollowed-out coconut palm trunks to explore this strange natural setting. At the end of our journey, weighted down with gifts of food and local products, I felt grateful to have accomplished something useful for my country.

A month later in June 1971, missing the village and the local people, I volunteered for a return assignment in Khin Mon. The goal of that second trip was to set up a village library, and I collected many books from friends and relatives. Irene accompanied me, along with a group of eight female students from Mandalay University. By then it was monsoon season, and the Chindwin River had flooded Khin Mon's sandy creekbed. We found parts of the village covered in muddy water a foot or two deep along the banks and perhaps ten feet deep in the channel. Reaching the village seemed an adventure, and I thought little about the local people's hardships when two village girls came to take us by boat to their house for lunch. I was in high spirits and shifted my weight to make us capsize in the middle of the village where the water was shallow and brown with silt. They laughed awkwardly to see our delight in getting wet.

Another time I asked a boat owner to row us outside the village where the water was deep and clear. Irene and I swam happily until we noticed the village girls' faces turning pale with worry and disapproval. I hadn't known they never swam and regretted my impulsiveness. Village council members registered a complaint about my frivolous behavior when the Literacy Campaign Committee next visited Khin Mon.

Those three months in the village sharpened my understanding of local conditions, and I saw that poorer families owned no land, no livestock, not even a plow. If a family managed to rent a small plot of land for cultivation, the parents worked in the fields or herded the landowner's cows while an older child took care of household chores and looked after younger siblings. Some parents sent kids as young as seven or eight to a local landlord, exchanging their children's labor for rice or money. Village youngsters worked hard. They also seemed intensely curious why I had no husband, since they often married at fifteen.

Irene felt happy and satisfied with our library project, but I wondered how much chance it had of success. Contraception was unknown, and rural women bore one child after another, assuring that even the richer families rarely had the chance to send their children beyond primary school. Daily labor in the fields left no time for reading, and I doubted whether the books we delivered to the small post office would find many borrowers, or whether university volunteers could hope to change the economic needs dictating the patterns of village life.

Despite my doubts, I joined the staff of the literacy campaign's magazine, *The Echo*, when I returned to campus, helping to promote volunteer work in the villages as a national duty. Still admiring socialist goals, I wrote an article with a strong socialist tone about my experience of village life, pleased to see my words in print for the first time. When I sent multiple copies of the magazine to Khin Mon, my enthusiasm drew the attention of the literacy program's organizer, a lecturer from the Pali department who asked me to participate in the campaign's 1971 awards ceremony as RASU's representative. He mentioned that I should be sure to wear Burmese dress on the occasion, so I arrived at Convocation Hall in a yellow blouse and a gray *longyi* with yellow roses circling the hem. The auditorium was filled with students from different universities, and when the announcer called my name I crossed the stage to receive the certificates and say thank you to the Education Minister. I could hear some students shouting "Shwe Ba" when they applauded.

The campaign's publicity efforts portrayed volunteer activities in such appealing terms that many students wanted to join. The RASU Literacy Volunteers' Organization Committee had many tasks, like making posters, providing forms, distributing notices and pamphlets. My classmate Aung Myint, an executive member of the campaign committee and a member of both the Lanzin Youth Organization Committee and the BSPP, soon asked me to join. As a committee member, I contributed regularly to *The Echo* and also to a weekly pamphlet that printed several of my early poems. When my classes ended for the day, I gathered with others to work in the campaign office, and often we sat talking in the canteen teashop until late afternoon. Our friendships grew strong, but the teashop had always been an exclusively male setting, so I received a friendly warning that my presence was not welcome. My reply that I drank tea at home and would also drink tea at school seemed to break the barrier, and soon other girls began to join.

In 1972, the literacy committee extended its program to include townships in Shan State and the Delta region. Most students wanted the chance to travel far from home, but my father's experience made me interested in rural life close to the capital. Nat Sin Gon on the Dala-Kungyangon Road was the campaign's base village in the Delta area, and I could make the round trip home by jeep and ferry in a single day. For two months, another student and I lived in the two-story wooden house of a classmate from RASU whose family owned paddy fields and a herd of gaunt white cows. Her elder sister managed the household for their widowed mother, but with a ten-year-old daughter and no husband, I could see that this young village woman faced many difficulties.

Street lamps lined Nat Sin Gon's main road, but the village had no other electricity. To the east stretched an expanse of paddy land, and behind my friend's house stood a bamboo grove. The famous Twantay Forest, a densely wooded area that served in the 1940s as headquarters for one of the insurgent groups, had once surrounded Nat Sin Gon, but people relied on firewood for cooking, and the local brick factory consumed quantities of wood. What had once been a forest was now only a stand of bamboo. As in other parts of the country, years of slash and burn agriculture destroyed most of the trees.

My main task was to help with women's affairs, which often meant listening to complaints from other volunteers about our living conditions. I also taught literacy classes every evening to as many as six students, writing my careful script on the blackboard under a dim kerosene lamp. But I could tell the villagers assigned to the class were not serious about their study. Tired after a day of field labor, they wanted to rest and knew that improving their ability to read and write would not change their lives. Uncomfortable in my role, I sensed more strongly the pointlessness of the literacy campaign. From the far side of the village at night, the brilliantly lit dome of the Shwedagon Pagoda glowed in the distance and I knew we lived in different worlds.

Most volunteers went home to enjoy the Water Festival celebrations, but I stayed as a campaign representative to take part in the local festivities. On the final day I watched a traditional procession led by a music troupe with a flute, two small drums, a cymbal, and a bamboo clapper. A dancer with provocative gestures drew teasing laughter, and several young women carried water pots on their heads to the monastery. I followed them to share in the tradition of shampooing the hair of the village elders, using a natural shampoo made from the dried bark of the yew tree mixed with boiled acacia soap. At a neighboring pagoda I also helped wash the Buddha statue and collect donations for the local monks.

After that volunteer assignment I wrote for *The Echo* about the difficult life in Nat Sin Gon. I described the gap between city and country and urged that the villagers' lives be improved, no longer sentimentalizing rural conditions. Quoting lines from poet Tin Moe, who edited our publication, I contrasted the darkness of the village, with its "Pitiful lanterns/Lights yellow and dim," to the shining Shwedagon across the paddy fields. To my surprise, some local people complained when they read my article. Proud of their village's relative prosperity, they felt insulted by my article. I had never considered that such heartfelt words could give offense, but their criticism reminded me how acceptance and resignation infuse Burmese culture. People humbly accept their circumstances as satisfactory regardless of any hardship, just as prison inmates squat and shout "everything is fine" when their names are read out in roll call.

The literacy campaign took me next to the ancient capital of Amarapura, eight miles from Mandalay and about four hundred miles north of Rangoon. As a campaign committee member, I joined a tour of several villages newly selected to receive university students. Again we traveled on a special train with two coaches reserved for a hundred volunteers. Setting off on another assignment renewed my optimism and also my spirit of adventure. Watching the child hawkers who crossed between cars peddling boiled eggs, snacks, drinks, and books, I decided to learn their technique. Checking to be sure there was no tunnel ahead, I stepped outside the carriage, grasped the car's iron handle, released my right hand and leg at the same time, and reached for the next car's handle. Once my right side was secure, I released my left hand and leg to move safely across the coupling. Other students watched me through the windows, and some shouted "Shwe Ba."

It was monsoon season in Amarapura, where we stayed at a BSPP cadre's residence. At a ceremony to mark the township's achievement of literacy, our supervisors from the university sat on the stage with the local officials, whose faces seemed uneasy. Because of our arrival, the township had hastily arranged literacy classes to provide work for the volunteers, but few people joined. We visited several homes and urged the adults to attend, but our encouragement had little effect. The government had already declared the township literate, they said. Having no useful function, we were sent off to swim in Taungthaman Lake, which swelled with water during the monsoons but became a fertile field in the dry season. Then we toured the ancient city and several nearby villages.

It was my first visit to Amarapura, known for its pagodas and monasteries, its skillful bronze casting, and its silk weavers who produce ceremonial *longyis* with intricate designs from the multicolored threads of a hundred shuttles. There Pe Pe had been arrested and tortured by the Japanese, so several of his comrades came to meet me. I also toured local industries, including a thatched shed that produced pasteurized milk, since imported condensed milk was no longer available. Battalions of flies swarmed over the milk that sat in large open pans on several woodburning stoves.

Observing the local conditions, meeting Pe Pe's friends, swimming, seeing the ancient capital, I tried to enjoy that trip. Back on campus, I struggled again to set my doubts aside, but despite my commitment to the program's goals, I could no longer avoid recognizing that the literacy program was essentially a propaganda campaign. I knew that Burma's rural education system did not improve through our efforts and that idealistic university students hoping to make a difference were simply deceived. We were being sent around the country primarily to create favorable publicity for the government.

During my last year at RASU, the junta's publicity efforts no longer focused on literacy but on the referendum announced for December 1973 that would approve at last the draft version of a new constitution. We had studied little about Burma's previous constitution, adopted in September 1947 and suspended after the military coup in 1962, and knew nothing about its ideals of social justice or its provisions for a legislature and a Supreme Court, but we were nevertheless expected to approve its replacement. This new constitution had been promised for more than a decade, but the BSPP had allowed years to pass while it consolidated its control. By 1973, more than half of its members and every high government officer came from the army, so the referendum's actual purpose was to secure popular endorsement for military rule.

BSPP officials summoned one member from every household to compulsory meetings, usually at the local primary school or the village monastery, and receive information. One of my younger brothers attended from our family, and all university students had to take part in similar briefings. We math majors gathered one morning in a large lecture hall to listen to an official presentation about the proposed constitution with its goal of a socialist society. The meeting unfolded like a concert. One person read out a portion of the draft constitution, then another person stood up to support it, and finally someone else offered support for the first supporter. That was called "double support." We listened to tedious explanations that repeated the word "socialism" with numbing frequency. Not only was socialism the goal of the state, requiring that all means of production be nationalized, but all power belonged to the BSPP, which would advise and instruct every level of government. Basic rights were said to be guaranteed to all citizens regardless of race, religion, status, or gender, even as Burma officially became a one-party state.

We were used to such orchestrated events. On public holidays like Peasants' Day on March 2, the date the Revolutionary Council took power, or May Day, commemorating workers on May 1, people were assigned to various assembly points, then marched more than an hour to reach the former racecourse, headquarters of the Lanzin Youth Organization, which held ten thousand people. Everyone knew General Ne Win, who was fond of horse racing, had shut down the track in 1963 to eliminate gambling. After that it was used for mass gatherings.

Sometimes I saw the holiday parades passing on our street with people shouting slogans, "Unity for nationalities' affairs" or "Burma Socialist Program Party—victory, victory." The ward leader required that at least one person from each household take part, and my younger brother, still in high school, represented us, believing the mass rallies a way to serve the country. For several years he marched in every procession until at one event he saw the parade organizer turn around before reaching the racecourse and head home. After that we hired a volunteer to fill up our quota. Money circulated around the city in many ways.

During my final semester at university, the Revolutionary Council announced it would enlist students to conduct a rural economic survey and assist the government with long-term economic planning. Literacy campaign committee members were asked to coordinate the survey project, and with perhaps a thousand other students, I attended two days of training. Unlike previous volunteer campaigns, this one started with an awards ceremony at the former racetrack. I was chosen by lot from several nominees to make a speech on behalf of the women students participating, my first time to appear in front of such a large audience.

The patriotic façade of such gatherings provided an opportunity for applause with ironic intent. Students often used large meetings to express indirectly their disapproval of the Education Ministry's authority, the continuing restrictions on education, or the socialist system in general. In fact, many students joined volunteer activities only to help their chance for a government job, so I hardly expected the assembly to be respectful. When the first official stepped onto the stage, students burst into laughter. Raucous comments continued during the speech by the Education Minister, who was my friend Daphne's relative. More applause mixed with loud shouting came when I was announced as the second speaker. The jeering continued as I launched into my prepared text about how the economic survey would guide plans for development, how students would learn about rural life, and how on their behalf I wanted to say we would do our best. Taking a risk, I fell silent, stared out at the crowd, then pounded my fist. My gesture might well have been ridiculed, but instead the noise stopped. Afterward the Education Minister smiled and said I certainly knew how to control my friends.

A few days later, the thousand volunteers left by special train for Upper Burma. To conduct the economic survey, we spread out to different parts of the country, even the most remote villages. With three classmates, also math majors, I was assigned to the large village of Wae Laung in Myingyan district, Thaung Tha township, about four hundred miles northwest of Rangoon in Burma's dry zone. Little rain fell even in the monsoon season, and each morning when we woke up early and rode by oxcart to even smaller villages, we stirred up a trail of red dust from the parched earth. Village authorities had ordered farmers to stay home for the survey, and our task was to record each family member's age, educational level, and occupation.

Most didn't know their exact birthdays, so one would say he was born in the year when the crops were ruined by insects, and another would say she was born in the year when the pagoda fair ended because of a fire. Rarely had their education continued beyond second or third grade, and perhaps 20 percent could not read or write at all, but the township had still been declared literate. They were all landlords, tenant farmers, or paddy field laborers, so we also asked their income, the size of their plots, what crops they raised, what agricultural tools they owned, and their average yield. In one village I met a landlord who had saved enough money to send his son to university where he became a math professor, but such achievements were rare. Another village was just a cluster of four or five huts with dirt floors and palm frond roofs surrounded by toddy palm trees. The occupants were all climbers who tapped the palm sap and refined it for jaggery, used commonly as a sweetener and substitute for sugar.

Our host was a member of the peasants' organization, and the oxcart that picked us up every morning also carried washing water to fill up his glazed earthen cistern. The day's supply was never enough for us to wash our clothing, so I tried fetching my own water. Village wells are deep, and the local people use light buckets made of bamboo or cane coated with resin from a lacquer tree. On the way to the rim, my bucket invariably tipped. When I finally managed to grab it, at least half the water would have spilled. Since the well water was alkaline, village girls walked every evening to a stream nearby to collect drinking water. I watched them dig a hole in the sand, then patiently catch the water in a coconut-shell cup attached to a bamboo handle. Filling a bucket took almost an hour, and they spent much time collecting firewood.

Using the survey techniques taught at our two-day training session in Rangoon, we filled out a twenty-page booklet for every household. If a village had one hundred households, we had to leave one hundred completed booklets with the village council. But the local people were reticent, perhaps fearing our information would bring higher taxes, so gathering information was difficult. Hoping to reassure them with a friendly tone and joking words, I practiced the local words for agricultural tools and measurements, trying to make clear that we were not government workers but students. Genuinely interested in people's living conditions, I asked about their daily food, sometimes even looking into their pots to see what they were cooking. My curiosity made some women uneasy, but usually they didn't mind explaining how they mixed broken rice with beans and maize for their staple food.

Over six weeks I gathered information about the income, education, living standard, and property of many families, most of them landless farmers who took loans and repaid the interest after the harvest. But while I collected what data I could, there was no way to verify their accuracy, and it seemed the government should hardly rely on such amateur efforts to plan the country's economic development. On our final day in Wae Laung, we four volunteers returned from the last village survey in somber spirits. Lost in thought, no one spoke. Only the rhythmic creak of the cart wheels and the oxen's hooves broke the silence. Darkness obscured the peanut fields, and stars dotted the night sky.

Knowing that classes had already ended for the term and that my university years were behind me, I had no idea how to face the responsibilities and uncertainties that lay ahead. When I contributed a final poem to the literacy campaign publication, I no longer praised the importance of serving the people but tried instead to capture the starkness of rural hardship.

> we find
> coarse food
> broken rice with
> millet and beans
>
> they ask
> why do you come
> here we have
> only trouble
>
> we see
> a rutted cart path
> thatched roofs
> filtering moonlight
>
> they tell us
> life is hard

CHAPTER SIX

~

Inside the Bureaucracy

Searching for a suitable job in July 1973 required registering at one of Rangoon's thirty-one township labor offices, where posted vacancies were mostly for day laborers. The office serving my neighborhood, a low wooden building near Royal Lake, offered shade but no relief from the heat as many people like me foolishly gathered inside. A long wait predictably brought disappointment. With no private factories, no independent businesses, and no foreign companies, the main option for university graduates was a government job. If I relied on my resume, I would most likely be posted as a primary school teacher in a village like Khin Mon, but I had no interest in teaching, nor did I like clerical work. My dream was to become a writer.

Delaying for an hour having to face my grandmother's inquiring gaze, I walked home instead of taking the bus. We had moved into her house in Tamwe township, which she bought when her husband retired from his job as an engineer at the government-owned jute mill in the early 1960s, soon after Pe Pe's death in 1965. Proud of my higher education, my grandmother assumed I would quickly find a responsible position, but her silent expectation caused me more discomfort than any of her childhood scoldings. More pressure came from my mother's hope that I could to begin contributing to the large household's expenses.

Some of my friends avoided a government job if their parents had small businesses that were still privately owned. My cousins in Sandoway made a steady income buying goods in Rangoon and carrying them home to sell at higher prices. They also toured nearby villages and offered advance deposits for purchases of rice, peanuts, dried fish, dried chili, and other local commodities, then sold those products from their home. My aunts' families had become the richest in their town, and residents said they couldn't avoid the chain of shops run by the grandchildren of my grandparents. I did not share the entrepreneurial instincts of my father's relatives.

When my trip to the state employment office brought no useful leads, May May decided to use her connections. Similar efforts had succeeded in finding work for my eldest brother Ko Gyi after he graduated from RASU in 1969 with a major in physics. Help from one of my father's friends brought him a job as apprentice press officer at a government printing and publishing company, Sarpay Beikhman, which had a distinguished history. The Burmese Translation Society was established in its headquarters on Theinbyu Road across from the Secretariat in 1947, and the first volume of the *Burmese Encyclopedia* was published there in 1954. But after the press became a state company, the BSPP officer placed in charge had a rank much higher than his ability, and on the regularly scheduled promotion exam, he scored lower than any of his apprentices. A repeat exam brought the same gap in scores, but the administrator alone received a promotion. That led my brother and another apprentice to quit. Ko Gyi began studying for a law degree while his friend joined the family's rice mill in a town seventy miles away.

Connections also helped my second brother find work. My mother continued to urge Ko Lay, at age twenty-four, to take care of his health, not to drink too much, and always to obey the Buddha's teachings. Wanting some measure of independence, he decided to join the merchant service, but May May at first refused to consider his request. The work of a deckhand was a job for those who were tough and uneducated, she insisted. Trying to help my brother, I said I would make the same choice if I were a young man, reminding her that Ko Lay had failed his tenth grade exams, that Burma offered him few choices, and that the merchant service provided many benefits. Sailors were required to send half their salaries home, and anyone who spent three months abroad received a permit to import a used Japanese car. The permit could be sold for cash. At last she agreed.

My brother visited the Sailors' Registry Office every morning to check the long waiting list. Applicants with good contacts jumped ahead in the serial numbers, and Ko Lay would see his number gradually go up to fifty, then drop the next day by twenty points. Once when his number reached above ten only to plunge down again, May May mentioned her son's difficulty to a visitor at our home, the son of the Transportation Minister who knew Pe Pe. With the help of this "socialist friend," Ko Lay was soon selected, and he signed onto a cargo ship headed for Singapore. Leaving Burma was already difficult in 1972, but sailors had only to submit the necessary documents, and a merchant seaman's certificate and passport appeared.

After Ko Lay went to sea, May May was happy to receive large sums of cash from his earnings and said proudly that even if her son wasn't educated, he was successful. He became our steady benefactor, providing a tiny link to the outside world, and we all felt overjoyed when he sent presents home. His first gifts were chocolate bars, T-shirts for the boys, and handkerchiefs for the women. We had last tasted chocolate in 1963, and we puzzled over the possible meaning of "T-shirt." One of my brothers thought the shirt had a T-shape, but someone else thought it was to be worn at tea time. Everything Ko Lay purchased had great value. A simple Sony radio cassette player seemed a treasure, while multivitamin pills were so precious that we reserved them for elders and monks. We knew that Burma's isolation had caused our country to be left far behind the rest of the world.

The only foreign goods available in Rangoon's markets came from Thailand. As Burma's economy declined throughout the 1960s, Thailand prospered by trading in teak, minerals, jade, and rubies and by utilizing cheap raw materials from Burma. According to law, no one could possess or trade illegally imported Thai goods, but regulations were rarely enforced, and the black market was thriving. People purchased imported clothing, electronic goods, and many other basic consumer items from Thailand, and we routinely saw carriers transporting, shops selling, and customers buying.

Domestic products of high quality were also in short supply. Before 1963, an Indian delivery man brought fresh milk to us daily in a metal pot. My mother boiled it in a special pan, just as she reserved other pans for sweet soup, sour soup, and meat, and for frying fish, cooking with green chili peppers, simmering fish paste, and frying chilis mixed with pounded dried shrimp. By 1970 milk delivered in the city was unreliable and sometimes diluted with water, so Rangoonians with money tried to buy scarce cans of condensed milk from Holland on the black market. When Ko Lay sent home both Nescafe and Coffeemate, we felt very fortunate.

Until the Revolutionary Council nationalized the coffee business, a huge coffee plantation produced a high grade of beans in Maymyo, once a beautiful British retreat, named after Colonel H. O. May, where colonial administrators built country houses to escape the Mandalay heat. Even when I was a child, May May preferred to purchase imported Nestle's coffee, but most Burmese drank the local B. T. Brothers brand until the coffee industry declined after 1963. The junta was not interested in coffee and preferred to expand the Defense Services Academy in Maymyo to train its military officers.

When it was my turn to find a job, May May contacted my father's first cousin, who worked for the BSPP as a compiler, researching and assembling data. The cousin contacted a friend of my father's from the Martaban Company who was department head of the BSPP's research section. Years earlier Pe Pe's friend had gone underground to avoid arrest as a leader of the Red Flag faction associated with the CPB, but by 1962 he was no longer in hiding and accepted a high-ranking civil service position that brought housing and security. Perhaps he was persuaded by Ne Win's frequent words that the army couldn't manage the country alone and everyone needed to work together, or perhaps he hoped to change the system from within. But by the time I met him, he was a central committee member of the BSPP.

Surrounded by thick leather-bound books in his apartment, he pushed up his reading glasses and asked whether I was interested in literature. May May replied that I was crazy about books and said I had been educated in a missionary school and had written articles for a university magazine. While they talked, I noticed the department head's modest lifestyle despite his high BSPP post and soon learned that he had seven children, all crowded into that small apartment. His soft voice and gentle manner reassured me, and his eldest daughter said I would meet a daughter of *Thakin* Tin Shwe and other political offspring if I joined the research group.

Pe Pe's cousin immediately filled out the application form on my behalf. My brothers quipped that I was always the first to criticize the BSPP, yet now I would join its staff, and during those days when my life was being planned by others, I hated not just Pe Pe's cousin but my brothers and most of all myself. Only looking at my grandmother's face consoled me. Giving favor to one's parents is a blessed thing, she said.

Submission to the elders remains a powerful obligation in Burmese culture. When one of my father's sisters married her boyfriend against the wishes of her elders, the whole family, except Pe Pe, refused contact with her for many years. Arakanese traditionally favor marriages between cousins, with one brother's son marrying his sister's daughter, and another brother's daughter marrying a different sister's son. Pe Pe believed in the progressive idea of personal choice, but most of his siblings bowed to custom. Three other sisters accepted arranged marriages, and when Oo Lay Kyaw refused to marry a first cousin, my grandmother ordered Pe Pe to come home, exercise his authority, and persuade his youngest brother to honor her request. Instead Pe Pe criticized her old-fashioned ideas and encouraged Oo Lay Kyaw to marry the woman he loved.

By the 1970s those attitudes had started to shift, but deeply rooted traditions take many years to change. Even in my generation, some of the male cousins on my father's side attended vocational college in Rangoon, met girlfriends, fell in love, but still returned home to marry young women chosen by the elders. My female cousins were less compliant, and one declared she would remain a spinster if the elders didn't allow her to marry her boyfriend. But guidance from the elders is difficult to resist, whether about marriage or employment.

As my fate was being decided, I had many misgivings about working for the BSPP. Joining the research office could lead me in a wrong direction, but my life wasn't like a math problem that allowed a simple correction. Years earlier when I read about the government's efforts to improve the lives of ordinary people, my heart would fill with expectation, but my experience in the literacy campaigns had shown me firsthand the conditions in rural Burma. After that, I could never become a BSPP believer. Several friends had started postgraduate courses or enrolled in a training class at RASU's recently completed computer center, but those options were closed to me. As a student I had devoted my effort to volunteer work rather than serious study and deferred thinking about my future, never directing my learning toward a practical goal.

The BSPP Periodicals and Research Departments on Pansodan Road occupied the two upper floors of a colonial-era brick building with flaking yellow paint. That first morning Pe Pe's cousin's wife came down to escort me to her office, where I saw men and women researchers sitting close together, chatting idly. Polite and helpful, she introduced me as her brother's daughter, but the noisy atmosphere reminded me of my high school English class. That evening at home I declared that I couldn't work in such a place where people just wasted time. My mother answered, "Do as you like," and turned away. Her silent treatment always brought my compliance, but I couldn't hold back my tears. My brothers calmed me, saying I could continue looking for another job while I worked as a researcher. With so little opportunity for initiative or accomplishment, they understood that any job brought frustration and compromise.

The next day, assigned to a different research section where the room was quiet, I found five other new apprentices who seemed more interested in reading than talking. Soon I established connections. The research officer third in authority was a friend's elder sister, and I met someone from St. John's Girls' School whom I had known years before. Her father was a high-ranking officer, and while she seemed unhappy at work, she told me it was an easy job and I would have a good chance to read. Meanwhile I made friends with two of the women apprentices, Aye Aye, a physics major from RASU, and May Thi, who graduated from the Institute of Economics.

I also liked one of the male apprentices, Ko Nyo, a relative of Pe Pe's friend who was the department head. Unlike many with high connections, Ko Nyo seemed ambitious but hard working, and he also had a gift for storytelling. I liked to hear his descriptions of life in the countryside, where every morning he pushed his bicycle along narrow embankments in the paddy fields to reach a paved road leading to the nearest high school five miles away. We all knew that he was fortunate. Many students had to travel even longer distances to school on foot.

My first assignment in the BSPP office was to collect data about economic planning. Every morning I read newspapers and marked relevant stories, mostly routine reports of departmental meetings or articles about the BSPP and the Central Committee. The section leader instructed us to take notes on index cards daily, but I could gather a month's clippings in a week, paste them on sheets of paper, write the required notes, and still finish my assignments before the deadline. After that I could read. In the afternoons I attended English lessons with other compilers, taught by a friend of my father using the long-outdated Nesfield English Grammar.

During lunch hours, freed briefly from the office, I strolled with May Thi and Aye Aye along crowded Pansodan Road, sharing lunchbox curries prepared by the elders. Sometimes we watched a magic show or a monkey dance, noticing how the monkey owner treated his pet like a son, asking him to dance or jump or cry, after which the monkey placed a tray on his head and walked around the ring, winking his eye and collecting money. But mostly we searched for whatever new foreign goods appeared in the street stalls. A bright-eyed toy tiger with a head that moved and whiskers that danced tempted me, but I preferred to spend my small earnings on books and cups of strong, sweet black tea.

Tea leaves grow abundantly along the hillsides in Shan State, so when we could no longer buy good coffee, I converted to tea. Lingering over tea and snacks is an important part of social life, a time to read newspapers, exchange information and rumors, or discuss personal and business affairs. In the colonial period, most teashops were run by Indians, but later Chinese and Burmese opened shops. Some customers like strong green tea but I prefer black tea with sugar and condensed milk, adding jaggery when sugar is not available. The salad called *laphet*, made from green tea leaves soaked in peanut oil, mixed with sesame seeds, peanuts, fried chickpeas, dried shrimps, and crisp fried garlic slices, has always been my favorite teashop snack. When green chilis are added along with garlic, tomatoes, lemon juice, and fish sauce, the pickled tea leaf salad becomes an even more savory dish.

Famous for its array of colorful activities, Pansodan Road offered many teashops and many stories. Swallowed up by the midday crowds, I tried to ignore the gay men, beautified with makeup and wearing women's clothing, who sang, danced, and solicited donations. Often they sold preserved citrus fruit pulp, a snack favored by women and children, and some were polite, but many were foul-mouthed and loose-tongued, making feminine gestures with their eyes and shaking their artificial breasts.

Rangoon's gay community was large and diverse in the 1970s. Gays operated most of the beauty parlors, ran tailor shops, or became money lenders. Some were rich, like the son of a prominent family that moved to Rangoon from Mogoke, the area known for high-grade rubies. Some were medical doctors who earned comfortable incomes, while others with few resources became hawkers. Discrimination against gay men reflected the traditional Buddhist belief that males have superior nobility. An effeminate man will be denounced for rejecting the noble gender that is his birthright, and like most straight men my brothers disliked gays.

From them and from the gay beauty parlor owner who cut my hair, I sometimes heard stories about conflicts over handsome men considered desirable lovers. To me it seemed a strange way of life, but a short story I read that year gave me more sympathy. The plot described a married man's difficulty finding a job that could support his wife and children. When he discovered that he could earn a living as a female impersonator, he pretended to be gay. The writer was well known, and the fictional circumstances seemed to reflect his own experience.

A daughter who acts like a tomboy in Burma is treated with more tolerance, since elders assume she will change when she meets an appealing man. It was common in girls' high schools to have a "favorite one," and sometimes a girl wrote a loving letter to a close friend. If the letter was accepted, they acted like boyfriend and girlfriend, caring for each other deeply. Such youthful feelings most often faded, but occasionally women lived together as couples, sharing happiness and sadness. Parents had great difficulty accepting gay children, but the strength of family ties usually overcame the disapproval.

At night, the character of Pansodan Road changed when prostitutes gathered at the railway station overpass. Trishaw drivers knew all the girls, usually teenagers who prowled like stray cats and sold their bodies to anyone offering money. They never received the full amount, as the head prostitute took a commission and also bribed the police. Roadside stalls along the main streets in downtown Rangoon sold condoms, but customers frequently refused to use protection, so sexually transmitted illnesses were widespread.

Burmese culture dictates that women maintain their virginity until their wedding night, but love affairs seemed common in the BSPP office. I often heard about an older married man pursuing a young single woman, as people gossiped and rumors spread. I was never interested in the details, so my coworkers turned their backs when discussing the latest news. But when Ma

Wah, the only woman in my section promoted to research assistant and my close friend, became entangled in an affair, I couldn't hide my concern.

Ma Wah was quiet and earnest, never flirtatious, and she wore loose Burmese-style clothing, but her conservative manner did not deter the approaches of a married man. Worrying how to respond to his overtures, she grew pale and lost weight. May Thi and I tried to protect her, but she rejected our concern. Believing that her circumstances were a reflection of some previous life, Ma Wah placed responsibility on fate. She rebuked me for opposing her choice and said the love affair was her destiny.

For several weeks I exchanged books with a man in my English class, until he started writing me notes. The first one I read, but the rest I returned unopened through a friend. Ignoring my rejection, he sometimes waited at the bus stop until I arrived, and one day he stepped close, grabbing my shoulder bag. Frightened, I asked him not to bother me, but he responded with a string of abuse. "Why do you borrow my books, why do you smile at me everyday, you are just a whore," he shouted. Pulling my bag free, I rushed inside the office. The news spread quickly, and our English teacher U Myint Tun declared that such behavior was an insult to both a father and a daughter, and because I was the daughter of my father, he would always protect me. My habit was to smile at everyone in the office, but my coworker's outburst left me upset, concerned that my friendliness could be misinterpreted.

Later my friendship with Ko Nyo, the apprentice who shared stories about village life, grew closer, and some friends guessed wrongly that we were a couple. Any Burmese woman who keeps company with the same man risks that conclusion, and I had only to walk together once with a man for gossiping office workers to assume we were lovers. Actually I did wonder if Ko Nyo might someday propose to me, but it became clear that he wanted a typical Burmese lady. Years later, when he rose in the bureaucracy, I came to realize the huge disparity in our views.

The approach of the constitutional referendum in December 1973 altered our daily office routine. Film stars and singers had started accompanying BSPP officials around the country to promote support for what was publicized as the first popular vote since 1960, and the BSPP headquarters announced frequent rallies. Staff members had to take part, so on specified mornings all 1,500 of us gathered outside. The leaders carried a large billboard declaring "Referendum 1973," and we marched around the block, then posted the billboard at our headquarters while everyone applauded. Party cadres at those rallies made speeches in pairs, with one person proclaiming how perfect the new constitution was, or how important the referendum was for our socialist country, or how the BSPP brought so many benefits to our lives, and the other person expressing support. Similar gatherings, always publicized in the newspapers, took place in ministries and townships throughout the country.

More than a decade of arbitrary military leadership had left little confidence that the new constitution's guarantees of individual freedom and state responsibility would be realized. What wasn't always clear is that the referendum's objective was simply to affirm the socialist institutions and values ostensibly guiding military governance. Seeing no alternative and just wanting a peaceful life, people obeyed when instructed. Burmese are easy to organize and eager to please, and the attitude of *ah na de*, a fear of offending combined with a desire not to impose, is widespread. Some recognized that others took advantage of their deference, but most Burmese had not yet learned the cost of complying.

A few days before the election, the section leader in my office urged us all to cast an affirmative vote, so I was surprised at the polling place to find duty officers saying we could vote for whichever color we preferred. Then I noticed the curtained voting booths close together, with a white box for votes in favor of the constitution and a black box for votes against. Monitors could easily observe who cast ballots in which booth and identify any negative vote. With only ten households assigned to a polling station, few dared to vote in opposition. Also, neighbors are friendly, and at least one neighbor was always a party cadre. Burmese look after each other, and no one wanted a neighbor to face difficulty.

Since both neighbors in the house beside ours in Tamwe township worked for the government, he as a municipal officer and she as a high school headmistress, voting booths were set up right next door. Assuming the only possible result from the referendum was 100 percent support, no one in my family bothered to cast a ballot until our neighbors called to us at 9:00 p.m. on referendum night, saying the booths would close soon. We obediently cast affirmative votes. Later we heard that residents of an ethnic minority village in Maymyo township who traditionally wore black had cast their votes in the black box because of its color. We also heard that the chief editor of a news magazine in Rangoon had pulled up the curtain and told duty officers to take note that he was voting in opposition. But "no" votes were few, and the referendum's outcome brought no surprise and little criticism.

As expected, the result was announced as 100 percent in favor of the military regime's civilian constitution, and on January 4, 1974, my country officially became the Socialist Republic of the Union of Burma. Even though the BSPP replaced the Revolutionary Council, General Ne Win and the army continued to rule in civilian clothing. With a new constitution adopted, the People's Assembly, called the Hluttaw, convened, but its representatives acted in concert even more conspicuously than those of us in the civil service.

By then my routine inside the BSPP bureaucracy had grown familiar, and I performed my duties in the research office automatically. If a Central Committee member wanted to know about a particular topic, I helped compile the available facts and figures for a report. If a trade delegation planned a study tour abroad to Japan or Singapore, I helped compile information about trade issues in those countries. The only benefit was that the research department maintained its own library with a wide selection of imported books, including the latest edition of the *Encyclopedia Britannica*, and my section leader, a graduate of the Institute of Economics, encouraged us to read.

As the weeks passed, I grew restless and dissatisfied. I thought about finding another job, as my brothers had suggested, and noticed that editors in the BSPP periodicals department, located in the same building, seemed quite busy. Most of its magazines were doctrinaire, like *Party Affairs*, *Economic Affairs*, and *Lanzin News*, but my generation had grown up with propaganda articles, and I knew that it also printed a few books like *Milestones of World History* and *Milestones of Burmese History* that were less steeped in socialist dogma. Also, its popular monthly journal *International Affairs* offered one of the few windows on the outside world after 1962, when contact beyond Burma's borders was cut off and even filtered foreign news was welcome. I considered requesting a transfer but then thought back to my work on *The Echo*. My days of writing socialist scripts had passed, I decided, preferring the routine work of a compiler.

Eager for some connection to Burma's writers, I next wondered if the Press Scrutiny Board on Pansodan Road across from BSPP headquarters might offer an alternative. Since 1963 all periodicals except for BSPP publications had to be submitted for approval from the Press Scrutiny Board, but some officers maintained respectful connections with writers. Perhaps there I could read current books in a less stifling atmosphere, I thought, and decided to meet the woman Pe Pe had hired in 1958 as headmistress of the school behind our house on Ma Kyee Kyee Road. Her husband was one of many former Communists who surrendered his position in the political underground and accepted a government post. As the chief editor of a Burmese newspaper, I thought he might help me, but again I dropped the idea of changing my job. Having to implement the regime's censorship regulations invited even greater unhappiness, I decided, and resigned myself to a research job with its small but steady income.

CHAPTER SEVEN

~

Crackdown and Compromise

The economy deteriorated steadily under twelve years of military-administered socialism, and the many problems facing our increasingly impoverished country could not be disguised. The British had left behind an efficient infrastructure and an educated citizenry, and Burma had fertile land, powerful rivers, and rich supplies of oil, timber, minerals, and precious gems. Yet the centralization of authority, the appropriation of resources, the privileging of military personnel, and the crushing of opposition had consumed both human and natural resources.

Inflation grew so serious that many workers and peasants could no longer meet their families' basic needs. The continuing propaganda about a socialist workers' paradise and the slogans promising "this is the age of our workers" or "peasants' affairs are our affairs" seemed a mockery. Anger at rising prices, combined with increasing hardships and no prospect of change, triggered a workers' demonstration in May 1974.

As the mood of protest spread, striking dockyard workers joined the cause in early June, marching through Rangoon's streets to demand more rice and better pay, joined by railway and textile workers. Government troops responded with force, and one of my maternal uncles who lived in an industrial housing complex close to a textile factory on the Rangoon-Insein Road heard the first shots. He watched from a window as strikers fled, noticing a party cadre in the opposite apartment taking notes. Informers were quick to provide names and details, which brought financial benefit and assisted careers. The first person shot to death was a worker at the Sinmalike dockyard whom I had met. I knew he was the sole support for his widowed mother.

When demonstrators marched in downtown Rangoon, my brothers wanted to observe, but May May insisted they stay inside the lottery shop. Their friend Maung Win, intent on learning what was happening in the streets, refused to heed her warning. He never returned. Official news reported more than twenty people killed and at least sixty injured, all routinely accused of Communist connections, but there were no reliable casualty figures. Eyewitness accounts spread quickly, and unofficial estimates placed the dead at two hundred. In the BSPP research section we shared information in whispers.

After Maung Win disappeared, May May worried that one of her children would be arrested. She could not forget Pe Pe's experiences in jail and wanted to protect us from that suffering. The crackdown was severe, with universities and schools abruptly closed. Maung Win spent a month in detention, but later told us how he had followed the crowd to the Secretariat office, not knowing that troops had already set up roadblocks at major intersections to trap demonstrators and also onlookers. Residents opened their apartments to those who fled, but just as he reached someone's door, soldiers pulled him down the stairway and dragged him away.

The government made more rice available after that workers' uprising, hoping to reduce underground political agitation and prevent further strikes. Its response hardly met the need. One of my university friends, Kyaw Zaw Oo, who was arrested in the 1969 Southeast Asia Peninsula Games affair and was the son of Pe Pe's military commander Kyaw Zaw, visited me in the BSPP office several times. He gave me leftist booklets and asked me to copy them, but what interested me most were the hand-copied poems. Some were just vehicles for political jargon but others captured the hardships facing ordinary workers. One described how people sacrificed their lives for rice and invested their blood, yet when more rice finally came, it was like feeding a handful of sesame seeds to an elephant.

Anger at the economic decline and the harsh crackdown on workers had not yet subsided when we learned on November 25, 1974, that Burma's most famous diplomat had passed away in New York after a battle with cancer. U Thant served as Secretary General of the United Nations from 1961 to 1971, and Burmese people felt great pride in his achievements. Many also knew that the Revolutionary Council had invited him to visit Burma only once, in July 1964, when Ne Win, resentful of U Thant's stature and ties with U Nu, reluctantly hosted a ceremonial dinner. A decade later the regime announced that U Thant's body would be laid out at the racecourse before his funeral, but news spread that no official delegation had greeted his coffin at the airport. People interpreted this as a sign of disrespect.

Always Burmese honor prominent people in death, and May May often told us how she waited in line in 1947 among thousands of mourners at the Jubilee Hall on Shwedagon Pagoda Road to view General Aung San's body when it lay in state. A quarter century later, tens of thousands waited along the same streets to honor U Thant's passing. At the BSPP office, people complained that U Thant would receive only an ordinary burial in Kyan Daw Cemetery, with no acknowledgment of his special stature. On December 5, students from various colleges marched to the racecourse grounds to deliver eulogies beside U Thant's bier.

Both my sister, by then a fourth-year botany student at RASU, and my younger brother, a first-year student majoring in Burmese, joined the huge crowd of mourners, estimated at fifty thousand. At home that evening they talked excitedly about the day's events, describing how a group of monks had seized the coffin and handed U Thant's body over to the students and how they had walked for almost an hour behind the decorated truck that delivered the coffin to the university campus. Along the route, people offered food and water to the marchers, and when the procession reached Convocation Hall, students and monks delivered speeches to loud applause, demanding an appropriate mausoleum. Eager to witness such historic events, I requested a day's leave from the BSPP.

At the side gate to the campus on Chancellor Road the next morning, students in charge of security searched my shoulder bag, and I recognized several men from the BSPP among the crowds, wondering about their purpose. Perhaps they would think I too had been assigned a task if they noticed me, I thought, and let myself be carried along in a human wave toward Convocation Hall. Not wanting to be conspicuous, I found a seat in the balcony. Again the speakers praised U Thant and stressed the country's economic decline, offering thinly veiled criticisms of the current regime. The audience clapped wildly. Meanwhile students outside had started moving bricks and cement from a construction project to expand the library, determined to build a mausoleum for U Thant on the site of the dynamited student union.

One of those giving instructions was my literacy campaign friend Aung Myint, who asked me to distribute packets of donated rice to volunteers working in the student union compound. My younger brother saw me and patted my arm with a smile, and I knew my sister was somewhere in the crowd. On Saturday I returned to the campus immediately after my half-day shift to find that representatives from different universities had overnight set up booths of bamboo and thatch along Chancellor Road. Crowds filled the campus, and I noticed two artist friends drawing posters. I joined another friend from the literacy campaign, May Su, who was helping medical students in an impromptu clinic across from the student union compound. The clinic was so busy I had no chance to listen to the speeches, but others said they celebrated U Thant's goals of freedom, democracy, and peace while directly criticizing the military regime's corruption and the people's economic hardship.

I returned with my sister early on Sunday morning, December 8, to find that students had completed the mausoleum. The situation was so tense that everyone expected troops to be called out after dark, but for two more days protests continued as newspaper editorials attacked the lawless gangs that had appropriated U Thant's body. Early Wednesday morning, police and soldiers raided the campus. Baton charges and tear gas quickly subdued the small groups who resisted, and U Thant's body was removed for reburial near the Shwedagon Pagoda. Hundreds of monks and students, including my two artist friends, were arrested.

In the BSPP office on December 11, I heard that crowds were smashing markets and cinemas, setting fire to buses, even threatening to attack a police station. Martial law was declared that afternoon at 4:00 p.m., the first time since Burma's independence. Demonstrators were identified and rounded up, and I learned that Nyo Maung, a friend from the literacy campaign, had been seized. Like me, he spent those days working in the medical booth, but he was falsely accused of riding in the truck that carried U Thant's body, making a speech, and shouting antigovernment slogans. Because he was a member of the Community People's Council established by the 1974 Constitution, the case against him was difficult to understand, but arrests were often arbitrary or based on inaccurate reports from informers.

I joined other friends to lend encouragement when Nyo Maung stood trial, amazed by his sense of humor. Somehow he managed to joke that his accuser must have had no problem singling out a short, slim, dark man like himself from that huge crowd. The two lawyers defending him, one hired by his family, the other by his friends, asked sharp questions but could not prevent a three-year sentence. His stepmother collapsed when the judge read the decision, but Nyo Maung never lost his spirit and waved farewell to us from behind the bars of a blue prison van.

The combination of political repression and economic hardship inevitably affected people's sense of morality, and the five precepts that form the core of Buddhist teachings seemed more than ever difficult to uphold. The precepts instruct us to abstain from taking a life, from taking anything that has not been given, from adultery, from telling lies, and from drinking liquor or using intoxicating substances. I had always struggled with the first teaching, as ants, mosquitoes, cockroaches, and termites cannot be avoided in Burma's tropical climate. As a child I killed ants by lighting them with a torch or sealing them with drops of hot candle wax and always wondered later if it was retribution when I cut myself accidentally with a kitchen knife. But the junta's violation was killing innocent bystanders. Other precepts were also ignored, as theft happened even within families, adultery was widespread, liquor provided an outlet for frustration and discontent, and lying had become ever more difficult to avoid.

Alcoholic beverages were readily available, and men found many excuses for daily drinking. They drank because they were happy or because they were sad, when they passed an exam or when they failed, because they were successful in love or heartbroken, because they were meeting with friends or lonely, because of a football match or because it was raining. Men who consumed alcohol said there were only four reasons to abstain, because someone had strong religious beliefs, or a health problem, or wanted to curry favor with a relative or official, or just didn't like the taste of alcohol.

Government-run liquor bars in the cities sold strong, cheap white spirits to men young and old who sat on stools at low outside tables and drank until dark. The elders didn't like me even to walk past those bars where the owners lit candles after dark and the customers continued drinking while women sold a variety of cheap snacks. The highest grade distilled liquor was produced by lepers in nearby Htauk Kyang village, but beer was also popular, as the British had established a brewery in Mandalay in 1886. In the countryside, fermented toddy palm juice was available everywhere at a low cost in earthenware pots with a small cup to serve as a scoop. Tapped from the tops of toddy palm trees in the morning as a clear, sweet liquid, the sap changed color by afternoon to become an alcoholic drink that Rangoonians called jungle beer.

More serious intoxication came from drug abuse, which spread through all levels of society, causing suffering for many families. As a child I heard frightening tales about how Burma's early kings prohibited the use of opium and punished offenders by having liquid lead poured down their throats, but under British rule the sale of opium became legal. The United States supported the opium trade in the 1950s to finance Chinese Nationalists who fled across the Burmese border, providing pockets of resistance against the spread of Communism. By the 1960s the drug trade had become the foundation of the economy in the Golden Triangle, the opium-growing region that includes Burma's Shan State and areas of neighboring Thailand and Laos.

As a university student I had learned from Po Shoke how easily heroin could be obtained in Rangoon, and in the 1970s everyone knew someone with a drug problem. My friend Aye Aye in the BSPP office faced constant difficulties because three of her four brothers had a drug habit and, like other addicts, took things from home to sell at any price and satisfy their need. Once they even stole Aye Aye's lunchbox when she forgot to lock it away. Fortunately my own brothers' rebelliousness took milder form.

Long hair had become popular in the mid-1960s, causing conflict between parents and sons, teachers and students. Elders forgot the tendency for young people to be contrary, and my eldest brother also failed to understand the impulses of youth or the desire for novelty. Taking his family responsibility seriously, he shared May May's view that boys with long hair looked like hooligans and ordered my younger brothers to get shorter haircuts. I knew they would wear their hair long for a time, then one day crop it short, but in the meantime they resisted Ko Gyi's authority, saying that not every long-haired boy was a hooligan. After lengthy arguments a truce was reached, and May May agreed my brothers were not ruffians, saying we should all be thankful they had never started using drugs.

Certainly lying had become more difficult to avoid because people disapproved if you told the truth. When you lied once you had to lie again, so both lying and truth telling were difficult. I didn't want to work in a government job or meet with people I didn't like or tell lies when the truth was unwise, but there were few alternatives. We had to do many undesirable things, so I stopped reciting the five precepts, knowing I couldn't observe them.

During those months, poetry provided the only outlet for my sense of helplessness and frustration. At work I often scribbled poems on scraps of paper, then carelessly slid them into books, fearing trouble if I copied them into a notebook. Friends suggested I submit my work to magazines, but I lacked confidence. Many of those early verses were lost, and another year would pass before I risked hand-copying a few poems to distribute to friends.

Not wanting to go directly home after work, I often walked the streets thinking and sometimes composing a poem. One that I wrote in 1974 described my longing for evening, freed from the office for the remainder of the day.

> time at last
> heading home
> rays of sun
> pour liquid gold
> mingling colors
> in clouds

greed anger folly
concerns of the day
mix with pride
and defiance
but float away
as evening wears on

staying someplace
you don't want to be
smiling at people
you don't want to greet
flattering some
you want to deride
avoiding those
you don't want to hate

on such worldly tasks
at last turn your back
it's evening now
bathe in gold
peaceful at heart

Looking for new direction, I tried my hand at translating English articles into Burmese for a respected quarterly journal, *Varieties of Knowledge*.
I relied on a dictionary and sometimes asked for help, but I felt proud to
receive even a small payment for something I wrote. My first published
translation was a twenty-five-line health story taken from *Time* magazine
advising people to eat less meat and more fiber. I gave my fee, forty kyats,
to May May. Next I decided to prepare for the Registered at Law (RL)
exam, following Ko Gyi's path, but no amount of wandering through
bookstalls in the afternoon or studying law after my duty shift or translating articles from English late at night relieved the deadening effect of the
BSPP office.

Sixteen months after I became part of the civil service system, I prepared
for the required compilers' exam that would determine which apprentices
qualified as permanent staff members in the research section. The exam required translation, a general knowledge test, an essay, and an interview. I
made one mistake in the sight translation of a short news story from English
to Burmese, but the department head, who had interviewed me initially, offered encouragement. My translations would improve when I gained more
experience, he said, and so in 1975 I became a full-fledged BSPP compiler

with a regular salary, qualified not just to gather information but also to write research papers.

All newly promoted apprentices had to attend a five-month training course in June at the Workers' College where I had attended lectures as a college student. Among those 120 research assistants, compilers, and Lanzin youth organizers, I studied socialist ideology and memorized jargon about class exploitation and the means of production, a tedious regimen. One requirement was more interesting. As practice for writing research papers, we submitted weekly diaries to the chief trainer, an ex-army officer who instructed us to write down our thoughts about what we encountered in class.

We had not yet settled into that routine when a demonstration broke out on the first anniversary of the June 1974 workers' affair. Hundreds of students joined workers protesting against rising prices and demanded release from jail for those still held after the U Thant affair. Days of protests included a march toward downtown Rangoon, and the inevitable crackdown brought more arrests and another closing of universities. But we BSPP trainees were not considered students and still had to report for instruction every day. After any riot or demonstration, troops were stationed in Rangoon's public buildings as a warning, and our chief trainer announced that soldiers would bivouac on the Workers' College ground floor. Women trainees should not be flirtatious with soldiers, he warned. Insulted by that remark, I recorded a string of complaints in my diary.

Weekly entries, submitted on Saturday, were returned on Monday with the signature of U Myint Tun, my former English instructor, now assigned as deputy trainer. First I wrote that I couldn't understand political science because of its lofty but impractical words. The next week I complained that the chief trainer's dismissal of a pregnant apprentice was wrong, elaborating at length and arguing that she had quit her previous job to take a compiler's position, they had known she was pregnant when they accepted her, excluding her would make her miss this important chance, her child's future was being denied before it was born, her handful of rice was being slapped away when it was close to her mouth, and so on.

The woman duty officer entered red marks in the margins of my diary to indicate her disagreement, and U Myint Tun cautioned me with a Burmese proverb, "Don't rely on fate where the tiger prowls." I replied that I wasn't relying on fate but had an invisible weapon called truth. When the chief trainer summoned me along with Saw Saw, also the daughter of a *thakin*, he accused her of using rude language in her diary but seemed cautious with me, perhaps because I had stated facts, even if I wrote bluntly. His announcement a few days later that the pregnant staff member would be reinstated brought applause from the whole class. After that small achievement I started passing my diary around. Some said I would become a writer.

As a full-fledged staff member I had a higher salary but no greater influence than before. Lower-ranking BSPP staff were simply cogs in the wheel of an inefficient, self-seeking, often resentful bureaucracy. Compilers were ordinary people needing jobs and income, and we had no access to inside information except knowing that the BSPP headquarters building downtown was less important than the compound on Highland Avenue, located in the seventh mile of Prome Road, where high-ranking party officials enjoyed a separate world of seclusion and privilege. Children of Central Committee members described movies shown in a special cinema hall before release to ordinary theaters, and told about a special book that allowed the purchase of consumer goods at reduced prices. They paid only two kyats for a tin of condensed milk that cost sixteen kyats on the black market. Such incentives encouraged people to advance in the government ranks, and we could see that personal values were changing because of the lure of official rewards.

As the months passed, I could recognize some advantages to my work despite the dreariness and discouragement. Staff members received a modest but steady income and a monthly ration of rice and oil, along with packs of cigarettes that could be resold. I also had close friends in the research section who were generous and helpful, and no one in my office gave trouble to others. By then I could distinguish between different types of people, those who were ambitious, manipulative, and compromising, and those who didn't strive for opportunity, cheat, or take unfair advantage of others.

Ko Nyo, the apprentice who arrived with me, had introduced a cooperative credit society within our section, and if someone needed an emergency loan, we used our collected savings to offer help. He also started a book club, and I became its librarian. Any member who failed to return a book on time paid a fine, and I collected the fines, then used the money to buy more books and magazines. Accustomed to the office routine, I finished taking my notes in the morning, which left the rest of the day for my own use. Sometimes I read two books in a single afternoon. I no longer carried my lunch from home to wander on Pansodan Road but instead joined my officemates to buy food at the special BSPP canteen for Central Committee members and staff. Their lunch schedule was earlier than ours, and when they finished, we could buy curries cheaply, no doubt eating their leftovers. One and a half kyats bought a decent meal, whereas outside I would spend at least three or four kyats for the same food.

Dismissed at 3:30, I often walked to 33rd Street to search for current magazines or new books. Wandering through bookstalls and past the few printing presses still privately owned, I always hoped to meet writers, but I remained an anonymous book buyer. I had not even met the writers who lived near my grandmother in Tamwe township. Directly across the street a privately owned publishing house printed entertainment novels and distributed several books each month penned by male ghostwriters who used the names of the printer's two daughters.

Those novels typically developed some version of a triangular affair, with the characters meeting, falling in love, quarreling, parting, and at last finding some way to resolve their conflict or dying of heartbreak. The slightly risqué plots appealed to ordinary people struggling with real-life problems, but often I could not get beyond the first page and preferred more realistic fiction, like the writing of Moe Moe, a friend who worked in the BSPP research section. Famous for her short stories, she had recently published a bestselling novel, based on her own experience, about a newly married couple facing difficult financial problems. The plot tapped into widespread anxiety about economic hardship, and the novel won the National Literary Award.

Chinese martial arts and spy books also sold well, and the demand for such lowbrow books, as well as for comic books with lively illustrations and humor, attracted black market businessmen and traders to the publishing business. Books issued with a colorful cover and appearing under a woman's name served a huge market, and entertainment publishers maintained friendly relations with the Press Scrutiny Board, so those books passed review quickly and could be printed in large runs. Martial arts novels, translated mostly by older Chinese men who lived in Rangoon's several Chinese temples, were also assured of commercial success. Publishers tracked down original knight errant adventures in Chinese, then recorded oral translations provided by the temple dwellers, sometimes issuing those tales in a series to increase profits.

Fiction appealing to a more educated audience also found eager buyers, often casting ordinary people in historical settings or recalling the British colonial period. But it was urban audiences hungry for entertainment who provided a mass reading public in the mid-1970s. Only 27 percent of Burma's population had completed primary school, but children learned to read in monasteries, and the literacy rate remained high even in rural areas. People found an outlet in fantasy and a diversion in formulaic plots, and they particularly enjoyed romances about the rich and fortunate that played out their own dreams.

CHAPTER EIGHT

~

Roads Leading Nowhere

So successfully did the junta institutionalize discipline, secrecy, and intimidation as methods of control that no one dared call attention to obvious injustices or errors. People chafed at the stifling of initiative, opinion, and morale, yet leading BSPP officers received only good news from striving midlevel bureaucrats. Isolated by the vertical hierarchy of top-down command, they remained willfully ignorant about the impact of their policies. Suddenly in July 1976 we heard shocking reports of an assassination plot against General Ne Win and other members of the ruling group. It was the first sign that opposition to the regime lurked within the military.

Newspapers provided daily coverage of the alleged plot for three months until a judge ruled that a junior officer, Ohn Kyaw Myint, bore responsibility for the coup attempt and was guilty of high treason. For plotting to assassinate state leaders, he was sentenced to be hanged. In addition, eleven captains and three majors received sentences from several years to life in prison. A publicity campaign trumpeted the harsh punishments in newspapers and on the radio, issuing a warning to any potential dissidents among military leaders.

In the BSPP office we exchanged information about the accusations in low tones. So serious was this affair that Gen. Tin Oo, appointed Defense Minister just two years earlier and considered the third-ranking member of the ruling group, received a jail sentence of seven years with hard labor for failing to detect plans for the coup. Many people believed Kyaw Zaw, Pe Pe's military commander, and Tin Oo would have taken charge had the junior officers' plan succeeded.

The coup attempt triggered a mass purge of the bureaucracy to root out further dissent, and a special Party Congress was convened to "halt the country's deterioration in the political, economic and social fields." The investigation identified many problems within the BSPP. Rules were not followed, errors were not corrected, criticism and self-criticism were not practiced, and factions had formed within party units. Every BSPP department conducted its own internal investigation as part of the cleansing of the party's ranks, and within a month more than a hundred Central Committee members had been dismissed.

Before the regularly scheduled Third Party Congress met in February 1977, the BSPP research department selected volunteers to participate in a training program. I was not chosen, but one who attended later said that they learned how to count votes, ate expensive meals, and had the chance to buy medicines, consumer goods, clothing, and other commodities at low prices set for government officials. Still the meeting did not proceed according to plan. Ne Win apparently received fewer votes for BSPP chairman than his former military subordinate ex-Brig. Gen. San Yu, and not even the careful coaching of the vote counters brought unanimous endorsement of Ne Win's agenda.

The unexpected results of that Party Congress caused investigators in the cleansing ranks campaign to redouble their efforts. The dossier of every BSPP staff member was scrutinized, including the résumé required at the start of employment. As job candidates we had to list any personal acquaintances among Central Committee members, army officers, or high-ranking government officials, and I had filled out that form carefully in 1973 without supplying names. Another compiler in the research section unwisely included among his acquaintances Ohn Kyaw Myint, the junior officer sentenced to death for high treason. Because the purging of party ranks sought to remove anyone with a peripheral connection to the coup attempt, that compiler was dismissed, as was former Defense Minister Tin Oo's nephew by marriage, a humble man who worked in another section of the research department and never took advantage of his powerful connections.

As the investigation gathered momentum, a number of Central Committee members, their assistants, and other influential BSPP members were not just dismissed but put on trial, including the high-ranking officer in charge of the party's logistics department. After so many former politicians were sacked, I wondered if I would also be caught up in the party cleansing. When the head of my section asked me early in 1978 to apply for BSPP membership, alerted by investigators that I had never joined even the Lanzin Youth Organization, I assumed my dossier was being scrutinized.

Anyone who was a Burmese citizen could visit a township BSPP office to ask for a party membership application form. Committee members from the local party unit would visit the applicant's home within a month to approve the application for candidacy, and full-fledged party membership followed within a year. Even if you were a farmer, worked at odd jobs, or were unemployed, you could become a member of your local party committee. If you participated actively, you became eligible for the state committee, the division committee, then the Central Committee, whose members were elected by the Party Congress. I ignored my section leader's request.

Still searching for relief from the BSPP routine, I enrolled in an evening class at the Fine Arts School where the headmaster, my father's friend and a BIA veteran loyal to Bo Let Ya, addressed me as *Tha mee*, daughter. Famous for his watercolor technique, he had shifted to commercial art because of financial need. I admired his ability and decided to spend most of my salary on stencils, styluses, compasses, and rulers. Next I bought drawing inks, pencils, and pens, then watercolors, brushes, and various weights of paper. Usually I worked with sepia tones, pleased with their rich brown hues, struggling to improve my freehand drawing skills. At home Ko Gyi borrowed my art supplies for his own sketches, and one younger brother started drawing graceful pagodas and intricate studies of lotus stems, buds, and blossoms. Both had natural ability while I continued to copy, whether drawings by local illustrators or sketches by van Gogh.

The evening lectures about method and theory were followed by studio sessions with a range of assignments. For still life compositions, I tried to convey an object's inner spirit. Looking at a bedsheet piled on a table, I saw a white mountain. For life drawings we used a young female model who needed money and lived in the school's staff quarters, but I could never capture her troubled spirit to my satisfaction. The instructor would add just a few lines or smudges and bring my drawing to life.

When I mentioned the evening art classes to U Than Win, the editor of *Varieties of Knowledge*, he assigned me work as an illustrator for the magazine in addition to my ongoing translations. And when the headmaster of the Fine Arts School learned I was translating articles, he loaned me art books in English. I started writing profiles of Western artists for the journal, eager to introduce Burma's readers to European masters like Picasso, van Gogh, Cézanne, and Henry Moore, surprised that I had grown more comfortable reading English and more confident as a writer.

Still the party cleansing dragged on. After tens of thousands considered unworthy or unreliable had been removed from party rolls and civil service jobs, I was not surprised when a senior officer in the research department notified me to appear at party headquarters. Arriving at precisely the time specified, I saw at least a hundred people already seated. Everyone was silent. The sister-in-law of one newly fired Central Committee member was crying, and the niece of another dismissed Central Committee member had a puffy red face. Dismissal meant not just political disgrace but loss of income.

As our names were called, we stood to accept a document announcing immediate discharge, until finally a Central Committee member concluded the meeting. He regretted to inform us we would no longer need to report to our offices starting the next day, he said, and we should all know by ourselves why this had happened. Back in my section a few staff members kept their distance from someone just rejected by the party, but my friends spoke encouragingly. They said I had been released from a burden, I would find other work, I could do anything, I was free.

The third day of the annual Lighting Festival that falls in the seventh month of the Burmese lunar calendar is usually an occasion for celebration and happiness. Colorful paper lanterns, candles, oil lamps, and strings of colored electric lights decorate pagodas and homes to commemorate the Buddha's return to earth after a sojourn in heaven. As children we always set off fireworks and presented gifts to our elders. May May selected the clothing and jewelry she wanted us to wear on that day and purchased cakes, fruits, condensed milk, sweets, towels, and *longyis* for us to deliver as gifts to relatives and elders like Bo Let Ya. We knelt before them to show respect, raising our hands to our foreheads.

By then my family had sold the house in Tamwe township, and we all lived together with my grandaunt in her house on York Road. Returning home earlier than usual on October 17, 1978, I saw my mother lighting candles at the main gate. According to tradition, we place candles beside the rice pot in the kitchen, in the bedroom, and on the ground as an offering to the guardian of the earth. I saw the moon rising and the light from the lamppost casting a dim glow across May May's face.

Searching for a calm voice despite my tight heart, I told her quietly that I had been fired. She asked why, but I could only shake my head and say I didn't know. When she replied that it couldn't be helped, I moved quickly into the shadow of a tree to hide my tears. At that moment, shame at my disgrace mixed with regret that I could no longer make a contribution to the household expenses, and chased away any relief at leaving behind the regulations and routines of the BSPP research section. That night I jotted words of discouragement in my notebook: "Any path I choose, never following to the end, always starting over, again and again." But I also remembered Pe Pe's words that the full moon is most beautiful on its first waning day, and then I wrote a poem.

sitting in that chair
couldn't last
no sadness
but lost earnings
only happiness
let it be

no job or father
caring or kindness
savings or dignity
yet courage
remains

failure brings
smiling and weeping
praising and denouncing
helping and attacking
gossip and comfort

so leave behind
carefree youth
innocent schooldays
let new journeys
bring strength

farewell 1978

Feeling obliged to honor May May's request that I tend her shop until I found other work, I soon became a full-time lottery ticket seller. Every day I walked to the storefront on Anawrahta Road, formerly Fraser Road, in a crowded commercial section of the downtown, never thinking of the British army engineer, Lt. A. Fraser, responsible for Rangoon's careful urban plan. Deprived of maintenance, the city's stately colonial buildings had deteriorated, but its spacious parks and tree-lined avenues still recalled an earlier era.

More than a century ago when Rangoon was a small but bustling port at the confluence of two rivers, British engineers arranged a grid of streets around the octagonal-shaped Sule Pagoda with its gilded dome, built two millennia earlier to contain a hair of the Buddha. After imposing Victorian structures like the Secretariat, the High Court, Rangoon General Hospital, the Central Railway Station, and Scott Market appeared, the city's infrastructure in the 1920s was said to rival London's. Meanwhile colonial administrators designed large houses with spreading lawns along Royal Lake, now called Kandawgyi Lake, and the leafy campus of Rangoon University arose on the banks of nearby Inya Lake. Soon the lush Burmese capital was called "the garden city of the east." That image was hard to recapture in the late 1970s.

Over the decades an influx of refugees displaced from the countryside by war and insurgency had strained the city's public services. Squatters driven by economic need built shanties, sometimes on public land, sometimes on private plots if the owners could not be found. The caretaker government started demolition of squatter neighborhoods in 1958, when it announced the development of satellite towns like South Okkalapa, North Okkalapa, and Tharkaytha. Some 150,000 huts were destroyed, their occupants relocated to outlying sites, usually cleared expanses of dusty land without shelter or sanitation.

On my daily walks to the lottery shop in 1978, I thought about the continuing plight of the urban poor. The small increase in rice supplies after the workers' demonstrations four years earlier had done nothing to ease their burden, and every morning I watched a stream of hawkers in narrow side alleys preparing to sell their wares. Men arranged goods for sale on raised platforms, while women prepared trays of vegetables, fruits, and flowers to offer passersby, but their life was like a tag game. No sooner had they set out their wares than the municipal police would appear, so they darted away. Sometimes the hawkers escaped, but sometimes their goods were confiscated or they were arrested and fined at the township police station. Even if they avoided such harassment for a day, a moneylender arrived in the evening to collect interest on their debts, calculated on a daily basis. I knew their children would likely inherit the hawkers' trade along with the parents' debt. I felt pity, but I couldn't help them.

To pass time in the lottery shop, I kept my dictionary beside me and a supply of books and paper so I could work on translations for *Varieties of Knowledge*. Every evening my brother Win Thaw relieved me so I could attend my art course. The kindest of my brothers, he changed the flowers regularly at the small Buddha shrine beside the store entrance. Slim with fair skin, curly hair, and May May's fine features, he always offered favor to others, leaving early for the morning market to buy food for the cook and taking on whatever housework the rest of us avoided, even heavy tasks like clearing the blocked drains during the monsoons. When a meeting or community affair required one participant from each family, Win Thaw was the only one who agreed to go.

Like my elder brother who joined the merchant service, Win Thaw had a keen intelligence but seemed not to care about university study and never finished high school, yet his English was superior to mine. I liked watching Hollywood films with him as he always followed the dialogue and explained the plots. Instead of regular work he helped out at home in the mornings while I minded the lottery sales, then at lunchtime brought me a container of rice with curries.

After we moved back to York Road, May May became the property's legal owner, but my family were not officially residents because we had not filled out Form #10 at the Immigration Department. That required procedure verifies the occupants of every house, allowing the regime to track the movement of its citizens. Another occupancy rule stipulates that when a visitor spends the night in another person's house, both owner and visitor must register. Usually the ward councilor notifies neighbors in advance of a check for compliance with the residency requirements and reminds them to register any visitors. But in 1978 we received no warning before the ward councilor, an inspector from the Immigration Department, two policemen, and several others, knocked at our door. Because we lacked the proper document, we were ordered to the township police station.

My grandmother, my mother, and my sister, then nursing her first child, were allowed to remain behind, along with my grandaunt and her husband who had registered as residents years before. My brothers and I spent the night in the police station, a five-minute drive from our house. Perhaps the ward councilor, who was also an automobile broker, neglected to notify us partly to show his power, but partly because we did not use his service to sell Ko Lay's car. Instead we chose a different broker, arranged by a relative. Except for a fine when I once crossed a street outside the designated white lines, that was my first encounter with the police.

Three men in shabby clothing stood inside the locked holding cell. We waited in the central receiving area, and I passed the time talking with others caught in the residency sweep. A well-known Chinese traditional medicine practitioner who lived on York Road and was gay said he was cited because he had a friend visiting that night. Another man had slept at his uncle's house because their conversation lasted late. Two medical students had studied together for exams, while another man had been about to leave his parents' house, a two-minute walk from his own home. The only woman, accused of prostitution, insisted she had been visiting her boyfriend. I also chatted with the two young policemen on duty who seemed unhappy at having to hold us for such minor offenses.

As the night passed, I rested my head on the table but couldn't sleep, and in the morning we visited the small food shop in the police compound to buy a snack for breakfast. The shop attendant looked surprised. Two years behind me at RASU, she had also been a math major and a member of my volunteer group during one of the literacy campaigns. I stayed to visit with her, and she brought water so I could wash my face. Later my brothers said they couldn't escape my friends, even in the police station.

After one of Ko Gyi's clients brought us money, we moved to the judicial office for a hearing, arriving hollow-eyed in our wrinkled clothes to see May May and my sister neatly dressed in the front row. Everyone stood to listen to the order read by the judge, who sentenced us to pay a fine. My mother had passed a sleepless night, worried about the consequences her children might face, especially her daughter, passing the night alone with many men. But compared with the huge problems facing others in our country, such a petty encounter with the police was a matter of no significance.

U Than Win's request that I write the introduction for Burma's first book on ecology, expected to reach at least twenty thousand *Villa of Literature* book club members, ended my lottery selling career. I left that work to my brothers and started searching libraries and bookstalls for information about the environment. My essay, completed within a week, explained in simple language why we humans need a safe environment since we have no place to inhabit besides this earth. Pleased with the result, U Than Win asked me to write a series of chapters on environmental topics. My first chapter used air pollution to illustrate the serious problems affecting the global environment, and next I wrote about deforestation. U Than Win seemed surprised when I provided detailed information, not knowing the BSPP once sent me to a forestry seminar or that I had loved trees and plants since childhood and often read about related topics on my own.

Caught up in finishing the book, I felt shocked and embarrassed one afternoon in the office when U Than Win announced calmly that he wanted to marry me. I knew he was unmarried, devoted to books, and generous to subordinates, but I quickly shook my head. I had no interest in love affairs, I said, and I could never make a good housewife. He told me to think it over and not give my answer until the next day. Admiring U Than Win as my mentor and supporter, I worried how to face him. When we met, I discussed my final chapter as if nothing had happened. He sat quietly, then quickly apologized, saying he felt sorry to have made my face so sad, telling me to forget his proposal. After that we communicated like before and never referred to that conversation. Nor did I mention it to my family.

Had May May not felt so unhappy telling her acquaintances I was unemployed, I could have been content with my unconventional life, reading until three in the morning, waking up late, lending some help in the kitchen, visiting the library or the *Villa of Literature* office to meet friends, just spending time. But my book on the environment had not yet appeared, and my mother's friends did not read *Varieties of Knowledge* magazine. They considered women office clerks and primary school teachers respectably employed, but not freelance writers. Sorry to disappoint May May, I wrote a poem.

following a trail
no special purpose
seeking an outlet

failure no regret
success just measures
one step forward

approaching thirty
still no beginning
never settled

without destination
tired from the journey
roads leading nowhere

no way to reach
the end of a path
just spending time

one day a new sun
one sun then a night
one night then a day

still another sun
still scorching

Attempting to find again a professional path, I enrolled in an intensive private course to prepare for the recently reinstated Higher Grade Pleadership (HGP) exam, suspended for five years, and also for the Registered at Law (RL) qualifying exam open to university graduates and government staff. I studied hard and received passing scores on both tests, which plunged me into a challenging two-year course that covered criminal law, criminal procedure law, civil law, and Burmese customary law. Had I taken the RL exam when I first started studying law in 1975 as a discontented BSPP staff member looking for a different job, I would likely have moved to another part of the low-ranking bureaucracy as an assistant in a government court. My life might have been more respectable, but I preferred my many detours as a translator, art student, and environmental writer. Rejecting a conventional role was my way to declare a small measure of independence.

That year I turned thirty. I knew May May did not want to continue supporting me, but I was startled to receive a proposal for an arranged marriage from a relative in the United States. If I agreed to marry the brother-in-law of one of my former teachers, I would depart for the United States for good, as had so many since 1962. I refused, but even the possibility of being married off to someone I didn't know and leaving my country pushed me to search harder for work. While I was busy translating articles and studying law, one of Pe Pe's friends suggested I apply for a job at a government-run magazine.

The News and Periodicals Corporation (NPC), a powerful government consortium overseen by the Information Ministry and supervised by a board of directors, published six newspapers, two monthly magazines, and three children's journals. All were scrupulously consistent with BSPP policy and therefore exempt from scrutiny by the censorship board. The managing director, a short man with sharp eyes, interviewed me briefly, then asked me to translate into Burmese a paragraph from the daily foreign news bulletin. Glancing quickly at my application, he wrote a note assigning me to the *Myanma-a-lin* newspaper, the *New Light of Burma*, an official organ of the BSPP.

People had few choices in finding employment, and by 1980 most of my university classmates had somehow accommodated to the limited options. They also grew experienced at avoiding the informers who reported in offices, factories, neighborhoods, and schools on signs of assertiveness or dissent. As an unsalaried newspaper staff member I would only earn daily wages, but at least my mother would no longer fret about my doing nothing and causing her burden. I hoped that assignment to the *New Light of Burma*'s foreign news section would be less deadening than compiling data in the research office of the BSPP.

Once again connections gave me access to a job. Before interviewing me, the managing director presented my contacts at a chief editor's meeting, explaining that his uncle, a brother-in-law of Aung San, was my father's friend, the administrative director was Pe Pe's former comrade, and the chief editor's children were among my university friends. Also, the husband of the headmistress at Pe Pe's school was a member of the NPC's editorial board. But while those personal ties and "socialist friends" provided an opening, they were not a guarantee. If I made a mistake, especially if I became involved in politics, no one could help me.

CHAPTER NINE

~

Reporting as a Woman

Control of the press tightened steadily after the military coup in 1962, and by the time the National Periodicals Corporation hired me in 1980, Burma's once vibrant media climate was only a memory. Thirty years earlier, after the country gained independence, thirty-nine newspapers were published, including twenty-one in Burmese and the rest in English, Chinese, and Indian languages like Gujarati, Urdu, Tamil, Telgu, and Hindi. My father subscribed to five newspapers during my childhood, each with a different editorial stance, but I grew up in an era of uniform reporting when the number of daily papers had shrunk to six, four in Burmese and two in English. Readers paid more attention to marriage announcements, condolence notices, and advertisements for movies or books than to the tedious reports of state visits and ministerial meetings.

The first newspaper to close was *The Nation* in May 1963, and two months later the government set up its own news service, called News Agency Burma. *Working People's Daily* was soon launched in Burmese, followed by an English version in January 1964. After that, newspapers closed one by one until the Revolutionary Council announced in October 1966 that all private news organizations were banned.

The *New Light of Burma*, founded in 1914, had a proud history as the country's leading daily during the independence struggle. It became a cooperative owned by its workers after the coup and managed initially to resist nationalization, while struggling to preserve its independent spirit. But in 1969, with revenues rapidly declining, it had no choice but to accept government control over news content, editorial opinion, administration, and personnel.

Most of its employees were relatives or fellow townsmen, but that close relationship among workers ended when the newspaper became an official organ
of the BSPP, and people from other dailies were transferred to its staff. Its
staid format and scant half-page of ads drew few readers. Having rarely read
the *New Light of Burma* myself, I had no idea what to expect when I rode the
bus from York Road to the press compound.

The deputy chief editor greeted me on my first morning. A tall man with
a cigar clamped between his teeth, he seemed friendly and gave me a tour,
introducing me even to the canteen owner. The general manager, whose
cousin was Pe Pe's friend, was less welcoming. There was only one toilet upstairs for the editorial department, he said. I replied politely that we didn't
use separate toilets at home and I knew the press was like a family, so he
seemed satisfied. Only two other women worked at *New Light of Burma*, both
downstairs in the administrative section, one as an accounting officer and
the other as a typist. I was the first woman to join the editorial department.

The assistant foreign editor arrived next. U Tint Lwin was a tall, slim Chinese man and a graduate of St. John Diocesan like my brothers. I was surprised to find him interested in journalism since I thought most Chinese in
Burma were businessmen or worked for the government as medical doctors
or engineers. He hurriedly explained all the tasks I would be assigned, confusing me with details. He even took out a file of newspapers to illustrate different typefaces, specifying 14 points, 13 points, 12 points before showing me
different headlines, some two lines, some three lines, some from a new system with two lines of white and three lines of black type.

Interspersed among U Tint Lwin's explanations were complaints that newspaper work was a man's profession and not suitable for a woman. He had requested an additional foreign news editor but expected a man; the managing
director must have no understanding of newspaper life; the few women editors
hired previously by the English version of *Working People's Daily* all quit because of the night shifts. Following each objection, he stated again that news
work was not suited for a woman. It was my first day so I said nothing.

The proofreaders and typesetters seemed to share his viewpoint, and their
style of address signaled reluctance to recognize a woman as their superior.
They addressed male editors as *Saya*, "teacher," but called me *A ma*, "elder
sister," or simply Ma San San Tin. I carefully used *U*, the polite term of address for an adult male, but no one called me *Daw*, the equivalent term of respect for a woman. Perhaps they thought I had found a shortcut to the press
when I knew nothing about journalism. That objection was justified, but I
learned step by step.

Later I met the foreign editor, U Naing Aung, who spoke encouragingly and opened a cupboard to offer me several journalism books. He was neatly dressed, carefully groomed, and good looking, perhaps half-Indian though he claimed to be Mon. He seemed outspoken, lively, and welcoming. I would understand the whole process within a month, he said. After that introduction, I began to work. When a complimentary copy of the newspaper arrived at my gate the next morning, my translated article, a few lines about the Palestinian leader Yasir Arafat, appeared on page three. U Tint Lwin complained again on my second day that a newspaper was not a suitable place for a woman. I replied that women doctors and engineers worked around the clock, and if they could manage night shifts, so could I. He looked surprised but never voiced those objections again.

The daily routine grew familiar. Every day the editorial department edited wire service reports received in English from agencies like Xinhua, Tass, Kyodo, Reuters, Agence France-Presse, and the Associated Press. Then a high-level group, called the marking board, met three times daily to mark the bulletins into four categories—compulsory, approved, ignored, or prohibited. After the foreign news staff received the marking board's decisions by telephone, our job was to translate into Burmese the wire service stories in the first two categories.

"Prohibited" was the most important designation, because if we mistakenly translated an article rejected by the marking board, we faced serious criticism. Foreign news articles about strikes, demonstrations, human rights, or ethnic conflicts, such as those between Turks and Kurds, fell into the "prohibited" category. "Ignored" stories were considered marginally acceptable, not initially translated, but occasionally printed if space allowed. Even for "approved" and "compulsory" stories, we often received instructions to delete words or paragraphs from our Burmese translations. On my second morning, U Tint Lwin was clearly testing me when he asked me to take the telephone report with instructions on which articles were compulsory or which paragraphs had to be deleted, knowing the Anglo-Burmese woman clerk from News Agency Burma would speak in rapid English. The details were difficult to follow, as I had no experience with spoken English, but I took care to repeat the information to be certain I had understood. U Tint Lwin seemed satisfied.

After the strict schedule at the BSPP office, the more flexible hours at the press made my life appear easygoing to my brothers, who didn't understand the daily pressure. I could arrive at the press late in the morning and leave whenever my work was finished, but as soon as the morning newspapers arrived at our home, I had to check every foreign story to see if I had made any mistakes. If three newspapers included the same information, the fourth could not deviate from the standard.

Top party leaders read the papers early and telephoned the responsible minister when they had complaints, suggestions, or denials. The minister contacted the managing director, who called the chief editor, who knew the mere ring of the telephone warned of a problem. Based on those early morning phone calls, everyone anticipated who would be criticized at the noon meeting when the NPC's managing director, directors, chief editors, and deputy chief editors all gathered to review the day's publications. If a question was raised about *New Light of Burma*, the managing director launched a chain reaction to trace responsibility. Any mistake kept many people busy searching the previous day's copy and the draft proofs, checking signatures and handwriting to determine responsibility for an error.

Nearly every day we faced some kind of problem simply because our staff made mistakes. Sometimes the problem was just a misspelling, attributed to the proofreader or the typesetter, but even then an official warning was entered in the employee's service record. Those notations usually had no immediate consequence, but when a person was considered for promotion, red marks on his record raised questions. Occasionally a mistake was more serious. When one of the township correspondents submitted a crime report about a murder on a train, officials in the Transportation Ministry objected as soon as the article appeared. News stories were expected to affirm the achievements of socialism, so unfavorable subjects could not be reported.

The city news section had its own obligations and constraints, as government officials never wanted to see stories that reflected unfavorably on their jurisdiction. The desk editor responsible for city news, U Ko Ko, had more authority than anyone besides the chief and deputy chief editors. He oversaw government-issued articles for the front and back pages, and even before the city news staff received its daily bulletins from the news agency's internal division, he had already been informed which stories to assign to what space in the paper. Following an established priority, articles about General Ne Win appeared at the top of the front page, with no other news ever appearing above his. Then came news about the Defense Minister, followed by the Home Affairs Minister and the Foreign Affairs Minister, always in a specified ranking.

My first regular assignment was to co-write weekly foreign film synopses. Since the Information Ministry's film department provided authorized summaries, I could write a brief article even when I nodded off during a screening. Occasionally I reviewed excellent American films like *The Adventures of Tom Sawyer* and *Kramer vs. Kramer* before their release to cinema houses and later to BBS TV, but the most important result of my reviews was earning respect from the printers and proofreaders.

Most Burmese writers use pen names, sometimes to conceal their identity out of humility, sometimes because of the need for protection, sometimes simply because they prefer a more poetic name. They might adopt the name of their native region, their university, or the magazine or newspaper to which they regularly contribute. U Naing Aung and U Tint Lwin had both used "Aung Aung Lwin" to write the foreign movie synopses, so I retained their pen name. For me, writing film reviews under a man's name seemed a counterattack when so many male ghostwriters assumed the identity of women.

I wrote my first actual news article on August 8, 1980, about the anniversary of the atomic bomb dropped on Hiroshima, explaining how that devastating explosion had destroyed human life and property, noting the terrible consequences of radioactivity. After that I wrote frequently, choosing my topics but knowing automatically what tone to adopt, always submitting my articles to the editorial board for approval. Sometimes I translated a foreign news article about the environment, as Burma's severe environmental problems could not be reported. My translations would suggest the causes of deforestation or the consequences of ozone depletion or the danger of wild life extinction.

Overtly political topics like party guidelines, economic planning, or the importance of Peasants' Day were assigned in rotation. When my turn came, I took a risk and claimed I didn't know how to write policy stories. I didn't want to lose my job again, and like all NPC employees I had agreed to carry out any assigned duty as a condition of being hired, but I hated the regime's propaganda. The deputy chief editor never complained that I was uncooperative nor did he again assign me to write a policy story.

From U Tint Lwin, who was a good storyteller, I learned the background of my co-workers. Always in a new setting we try to establish connections, and it didn't take long to discover that his sister-in-law worked at the *Villa of Literature* and his niece was my university friend. He spoke proudly of his father-in-law, a BIA officer killed by the Japanese whom he had never met, and since the city desk editor's father-in-law was also a BIA officer, U Tint Lwin said we three were comrades. Our professional relationship grew more relaxed, and soon he started asking me to join him at the press canteen's teashop. I never minded being the only woman in that setting, but someone lodged a complaint, prompting the managing director to request that I refuse any further teashop invitations from U Tint Lwin. The suggestion that we were having a love affair made the deputy editor's face turn red with anger and embarrassment, but I assured him people would come to know my character. Later we resumed our visits with no further criticism.

Personal contacts at the press were always subject to public scrutiny, and people routinely gossiped about each other. Late shifts placed strains on family life, and U Tint Lwin told many stories about married men taking mistresses or second wives, making a rough calculation that perhaps 70 percent of the NPC staff engaged in love affairs. Everyone knew that our photojournalist had two wives, as the first wife would pass through the inner newsroom without a smile or greeting, heading to the darkroom at the rear to collect money. One day when the photojournalist introduced a woman who worked in the darkroom as his wife, I joked that she didn't look like the mother of his son. From my grandaunt's experience, I knew that a husband could conduct a double life for years.

A popular short story described a man who worked for a newspaper and secretly maintained two wives. Each believed her husband had taken an additional job at a private press to supplement the family's income. One wife thought he was assigned to day duty while the other thought he worked at night. After he suffered a heart attack in the newsroom and died on the way to the hospital, both wives attended the funeral and only then discovered his infidelity.

During my first weeks at the press, I also learned the important role that drinking plays in the daily routine of many journalists. Bars served as a meeting place where correspondents from other cities could talk about their stories with local news staff and exchange information freely, saying whatever they liked when they got drunk. Sometimes night editors, unable to join those visits to the bars, kept their own bottles of rum in the newsroom, and many of the typesetters also liked to drink. I developed a different habit. When someone else in my office chewed a quid of betel, I began to crave it.

The mixture of betel leaf, lime, chewable areca nut, and aniseed, popular throughout Southeast Asia, has a special flavor. In Burma's villages, both men and women chew betel, but in Rangoon it is a rare practice for an educated woman. Hawkers in many neighborhoods and at crowded bus stops sell quids of betel along with cigarettes and cheroots, and people often have a favorite shop where they buy a particular blend. Those who chew regularly prepare a lacquerware betel box to display at home and present to visitors. Inside are small containers of white lime paste, areca nut, tobacco, licorice, aniseed, cardamom seed, and cloves.

Chewing betel has been popular in Burma for centuries, but the spittle leaves dark red stains that never wash out. When people prepare a quid of betel, they first paste lime on one or two betel leaves before adding other ingredients with their index finger. Then they wrap the blend and start to chew, wiping their finger on a nearby wall or pillar. Most public places provide spittoons, but people often spit wherever they like, and Rangoon's whitewashed walls show the ugly marks of betel stains.

Burmese folk tradition preserves a story about an ancient king who governed in accordance with the ten precepts for a ruler, practicing charity, religious devotion, benefaction, fairness, gentleness, keeping the sabbath, benevolence, patience, and avoidance of cruelty and conflict. Concerned that lime marks on the teak pillars marred the beauty of his palace, he issued an order decreeing that anyone who left betel stains would have his index finger cut off. The first to wipe his hand absentmindedly on a pillar turned out to be the king himself, who noticed the new stain and demanded that his ministers disclose who had ignored the decree. A brave minister replied that if the king killed him, he would die, and if the king let him live, he would live, but the one who had committed the crime was the king himself. Announcing that he would abide by the law, the king cut off his own finger. Through that folk tale we learned about integrity and the ideal conduct for a ruler.

When I first started the habit of chewing betel, I recalled the king's decree and disciplined myself to spit carefully into a spittoon. But I was a novice, and sometimes instead of hitting the receptacle neatly, some drops of spittle stained my blouse. I liked the dizziness that resulted from chewing but tried never to accept a quid of betel mixed with tobacco, which left me feeling intoxicated. No one openly criticized my new bad habit, and some men from the press even encouraged me. Later when my teeth started turning red and some of my clothes had permanent stains, I started chewing gum instead. The elders hadn't objected that I chewed betel, but they thought it disrespectful to chew gum, which was a foreign practice. I continued for almost a decade.

My position at the newspaper changed in 1981, when U Naing Aung was suddenly reassigned to the city news section and a new foreign news editor, U Tun Tun, well known for speaking out at editorial meetings, arrived from *Working People's Daily*. Also a graduate of St. John's, he had a bald head, bent shoulders, and excellent English, along with a clear, straightforward Burmese style. An able translator, he tried to make news engaging and informative even in our carefully scrutinized work environment where independent-minded journalists had to remain cautious and compliant.

One Sunday when we were on duty together, I finished a news story about floods in China and couldn't think of a suitable headline. The translated article mentioned how many people had died because of the floods that year, and U Tun Tun told me to include the number of casualties in the headline. The next morning our chief editor received a phone call, and a worker waited at the front gate to alert me that my story was being examined at the noon meeting. U Tun Tun quickly checked the original wire service report and insisted there was no mistake, but the other newspapers had printed a lower number, and NPC headquarters declared that *New Light of Burma's* China flood casualty figure was incorrect.

The variation in numbers was easily explained. The first paragraph of the wire story stated first the number of deaths in one province, then the total number of deaths that year throughout the country. Other papers simply reproduced the number of provincial deaths, but I changed the sequence and put the total number of casualties in the lead paragraph to convey the scale and scope of the disaster. U Tun Tun announced that he had selected the headline, so he would assume responsibility. In the end we did not receive warnings, but I learned that U Tun Tun had strong principles and that he stood behind me.

Many people found him peculiar because he didn't like flattery, bluffing, or seeking advantage, and he spoke frankly when someone displayed those traits. His outspokenness caused tension with other staff members, and often he stopped at a bar on his way home, easing his frustration with cheap, strong white liquor. Also a heavy smoker, he was hospitalized in 1981, then had to retire after twenty years of service. That brought U Naing Aung's transfer back to the foreign news section and my appointment to an editorial staff post.

In September 1982, I had worked almost two years at the newspaper with various assignments when one of my poems appeared in a private monthly literary magazine, *Moe Way*. Critics paid attention to poetry published in that influential journal, so I knew my work would draw notice. My poem described a dream in which I longed desperately for a soulmate, yet feared to meet him and dared not weep at my desolation. Some critics attacked its trivial emotion and lack of social relevance, but the editor recognized my suggestion that people live in fear and darkness, yearning for something lost. He knew this was more than a simple love lyric, and soon *Moe Way* published another short poem, called "Enjoyment."

> seeking the shade without breaking a branch
> plucking a bloom without harming the buds
> picking a fruit without tearing its leaves
> taking no more than I need
> I find beauty

By then, my book about the environment had been widely distributed, earning royalties of twenty thousand kyats, but *Moe Way*'s payment of thirty kyats for that first published poem brought far more satisfaction. The book's success showed my research ability, but having poems appear in that particular journal confirmed my literary taste. Even so, I wouldn't claim the term "poet," which I reserved for writers of more traditional verses describing love or the passing seasons, many of which I had copied into my notebooks ever since high school. The poet I most admired was Kyi Aye, who left Burma for good in 1972 at age forty-three and settled in the United States. I thought we had no contemporary woman poet to equal her, so deftly did she find subtle words to convey inner depths without sacrificing rhythm. Some critics asked why we missed Kyi Aye when she didn't love her country and left Burma behind. I believed she contributed uniquely to our literature.

When I sat for the NPC's scheduled promotion exam in 1983, I prepared to answer general knowledge questions, write a local news story, and provide a translation. One requirement I ignored. The exam also obliged me to list the many types of writing, like Kyi Aye's poems and novels, considered detrimental to the socialist program and the socialist economy. I had never memorized the official censorship categories, called the seven principles of literature and journalism, so when my editor notified me of my failing score, and chastised me for my carelessness, I assumed my failure to list the junta's journalism principles had disqualified me for promotion. I apologized to my editor, but when he checked the test results, he found that my test code number had been wrongly recorded. My failing grade turned out to be a simple mistake, an indication of how carelessly the promotion system was implemented, and in fact I placed first, despite my neglect of the journalism categories. And so in mid-1983 I became a full-fledged reporter with a salary increase and advancement to a junior officer's grade in the government bureaucracy.

Pe Pe (Bo Ba Tin) and May May (Daw Kyi Kyi), 1943

Pe Pe (Bo Ba Tin), 1954

May May (Daw Kyi Kyi), 1958

San San Tin (right) and Ma Ma, 1957

Children, Ma Kyee Kyee Road, 1959 (San San Tin, second from right)

Family portrait (San San Tin, second from left), 1963

Mother and daughters, 1965 (San San Tin, left)

Discharge certificate for Pe Pe (Bo Ba Tin), 1945

The Mirror *newspaper, January 31, 1959*

St. Philo's school concert, seventh grade, 1964 (San San Tin, second from right)

San San Tin, while waiting to attend university, 1968

San San Tin (second from left) and three classmates, Rangoon Arts and Sciences University, 1969

San San Tin, Convocation Hall, Rangoon Arts and Sciences University, 1970

San San Tin (back row, right) with literacy campaign volunteers, beside Irrawaddy River with Sagaing Hills in distance, 1972

San San Tin (center) and two friends with literacy campaign exhibit, 1972

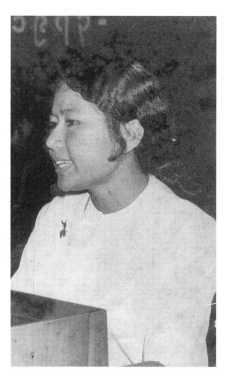

San San Tin, giving speech representing women students from Rangoon's universities, 1973

San San Tin, Temple of Heaven, Beijing, 1986

San San Tin (right), interviewing Moe Moe, 1987

San San Tin (right) with poet Tin Moe (1933–2007), Chinatown, San Francisco, 2000

CHAPTER TEN

~

Mounting Costs

Prices continued to rise in the early 1980s, with devastating consequences. Government salaries were never adequate, township clerks struggled to find extra income, employees at state-owned shops made connections with the black market, and printers from the NPC worked extra shifts at private presses to cover daily expenses. As shortages of basic commodities increased, "profiteers" stored anything that could realize a profit. The gasoline quota set by the government was never sufficient, so all private transportation relied on the black market. Entrepreneurs stored many tons of black market gasoline in fifty- or one hundred-gallon drums, sometimes with dire results. When a fire in a black market gasoline shop in Mandalay burned out of control in 1984, much of that ancient city turned to ash.

Most of Mandalay's houses were built of wood around tamped earth courtyards, and ordinary families typically lived in a named compound where close neighbors acted like relatives. The fire that destroyed Mandalay's neighborhoods also destroyed the traditional way of life in Burma's second capital. Long-term Burmese residents initially borrowed money to rebuild but later had to sell their plots of land when those loans were foreclosed. They could not compete with Chinese who had money to invest, sometimes from the sale of jade or drugs. Wealthy Chinese became the new landowners in Mandalay, rebuilding the city almost as a Chinatown, and newly opened restaurants, goldsmith shops, and printing presses were inevitably festooned with Chinese red streamers. But while Chinese were moving into the country seeking economic advantage, most Burmese struggled as inflation consumed their income.

To describe the mounting hardships, I drew ideas for a short story from my mother's daily account book. May May methodically kept track of every source of income and every expenditure, recording whatever money she spent, whether for a gold ring or the boiled peas and fried rice we warmed in oil for breakfast. Comparing her figures year by year, I saw that in 1965 cooking oil cost 4 kyats for a *viss* (the equivalent of 3.5 pounds), while in 1980 the price had jumped to 140 kyats. I wrote "A Thirty-Year Journey" to show how personal difficulties accumulated over three decades as a result of mounting costs, using a fictional narrator to describe the change in people's daily experience.

In 1955 when the narrator was in primary school, his mother gave him twenty-five *pyas* a day as pocket money, so he ate *mohinga* with fried peas and bought an ice pop coated with canned condensed milk, or sampled other treats his mother told him not to eat, like preserved fruit mixed with salt and chili powder so hot it made his tears flow. In 1965 when he was in high school, his mother gave him one kyat as pocket money, and he ate *mohinga*, paid the borrowing fees at a bookstall, and sometimes bought a book. In 1975 when he earned a daily wage of over three kyats, he ate *mohinga*, drank a cup of tea in the morning, and bought the latest issue of a magazine.

But in 1985 when he earned a junior officer's salary of 320 kyats, he could support his family only with the help of his wife's earnings at home using an old Singer sewing machine. He no longer ate *mohinga* or drank tea in the morning, and when he passed foodstalls and teashops, he had to swallow his longing. But his love of reading remained strong, so occasionally he stretched his earnings to buy an outdated magazine. Returning home one night eager to read, he searched in vain for a candle after the power went out. When his wife complained that he didn't understand the cost of a single candle, he went to bed in darkness, passing a sleepless night.

The story might well have been censored if *Moe Way*'s editor had submitted as illustration the drawing of a soldier's boot provided by a contributing graphic artist. Illustrators were sensitive to writers' intentions and recognized underlying meaning, but editors exercised caution. Instead, a bland drawing of a five-year-old boy wearing a school uniform accompanied my story, which passed the Press Scrutiny Board's review and appeared in the magazine in 1985.

As an established writer at last, I moved between two worlds. Working at the NPC was my job, but contributing regularly to private magazines was my choice. I worked on my writing only late at night and on my days off, but even as I was employed by the government press, I also maintained close ties to private publishing circles.

By then, thirteen private monthly magazines provided an outlet for independent writers' work, five owned by ex-army officers who had useful connections and a sense for market opportunities. The most established journals drew the greatest respect, so I sent my poems and articles only to the two longest running private magazines. In 1985 the editor of the oldest literary magazine asked me to contribute a regular monthly article, and I began writing about varied topics that appealed to reader interest. One article described the Statue of Liberty, another reviewed a friend's art show, a third reported on government-sanctioned trips to China. Sometimes I just translated stories about Hollywood stars, trying to give that popular subject a literary flavor.

Private magazine owners liked to hire moonlighting government press workers who knew how to make printed materials conform to authorized standards of language usage, specified in a handbook published by the Burmese Language Committee. Even though professional expertise had been marginalized for two decades, Ne Win turned common understanding into official usage when he made a widely reported speech to the language committee early in the 1980s. Everyone noticed that he pointedly altered a common phrase, *lu-taw lu-gaung*, meaning "smart and good," by reversing the word order to *lu-gaung lu-taw*, meaning "good and smart." His phrasing conveyed a message that intelligence was a liability while obedience was an essential trait.

In 1985 my articles appeared almost daily in *New Light of Burma*, whether foreign film synopses, translated stories about the global environment, or feature articles on foreign science topics, like the inhalation of second-hand cigarette smoke. By carefully choosing my subjects, I tried to use the heavily restricted foreign news to suggest how Burma shared the outside world's concerns. Alert readers could understand that a story describing deforestation in India as the cause of the Brahmaputra River's flooding pointed also to the frequent flooding of the Irrawaddy River within our own borders.

I worked simultaneously as a writer and an editor, routinely reading News Agency Burma bulletins and deciding which approved stories to place at the top of the news, calculating the layout, and providing copy with suitable headlines to the typesetters. I always chatted and joked with the staff and took small pleasure in the smell of newsprint and lubricating oil, remembering the printing press behind my aunt's home on York Road during my childhood. Often I reported to work when other editors were ill, skipping my days off, and usually I wandered through the streets when my routine tasks were finished. If I discovered a rare book about Burmese culture in a roadside bookstall, I was briefly happy. And as long as I didn't think about the fact that identical news items appeared every day in every newspaper, I was content with my work, grateful to have some limited access to what was happening beyond Burma's borders.

Personal disputes and antagonisms played a role in the newspaper's staff assignments, and late in 1985 I was abruptly transferred to the city news section. Piecing together what people told me, I learned that a woman editor who worked together with me in the foreign news pool had complained to the NPC managing director about an insult from a male editorial writer. Annoyed by the petty problem, the managing director apparently said women caused too much bother and moved all four women to different units. My new job was to edit reports filed by local correspondents around the country.

Most local news items concerned activities of district or township BSPP organizations, and I wrote those daily articles about People's Peasants' Councils, People's Workers' Councils, Cooperative Associations, Lanzin Youth Organizations, and township party units without ever attending a meeting. All I needed were the names of the chairman and the secretary to report which town held what organization meeting at which township office on what date attended by whom. Then I added that the chairman of the organization delivered an address on the occasion and a general round of discussion followed. The formula never varied.

More interesting was editing human interest stories for page six. People liked to read about criminal cases or personal tragedies, so those articles were popular. Once I reported on a villager who climbed into a deep well for routine cleaning, and when he didn't emerge, another man climbed down, followed by a third, and all three suffocated from lack of oxygen. Another local story described a stabbing that occurred when a pedestrian stopped a car in Shan State, then stabbed and robbed the passenger. Angry that he found only twenty-five *pyas*, which did not even pay for a cup of tea after the price rose to one kyat, the robber told police he couldn't stand being so poor. Compared with official news articles in the city section, these local stories had much greater interest, allowing Rangoon readers to glimpse a way of life different from their own.

After several months I began editing crime reports covering Rangoon city. One story reported on a theft of iron rods from a dockyard, and since I knew the columnist was from Dala, I mentioned the location of the crime. The next day the foreman alerted me there was a problem. Authorities at the Dala dockyard had complained, worried that readers would realize one person alone could not steal heavy iron rods, which meant there was likely a group involved in the theft of public property, possibly an inside conspiracy. The chief editor ordered an investigation to identify the editor responsible, but the printshop workers had recognized my handwriting and claimed the original draft was lost.

Ne Win's official visit to Beijing in 1985 put Burma's new relationship with China on full display. Government-to-government connections had started to improve after Deng Xiaoping became head of state in 1978, with the opening of border trade bringing economic benefit to both sides. During those negotiations China also agreed to stop its long-term financial and political support for the CPB, and we all watched when official BBS TV showed Deng smiling and greeting our general warmly, bringing an end to any lingering strain from the Cultural Revolution. Before the riots in1967, we sometimes said that Chinese and Burmese were "kin," but after relations soured, we referred to our neighbors only as "Chinese."

As bilateral exchanges increased, a flight from China landed at the Rangoon airport on Wednesdays, and it seemed as if almost every week we read newspaper reports about an official Chinese delegation arriving from Beijing and an official Burmese group departing for a reciprocal visit. Journalists accompanied a foreign delegation to provide publicity only when a top leader traveled, so being chosen for such a trip was compared to being a lottery winner. Delegation members could bring back consumer goods to use or resell, and the most enterprising even purchased industrial products like the corrugated metal sheets in great demand for building construction.

When an Information Ministry trip to China was announced in October 1986, we learned that the deputy chief editor at the English version of *Working People's Daily* would lead the delegation. As a public relations gesture, NPC directors decided to include women journalists, but the NPC had only five female newspaper editorial staff members. Along with one other woman and five male editors and chief reporters, I was allowed this chance for foreign travel. To obtain a passport and other necessary documents, I filled out pages of paperwork, including a résumé with a list of my every activity from primary school to the present. Having heard stories about flights that returned to the Rangoon airport before leaving Burmese airspace if someone onboard was suspected of past wrongdoing, I worried that even at the last minute my trip could be denied. But I also worried that it would be approved, as my writer friends criticized any journalist who participated in these official cultural exchanges. After the delegation landed safely in Beijing, my worry did not end, as each member's behavior in China was closely scrutinized.

For two weeks, accompanied by a pair of liaison officers and a photojournalist, my group followed a set itinerary and visited tourist sites in six cities. In Beijing, hosted by Xinhua, China's official news agency, we visited first a Buddhist temple containing a tooth relic, then later toured the Temple of Heaven, the Forbidden City, and the Great Wall. We also visited the official newspapers *People's Daily* and *China Daily*, and after a meeting at the Great Hall of the People, were ushered to the head of the line at Chairman

Mao's mausoleum. I remembered my earlier idealized impressions of China's socialist construction as I gazed at the waxen leader encased in glass.

Still influenced by Chinese short stories from the 1960s, I somehow expected people on the streets to wear drab jackets in blue or gray. I found instead a colorful China with high-rise hotels that welcomed foreign tourists and state-run department stores that reminded me of my childhood when Burma's shops had also been stocked with goods. The China I saw bore little resemblance to the revolutionary society I imagined when I read a translation of Edgar Snow's *Red Star over China*, admired Chinese short stories, and proudly wore my Mao badge. That romanticized place had disappeared along with my own glorified vision of socialism. Even my copies of Chairman Mao's book of quotations had gone because May May had burned them to get rid of an infestation of white ants.

Even if China's economic reforms brought consumer goods and tourist facilities unknown in Burma, I saw other similarities. On the train from Nanjing to Hangzhou, we two women editors were given second-class seats facing two young Chinese men who started a friendly conversation. They asked where we were from and whether they could practice their English, but almost immediately the Xinhua liaison officer ended our exchange and rebuked them in Chinese. Throughout the tour we stayed in luxury hotels, separated from ordinary people except for one meal at a modest restaurant. There we sat among regular customers until an argument broke out at the next table and the liaison officer rushed us outside before we had finished eating. Just as in Burma, the real life behind the façade was concealed from visitors.

A final overnight stop in Hong Kong brought a much awaited opportunity for shopping. I had little interest in spending money abroad but agreed to contribute my small amount of cash to a pool with two other delegates who purchased a television set for resale. Back in Rangoon many people said I missed a good opportunity by not bringing more items home. But letters of complaint were common after a foreign trip, as someone not selected might lodge a public grievance about gifts improperly accepted or goods excessively purchased. I felt relieved when no complaint letter attacked my delegation after our return.

Almost a year after my China trip, a different complaint was lodged that brought a summons to the headquarters of the Bureau of Special Investigation. It was monsoon season in 1987, and the rain had soaked my clothing when I arrived. I wore a windbreaker, unusual attire for a woman, and the investigating officer watched as I pulled off my drenched jacket and shook my head to clear the raindrops from my cropped hair. Burmese women always wear their hair long, but I had recently cut mine very short and also changed my style of dress. Instead of wearing a traditional Burmese blouse to work, I usually wore a T-shirt. To attend meetings, I put on a Western-style shirt with a collar instead of a close-fitting open-necked Burmese blouse. If asked, I said that I couldn't afford to buy clothing with my salary, but in fact I wanted to strip away any signs of femininity.

By then I was thirty-seven, and for years I had ignored conventional feminine behavior. Raised with many brothers, I felt comfortable with male companions and sometimes sat for hours with a male friend in a teashop or walked with a man alone around the city, even at night. But I hated having men stare at me or signal their interest, and three men at the NPC had approached me during that year. One sent an anonymous personal letter by post while two others made more direct advances, stroking my leg as we sat together and inviting me to a movie. Since all the men were married and knew me well, I wanted to make certain my open manner did not invite overtures. Changing my style seemed one way to prevent misunderstanding. I had worked at the press with long hair for seven years, so people noticed when I cropped it short. I never explained my altered appearance.

An unmarried woman cannot avoid challenging society's norms. Even though women in Burma face less discrimination in education and some forms of employment than in neighboring countries, they encounter strong pressure to conform to traditional ideas about dress and demeanor. Women can pursue independent professional careers in medicine, law, or business, but their appearance and their relations with men receive close scrutiny.

The investigating officer looked surprised by my short hair and bulging woven shoulder bag, as most women prefer a slim pocketbook, often foreign made. Because of the heavy rain, I wore my bag slung behind me like a backpack, and he seemed startled as he watched my every movement, especially when I said excuse me and spat out my chewing gum. Instead of asking political questions, he queried me first about my lifestyle, my work responsibilities, and my trip to China. Finally, I learned that a complaint letter had accused the NPC managing director of giving special access to women in exchange for sexual favors and had mentioned my inclusion in the group traveling abroad as an example of such privilege. The investigating officer was apparently convinced not only by my answers but also by my appearance that I was not a likely target of womanizing. Half an hour later he apologized for troubling me, then said my rank seemed lower than my ability.

Such petty concerns lost significance when Burma applied for Least Developed Country (LDC) status from the United Nations to gain relief from its foreign debt. Everyone's attention focused on the economic crisis. The country's foreign exchange reserves were depleted, and already Brig. Gen. Aung Gyi had written open letters to General Ne Win advising that the dire economic situation could trigger unrest, recalling the rice riots in 1967. Ne Win appeared to heed the warning and acknowledged in a radio speech on August 10, 1987, that our economy was in decline. Although he insisted that shortages of rice and essential goods were rare, this was the first time an official statement had confirmed so bluntly the failure of the Burmese Way to Socialism.

Three weeks later, on September 1, 1987, everyone felt encouraged to hear an announcement easing regulations controlling the transport of staple foods like rice, beans, and corn. Rice had become a restricted commodity in the 1960s, which brought a rapid decline in the productivity of Burma's fertile paddy fields. Transport regulations limiting distribution were strictly enforced, which maintained an artificially high price that contributed to shortages. Merchants could distribute rice within one state or division, but transporting it to another region was prohibited. If they crossed the Iva Bridge over the Irrawaddy River, leaving the Mandalay Division and arriving in the Sagaing Division, transporting rice became a crime. Sometimes even a single bag of rice intended for a monastery would be confiscated if it was carried from one division to another.

I observed at first hand the consequences of transport restrictions when I returned by bus in 1980 to Rangoon from Prome, a commercial city surrounded by paddy land. Rice bags were stacked on the floor and roof of the passenger bus after traders received a tip that this route was clear for a week, with no inspection. Instead of passing directly north from Meikhtila in the middle of the country, where rice grown in the Delta was collected, the bags of grain traveled south to Prome, then further south to Rangoon. From there they made a lengthy journey to Mandalay, either by bus or train, whichever was considered safer, then on to Lashio in northern Shan State, and finally across the border to China, their final destination. I knew that merchants were urgently transporting as much rice as they could carry, even though the added transport costs raised the price significantly. If these "profiteers" were caught, their rice bags would be seized and they would likely be jailed.

The sudden relaxation of transport restrictions seven years later raised some hope that Burma's economic difficulties might ease. The opportunity to sell and transport crops freely made commodity prices fall, and merchants collected any available cash, using every means, to start new business ventures. But the initial relief ended four days later. On September 5 the government announced its sudden decision to demonetize, allegedly to restrict the black market and solve the insurgency. It was the third time our existing currency had been cancelled, and the news caused outrage and a sense of des-peration. In 1964, the alleged targets of the regime's demonetization had been wealthy merchants who manipulated market prices. That announce-ment came when my family was returning from a holiday.

Six of us had traveled with my father by train when the Trade Ministry sent him on an official inspection tour. In Taunggyi, formerly a British hill station and the capital of Southern Shan State, I noticed that products displayed in the stores often seemed unsuited to local needs. Hill tribe people never like to eat fish paste, yet the stores had a fish paste quota they had to sell, and in one large village in Kayah State where there was no electricity, local shops sold ex-pensive electric rice cookers. But for us that trip was like a shopping spree. May May and her cousin stopped at every people's shop run by the Trade Min-istry to buy goods not available in Rangoon, even imported handkerchiefs, al-ways paying the special reduced price for officials. Later I thought about how my family benefited from those special privileges, and I also wondered if my parents had known some of their currency was about to lose its value.

The next demonetization in 1985 allowed the wealthy to profit at the ex-pense of the poor. As in 1964, the junta announced an interval during which some cancelled currency could be exchanged for compensation. Anyone with a valid state ID and family unit document could redeem up to five hun-dred kyats per family, but most of those who benefited were businessmen. They managed to salvage much of their cash by paying ten percent to any family that would exchange its otherwise worthless kyats.

The third demonetization was announced on a Saturday morning while I was visiting a painting exhibition in Judson Hall across from Rangoon Uni-versity, preparing to review the show for a private magazine. Just before en-tering the Judson compound, I noticed a minister's escorted car traveling through the streets with his golf set visible through the window. High-rank-ing officials frequently made business deals at Rangoon's Danyingone Golf Club, which served almost as an extension of their offices, but it was rare for them to leave the club before noon. Then I noticed artists at the exhibition unusually busy making sales and one woman who clearly knew little about art buying many paintings. When she said that the 11:00 a.m. news broadcast had announced a demonetization, I understood not just her buying spree but the minister's early interruption of his golf game.

So severe was Burma's economic decline in 1987 that rumors of a demon-etization had circulated. The government issued sharp denials, concerned that even the hint of devaluation would produce panic. After the 1964 demoneti-zation, the Information Minister was dismissed and sued for exchanging cur-rency based on prior knowledge, and the Post and Telegraph Commissioner

committed suicide after being sued on similar charges. Ne Win knew better than to provide prior information even to his inner circle, and earlier in
1987 newspapers had publicized a new policy to arrest anyone accused of
spreading dangerous demonetization rumors. Then on September 5, without
alerting even his cabinet, Ne Win passed a sealed envelope to the Information Minister. Inside were instructions to broadcast the enclosed announcement at 11:00 a.m.

I listened to the 1:00 p.m. news on a car radio outside the art exhibition.
When the announcer said government employees would receive 450 kyats as
emergency funding, I knew our kyat notes in denominations of 75, 35, and
25 had all been instantly devalued. At home that afternoon my family members gathered to pool our currency. Ko Gyi had received cash payment from
a client on Thursday, all in 75-kyat notes, and I had not yet opened my two
most recent pay envelopes, one containing my salary, the other my bonus,
also dispensed in 75-kyat notes. My brother and I together had only 25 kyats
in 10- and 5-kyat notes. Our other cash was useless. On Monday I received
my 450 kyats from the NPC in the new official denominations as emergency
funds and gave it all to May May.

The abrupt demonetization made clear the severity of the country's spi-
raling economic problems, but in one way, I thought ruefully, the demonetization was useful. Calculating purchases in 75-kyat and 35-kyat notes had always been difficult. The sum of the two notes added together was 110 kyats,
while the 75 and 15 denominations added up to 90 kyats, always difficult to
relate to the metric system. Burma's unusual currency notes had made every
financial transaction cumbersome.

For some reason I remembered May May asking Ko Gyi to buy duck eggs
when Pe Pe was in prison. Somehow my brother lost her 1-kyat note, and
I watched him retrace his steps in the front yard, staring intently at the
ground. For that 1 kyat in 1958 he would have bought 11 duck eggs, but in
1987 a single duck egg cost 2.5 kyats. Inflation had made our lowest currency
denominations so useless that small coins essentially disappeared from circulation, causing difficulty when we tried to follow the traditional funeral custom of placing a 25-*pyas* coin in a dead person's mouth.

Still hoping for compensation after the demonetization announcement in
1987, some people hoped to make a quick profit. Expecting a grace period,
they started collecting 75 kyats by paying 50, then collecting 30 kyats for the
same amount, then 20, until finally, when no followup news came from the
government, they realized they had lost everything. Two-thirds of the total
currency in circulation became useless paper, and ordinary citizens lost their
entire savings. Even the beggars suffered.

The situation seemed far more dire than in 1985, and on the afternoon of September 5, several hundred students from Rangoon Institute of Technology (RIT) staged a protest, taking to the streets, smashing street lights, and burning a government jeep. The outburst was quickly controlled and all universities shut down, but the damage from the demonetization could not be so easily contained. When I wrote my review of the art exhibit, my last lines described a painting that showed a duck egg lying broken on the grass.

CHAPTER ELEVEN

~

Political Training

According to BSPP rules, all government staff members had to attend the training course for the civil service established in 1965 as an instrument of the military's expanding control. For twenty years, newspaper staff remained exempt from that requirement, but after 1985 not even senior editors escaped political training. Soon after the September demonetization, I received notice to prepare for a four-month compulsory course at the Central Institute of Civil Service in Phaunggyi village, Hlegu township, some fifty miles from Rangoon.

Training sessions were directed at newly hired government staff, especially recent university graduates who accepted government jobs. Had I been forced to attend fifteen years earlier, perhaps I would not have felt so distraught, but at this later stage of life, I dreaded the requirement. I could not respond like a twenty-two-year-old undergoing physical training, running and jumping in response to a string of commands. At my age and with my years of work experience, I had no patience for military-style discipline, which required waking up before dawn every morning and living in communal barracks. But while I hated the idea of physical training and political lectures, what distressed me most was the regimentation.

Trying to accept the unavoidable, I traveled again to Kyaikhtiyo Pagoda in Mon State. Buddhist practice could not prevent misfortune, but it could bring peace of mind, and over the years I had traveled often to that place of rest and beauty. But I remembered how three villagers nearby had asked me to join them for a faith healer's consecration of the ground for a new pagoda.

For several hours I walked with them through open fields stretching toward the sea, passing small villages of thatched huts, finally reaching a square space marked off by a bamboo fence.

A thread over which Buddhist sutras had been recited twined through the fence to ward off evil, and at each corner offerings of bananas, coconuts, betel leaves, and tea leaves were carefully arranged. As a woman I could not enter the consecrated area or observe the faith healer performing his rituals, but when the villagers emerged, they complained that the faith healer had collected their donations, then disappeared. I wasn't surprised, as stories often circulated about charlatans who posed as faith healers, sometimes enticing village girls to have sex, then running away.

Several peaceful days at the Kyaikhtiyo Pagoda failed to ease my resentment, and back at home I was so irritable and rude that my brothers hardly dared speak to me. I spent weeks filling a large military trunk with an excessive amount of food, clothing, boots, sandals, and toiletries, taking a loan from the Cooperative Credit Society to cover the cost. As a permanent *New Light of Burma* employee, I had automatically become a member of the Workers' Organization, the Workers' Welfare Association, and the Cooperative Credit Society in 1981, requiring me to attend at least three meetings a year. For the first time one of my memberships proved useful. On December 9, 1987, my departure date, I knelt on the floor and raised my hands to my forehead to pay respect to my grandmother. She was alone in the room, and suddenly I felt a sense of foreboding.

The newspaper sent a Nissan pickup truck to drive me to the training course since my travel was an official duty. Along the road to Pegu stretched paddy fields where rice fronds drooped under the weight of golden kernels, but my spirits never lifted. I stared out the window, unable to enjoy the landscape or even to feel compassion as we passed through impoverished villages. My only thought was how to avoid the training school. A friend in Rangoon had told me a trainee once fled the barbed wire–enclosed compound but was quickly caught, so I pushed aside my brief fantasy of a Shwe Ba–style escape.

Seven workers from my newspaper had requested leave to accompany me, partly showing their friendship but partly to enjoy the fresh toddy palm liquor available along the route. They seemed in high spirits as we followed smooth tree-lined roads, then bumpy tarred roads, finally dusty red dirt roads, passing villages, paddy fields, monasteries, and police stations. At one intersection I saw many people waiting for a bus to visit a detention facility called the Ye' Bet Center, a prison labor camp. Had we turned right at the final intersection before reaching Phaunggyi, we would have reached another detention center at Min-gone.

A two-hour drive brought us to the training center's main gate. At the women's compound, a guard halted our truck, warning that vehicles could not enter, and a uniformed woman in the guardroom assigned me to Number 3 barracks. Two of my co-workers carried my heavy trunk toward my lodging, but another blue uniform clapped her hands and shouted that men could not enter. My fellow workers drove away with troubled faces, but I knew they would soon relax at a toddy palm shop, sitting in a circle on the ground, passing around coconut shell cups of strong, clear liquor. Few women in Rangoon like that sharp, fermented taste, but I would have joined their circle, using my own cup.

The only option seemed to be opening my trunk outside the compound, carrying my things one by one, then dragging the empty box behind me, but I saw another woman looking helplessly back and forth and suggested we carry her trunk in first, then mine. Inside the barracks I read many rules and regulations, which specified only one shower a day however hot the weather. I was grateful that my bed was close to a window.

Most of my barracks mates were newly appointed university tutors and lab assistants or junior judicial officers. I was the fourth oldest woman and the only one from the Information Ministry. Judicial officers had previously attended their own training course, but their grades in this subsequent session would determine their assignment to posts in various townships, so again I was happy I had not passed the Registered at Law exam in 1975. Low grades in the training course would result in postings to less developed areas or places with no opportunity for extra income, so the judicial officers were eager to succeed. The rest of us attended only because it was required.

An introductory briefing stressed the requirement to salute our trainers. They referred to us by number, and I was trainee 62. Then they distributed three dark blue uniforms, one new and two used, including boots, hat, belt, and a small kit bag identical to those assigned to the Fire Brigade. The used uniforms were for ordinary wear, but on opening day we would appear in the new outfit of pants and long-sleeved dark blue shirts, cuffed neatly at the elbow. We also had to sew bright red and yellow cotton badges on each arm, the insignia of the training school. One was a cog wheel and the other an ear of corn, emblems of solidarity with the workers and peasants. My neighbor in the barracks, who was married and had left a three-month-old child behind, offered to sew on my badges since I had no skill with a needle and thread. She also helped me fold my blankets and mosquito net to meet military regulations.

At the opening ceremony we sat in matching uniforms like three hundred identical robots while the training school's top leader gave a speech. I had noticed his Mazda 929 sedan parked outside the hall, a sign that his status was equivalent to that of a minister. When he finished, we clapped our hands in unison, a set number of claps, all with the same timing. I could not find my bearings in such surroundings.

Assigned to clean the lavatory, I moved in a daze. Not noticing water on the steps, I slipped and fell hard, wrenching my back, almost grateful for the pain, as a medical checkup might earn me the coveted status "return to unit." Instead the clinic doctor said I would recover in a week and should meanwhile report to the clinic each morning. Excused only from physical and military training, I would still have to attend classes. From my bed on the second morning, I heard the roll being called for physical training with the report "one absent." That meant I had already lost one point. Everyone started with a total of twenty-five, but if you took leave, broke a rule, or made a mistake, like leaving a strand of hair on the bed or folding the blanket or mosquito net incorrectly, you had a point subtracted.

For the first weeks, those who had received previous military training at a Lanzin Youth course in high school or university were appointed as our company and platoon leaders. They knew by heart the paragraph titled "Our Belief" emblazoned on posters and billboards throughout the compound. That same declaration stating our principles as a socialist state appeared as the preface to every book published by the BSPP. We trainees recited it in the morning before class and in the evening before study hour. I knew only one sentence by heart: "If you are hungry, you can't observe the precepts."

Altogether about a thousand people trained in Phaunggyi at one time, and of the three hundred trainees in my course, eighty were women. Two other courses were conducted simultaneously. Ours was called Zeya Company, while the course for government clerks and office workers was Bala Company. The training school was run like a military camp, and trainers all had an army rank. Most had grown up in a military or police barracks, so their lives had long revolved around commands. Every morning we got up at 4:30 a.m. to perform housekeeping duties, sweeping the barracks inside and out, or filling water storage pots. After calisthenics we headed in formation to the canteen for breakfast and at the end of morning classes on workers' affairs or peasants' affairs or leadership goals, we marched back to the canteen for lunch. Whenever we passed a trainer with one or more stars, our company leader interrupted his shouts of left-right, left-right, and ordered us to salute.

At 1:00 p.m. we reported for more classes, sometimes on agriculture or animal husbandry, after which we had practical experience, like plowing a patch of dusty field to plant rows of rosella, a fibrous plant used in place of jute whose first sour leaves sometimes flavored our soup. In the classroom where a low roof trapped the fierce midday heat, I poured water on my chair seat, which dried in ten minutes, so I stood up to drench it again. The afternoon ended with military training. Then we jostled for space in the communal showers to wash away the sweat and dust, marched to dinner, reported at 7:00 p.m. to study hall, returned to our barracks at 9:00 p.m., and waited for lights out at 10:00 p.m. sharp. For the first month we rotated on two-hour sentry duty every night. The last shift started at 2:00 a.m. even though our daily routine began again at 4:30. Regimentation seemed one way for the government to show its contempt for intellectuals.

Nights in the barracks brought isolation and discomfort, especially after a heavy rain when all thirty women tried to dry their heavy uniforms inside. I stayed near the window until the lights went out to escape the dank, musty smell of wet clothing. A plague of mosquitoes and other insects in that tract of undeveloped land brought instructions every evening to tuck our netting securely beneath our mattresses before dark. I rarely paid attention. Sometimes my neighbor prepared the netting for me while I sat outside, grateful for the fresh air, relying on my insect repellent stick to fend off mosquitoes. Gradually I grew used to seeing centipedes inside the barracks, but I worried one day when a trainee killed a scorpion and also when trainers warned about blood-sucking leeches. Built on a former paddy field, the compound had no proper drainage system, and during the monsoon season, leeches collected in standing puddles of rainwater or clung to the brush and grass.

When I had trouble falling asleep, I sat outside under a lamppost to read a book and light a cigarette. One night a trainer on her rounds told me to stay inside the barracks whether or not I wanted to sleep, and the next day she announced a new regulation—everyone must remain inside the barracks after lights out. From then on, I drank spirits in the darkness after others fell asleep. The men's wooden trunks were regularly searched for alcohol, but no one bothered to check our barracks because women generally did not drink. The local distilled liquor was easily available, and some trainees used it as a liniment for the joint pains that followed our strenuous physical exercise. Several barracks mates offered their liquor if I needed more, but I always declined. If my disregard for regulations caused a problem, I wanted no one else to be implicated.

I smoked a lot in Phaunggyi, and when I ran out of cigarettes asked for cheroots from a male classmate, a BSPP friend who disapproved of my behavior. I knew that everyone from government offices and factories received a monthly allotment allowing them to buy the local Duya or Khapaung brands, which some staff members sold to make a profit. Smoking harsh cheroots gave me a chronic sore throat, so I wrapped a scarf around my neck when cooling temperatures in the evening brought early morning mists before the heat of midday. One trainer reprimanded me for violating the uniform code, but I argued that no rule prohibited wearing a scarf. Thereafter I was allowed to wrap myself in a scarf only when I was inside the women's compound.

Gargling eased my sore throat, and I also cut back on smoking, thinking about Burma's villages where both men and women smoke even cruder cheroots. If they have no access to corn husks or leaves from the tropical aloe-wood tree, they use pages from newspapers, ignorant of the danger from lead in the newsprint. Often they ask their children to light their smokes, passing the habit on to the next generation. One of my paternal aunts in Sandoway owned a small cheroot factory, and she and her sister-in-law would sit together smoking while they rolled a mix of chopped tobacco stems and other ingredients. After smoking for several decades, she died like my father from lung cancer, followed six months later by her sister-in-law.

Three weeks had passed when I noticed my barracks neighbor weeping. It was Christmas morning, and she was a Christian. To cheer her, I made a card to give her as a gift. I had only a few soft pens, but with those and some white paper, I drew a Christmas bell. Others surrounded me, asking if I would draw pictures for them. Making those amateur holiday cards helped me forget that on Christmas Day in Rangoon I would have joined my Christian friends to share their festivities. That night when my neighbor and I were assigned together to guard duty, we sat on low chairs outside the main door of the barracks, gazing at the night sky, and she started quietly singing "Silent Night." Then together we sang one Christmas carol after another, mingling our voices and tears with the stars and the darkness. We didn't stop even when the duty officers ordered us to sing Burmese songs, as I said the only one I could sing from beginning to end was the national anthem.

Petty rebelliousness was my way of preserving some shred of independence. Study hall rules specified that we could read only assigned documents, but I carried my own books in my shoulder bag. When the duty officer made her rounds, my neighbor placed a document in front of me, not wanting me to get in trouble. I pushed it away, and the duty officer pretended not to notice. Another night a different duty officer asked why I wasn't studying, then asked what was in my bag, so I turned it upside down to show her the contents. She ordered me back to the barracks to bring the books I had been issued, like *Milestones of Burmese History* and *World History Milestones* published by the BSPP. Then she made a new rule just for me. I had to study course materials during study hall. After that I opened an assigned book but never read a line, and the duty officers

said nothing more. Wasting precious time in such a meaningless way made me
always sad, and one day I wrote a poem.

> these wings
> fly not
> though I yearn
> to spend
> long days
> with you
>
> those songs
> sound not
> though I long
> to sing
> always
> to you
>
> this pain
> eases not
> though I hope
> to catch
> poems
> that flee
>
> no songs
> no words
> faded sunset
> wilted flower
>
> without you
> this bird alone
> yearns

My resistance extended to the canteen. Food was ample at the training
school, but lining up for a meal made me remember visits to my father at Insein Prison. We entered the building to receive our trays from a trainee assigned as leader, and when everyone from the three companies was seated, a
senior company leader requested permission from a trainer to start the meal.
Then everyone except me recited the oath pledging to be loyal to the state
as we ate the food it provided.

For the first weeks I rarely touched the food at those communal meals. On
Sunday, Monday, Wednesday, and Thursday we were served yellow bean

soup, sometimes with a few pieces of duck or fish curry, but I could think only of my father's description of watery bean rations at the penal colony on Co Co Island. Even when the canteen served fried rice mixed with boiled garden peas for breakfast, or tea with sugar and sweetened milk alongside cookies, or deep-fried twisted dough sticks, I took just a couple of spoonfuls and gazed at the others. Some trainees said the meals were better than at their university hostels, but I preferred to wait and later mix boiling water with instant coffee, adding packets of powdered milk from my trunk to accompany the snacks I had carried from Rangoon.

In those surroundings my provisions stood out as a luxury, and soon I felt self-conscious, noticing that only a few of my barracks mates could afford to drink coffee. Not wanting to set myself apart, I started drinking the low-quality tea in the dining hall along with the others. When one of the friendliest trainees offered words of criticism during a meal, I felt ashamed. Looking at my unhappy face and noticing my refusal to eat low-quality rice and tasteless curry, she asked how I could know the people's life as a writer if I didn't eat such foods. Her words forced me to eat a bit more of the canteen fare. Soon I stopped carrying the packs of soft tissues bought in Scott Market and Chinatown to use instead of a coarse toilet roll.

Finally after the first month of training, we could request overnight leave and return home. The fifty-year-old bus from Phaunggyi to Rangoon traveled much too slowly, and I stared out the window at the people and the city buildings as if I had never seen those sights before. I felt changed, having learned how to live together with many women, how to deal with trainers, how to survive regimentation. One trainer encouraged me, saying that I would form the habit of getting up early in the morning. I doubted that pattern would continue, but I did resolve after washing my heavy uniforms by myself to do my own laundry in the future and not leave it for a maid at home.

With my hair still short and my skin darkened by the sun, my brothers hardly recognized me. First I slept, then wandered in the streets buying snacks and fruit to last for another week. The training course was a kind of test for me, I thought on the bus back to Phaunggyi. I saw myself as one of those weighted dolls that rights itself whenever it is knocked down and determined to try harder to detach myself from life's changing circumstances. During a political class that week I wrote a poem, and on my next home pass offered it to a private magazine, *White Jasmine*. It appeared some weeks later, in March 1988, the month of Resistance Day.

never caring when cast aside
when shouted at
or cheated

never proud when praised
fearful when threatened
exalted when lifted high

never falling when battered down
but standing firm
facing challenge

boldly claiming
righteous grace
in the proper place

unflagging when cast aside
steadfast when flattened down
never prostrate

standing firm
in this harsh life
one continues

The second phase of training taught us to handle weapons, and we marched each afternoon to the arsenal to receive decommissioned rifles. After two hours of holding the rifle butt against my shoulder the first day, my upper arm ached sharply. I understood why some women had folded small towels under their shirts as cushions, and the next day offered to help my neighbor carry her rifle, as she was still weak from childbirth. Soon I preferred carrying two guns, which allowed me to follow behind the company rather than marching in regular formation. Even with the extra weight, I preferred walking by myself at the rear.

Allowed to select our company leaders, we chose Naw Naw, the friendly barracks mate who had urged me in the dining hall to eat the food provided. If she needed volunteers, she always asked me and one other woman to help. When others saw me sweeping up fallen mango leaves in the compound, they joined, saying that if the older one helps, the younger ones could not avoid pitching in. Growing accustomed to the petty regulations, I stopped wasting energy resisting and followed most of the rules.

As the weeks passed, I sat through lectures on political science, history, law, economic planning, health education, accounting, administration, public relations, office correspondence, and many other topics quickly forgotten. No one could master so many subjects so I let my mind wander during classes, pretending I was taking notes while I drew a picture or wrote a poem. I started chatting with those lecturers who were from civilian departments, remembering my days in the BSPP office and understanding that some performed their jobs simply out of obligation.

Union Day, February 12, fell on a Friday in 1988, and I arrived in Rangoon on a holiday pass on leave, so tired that I lay on the floor of our sitting room exhausted. I didn't notice that my grandmother, then eighty-seven, no longer had her usual talkative manner. When I helped her in the bathroom, she said softly that she was useless now and would like to die. That afternoon my sister called me to say something was wrong. I quickly checked my grandmother's breathing but did not find a pulse. The doctor who looked after our three widows, my grandmother, my grandaunt, and my mother, confirmed that she had passed away. Perhaps she waited to say goodbye to me, but then death came fast.

Wanting to take part in her last journey, I asked that the cremation take place on Sunday morning before I returned to Phaunggyi after my weekend leave. Ko Gyi started arranging for cemetery costs and ordering small snacks like roasted watermelon seeds to offer visitors, and everyone at home grew busy with many tasks—applying for the death certificate, placing news announcements, renting buses to carry guests, informing monks about the offerings, ordering fans for the funeral attendants. Receiving special permission, I returned home on Wednesday afternoon, in time to greet relatives and a few guests from the NPC who attended the seventh day alms offering. Grief shadowed my next weeks at Phaunggyi as I remembered my grandmother and tried to absorb my family's most recent loss.

CHAPTER TWELVE

~

Confrontation

Despite its fertile land and abundant natural resources, the Socialist Republic of the Union of Burma in 1987 had officially become one of the world's poorest countries, ranked economically alongside Bangladesh and Ethiopia. Designation by the United Nations as a Least Developed Country meant that Burma's per capita income was below $200 and its ratio of manufacturing to gross domestic product below 10 percent. Shocked by the country's diminished stature in the world, Burmese people felt shamed and angry.

On March 14, 1988, I overheard shocking news at the Phaunggyi training center that students from the Institute of Technology (RIT) were again demonstrating in Rangoon. After evening study I regularly went to the common room to read newspapers and that night overheard a trainer say that protests had been reported on the radio. Eager to verify her information, I listened on the farthest, darkest side of the compound to the 9:15 English news on a transistor radio kept illegally by a newly arrived trainee. Hearing the disturbance mentioned on the official BBS broadcast, I knew it must be serious. The next day the whole training school talked about the student protests.

Overnight passes were denied that week, but from visitors and other trainees, I pieced together what had happened. On March 12 local youths had quarreled with RIT students in the Sanda Win teashop, named for Ne Win's favorite daughter. The son of a BSPP official had started a brawl that left one student, hit in the head with a chair, seriously injured. Police arrested the instigators but quickly released them, and the next day students surrounded the local People's Council office to protest the injustice and obvious police favoritism. Riot troops suppressed the demonstrators with force on March 13, killing RIT student Phone Maw.

Another student, Soe Naing, had apparently died while in the hospital after gunshot wounds. People said he was refused medical treatment because he would not state that his injuries came from climbing over barbed wire and scrap iron. When a second wounded demonstrator, Myint Oo, also died in the hospital, outraged RIT students distributed leaflets and posters to other universities to protest the deliberate medical negligence. That brought soldiers and riot police to raid the RIT campus where hundreds were arrested. The news I heard at Phaunggyi on March 15 was the BBS announcement that the RIT campus was again under control.

On an overnight pass to Rangoon the following weekend, I saw two open trucks on the road to Hlegu carrying prisoners with newly shaved heads and dirty white uniforms, most likely headed to the Ye' Bet Center prison labor. At home I tried to gather information about the shocking violence. Rangoon University students, determined to march to the RIT campus some five miles away on March 16, had been blocked from both directions on the sixth mile of Prome Road by special forces soldiers and riot police, called *lon-htein*. Wealthy people's homes with large gardens and high fences lined one side of that broad boulevard, and on the other side a high embankment bordered Inya Lake. That was where the combined troops attacked. With escape routes cut off, some students managed to climb over the walls and gates of private homes. Police chased others up the embankment, and a number drowned in the lake, apparently beaten unconscious by the *lon-htein*.

When I returned to Phaunggyi on Sunday evening, one trainee who lived near RIT showed me a photograph of Phone Maw, saying he was cremated secretly on March 17, ahead of the funeral plan arranged by his family. She told me anger was seething among the thousands of sympathizers who planned to attend Phone Maw's funeral. We also heard rumors that universities would remain closed, that students were being brutally beaten in jail, and that the *lon-htein* had raped girls in detention. Hearing similar stories from different people left me in no doubt about the soldiers' brutality.

By then I was counting how many full moon days I would watch from the Phaunggyi compound. On April 29, the last day of the training course, I marched in a military parade to receive my certificate. Then I was free. The newspaper office sent a pickup truck with several staff members who requested leave to meet me. We stopped at three toddy palm liquor shops along the road to Hlegu. The workers, passing around a coconut shell cup, spoke angrily about the treatment of a *New Light of Burma* driver swept up in a prison van along with a crowd of demonstrators on March 16. No one had received water in the stifling heat, but the driver survived and was taken to a detention center, then released. More than forty people died from suffocation inside the locked van. Such stories of police brutality hardened the mood of protest.

I returned to work on May 1. Never had I seen Rangoon so tense. People shared rumors about student leaders establishing a network of small, secret groups in which members knew only one person in the larger organization, and by the time universities reopened on May 30, we heard that pamphlets circulated among students, and speakers demanded the reinstatement of those expelled and the return of anyone still in detention after the March protests. Accounts of torture and rape from classmates already released were provoking heated campus meetings. University and high school groups were said to be organizing together, and the names of student leaders like Min Ko Naing and Moe Thee Zun, who emerged as spokespersons, soon became familiar. The Education Ministry's response to continuing demonstrations was to close down Rangoon University again on June 17.

Somehow people still dared to protest, and the sound of shouting voices drew me to the front gate of our house on York Road four days later where I saw a crowd of onlookers cheering and clapping in support of marching demonstrators. Students waved banners displaying their slogans, penants with the fighting peacock logo of the abolished student union, old national flags that evoked Burma's independence struggle, and posters with Aung San's photograph. The protest was peaceful, but when I saw the marchers, I wondered if the point of toleration for the country's decline had passed.

As I watched and worried, my eyes filled with tears to think about the courage required for such public demonstrations. Ignoring May May's urging that I stay at home, I left for the newspaper office, where a cluster of workers talked excitedly outside the gate. The demonstration had started at the Institute of Medicine on Prome Road, they said, more than an hour's walk from downtown, and along the route high school students, monks, and ordinary people had come out to support the medical school organizers. Confrontation seemed inevitable.

Before I reached home late in the afternoon, security forces were already firing tear gas and bullets into the crowds. One of my brothers watched a sharp clash between protesters and police, and said that a fire truck carrying six dead policemen had been torched. The violence escalated quickly, and a curfew was announced. Foreign diplomats later estimated that more than eighty civilians and twenty policemen were killed in Rangoon on June 21.

Every newspaper, including the English edition of *Working People's Daily*, carried the curfew announcement:

It is hereby made known to the working people of the Rangoon City Development area that, commencing 12:30 hours on 21 June 1988 in some townships within Rangoon City Development area, crowds bent on causing disturbances and violence refused to follow and obey the lawful, peaceful and unarmed endeavours of the members of the security unit of the People's Police Force to desist but to the contrary resorted to violence with attacks with sticks, dahs (knives), catapults and jingles (catapult arrows). . . . Considering that such acts are a threat to peace and security and may lead to conflicts and civil disturbances, the Rangoon Division People's Council Executive Committee has hereby issued this order . . . banning people from going outside from 6 a.m. to 6 p.m.

My family's house, close to City Hall and the Rangoon General Hospital, became a meeting place. Friends dropped by to tell what they had seen, adding to May May's worry. Like other parents with strong memories of earlier student protests, she pleaded with us not to get involved. Venturing outside our gate was the same as preparing for battle, she said. My grandaunt, expecting a shortage, headed to the market to buy supplies of dried and preserved foods. Things were happening quickly, and no one could guess how an open clash between the government and the people might unfold.

Burma seemed like a tinderbox waiting for any spark to ignite further unrest. Protests spread beyond Rangoon, and on June 23, police opened fire on demonstrators in Pegu, about fifty miles north of Rangoon. Two weeks later on July 9, the curfews imposed in Rangoon, Pegu, Prome, and Moulmein were lifted, but the spark soon caught fire again when a riot erupted between Buddhists and Muslims in Taunggyi.

A flood of rumors had apparently circulated accusing a Muslim of harassing a Buddhist novice and claiming that a Muslim teashop owner's son who attacked the young monk had been arrested, then released when his father offered a bribe. Monks protested the insult, and a mob burned down the Muslim teashop. When police took no steps to safeguard Muslim property, rioting spread unchecked for two days.

Clashes between Buddhists and Muslims in Burma had a long history, and political tensions could easily trigger religious conflict. I knew that after the Japanese occupation in 1942, Muslims in my father's native Arakan State, bordering what was then East Pakistan, had remained loyal to the British. The Japanese military authorities later encouraged the mostly-Buddhist BIA to attack Muslim villages in southern Arakan, and the displaced Muslim residents in turn attacked Arakanese villagers as they fled north.

The same religious bias had surfaced many times. Given the Burmese prejudice against Muslims based on race and religion, everyone knew that the military regime could easily provoke an incident, and some people assumed the monks involved in the Taunggyi conflict were actually soldiers with shaved heads. People also recalled how looting and violence had flared after the regime prompted anti-Chinese sentiment in 1967. Two decades later it seemed likely that religious hatred was again being deliberately aroused. A curfew was imposed in Taunggyi, but the mood of unrest spread, and rioting broke out also in Prome.

On July 22 the chief editor at the *New Light of Burma* called an emergency meeting to announce that after twenty-six years of state planning, the government's policy of economic centralization would be modified to include a market orientation. His voice sounded strained as he conveyed the official directive. Appointed only a year earlier, he had worked for *The Guardian's* English newspaper before receiving this promotion and seemed a quiet man with a kind heart. He was said to be fond of reading English books and was well liked by my friends at his former newspaper. A Karen and a Baptist, he was a widower and lived in the nearby town of Insein with his daughter in a compound beside the church built by his ancestors. That day his remarks seemed halfhearted. The government would remain in control of radio and television, he said, but private newspapers and privately run cinema houses would open soon. He kept his face utterly blank when he issued a final instruction ordering us not to publish any positive news about Britain or the United States, obviously a retaliation for criticism of the BSPP from both the BBC and the VOA in their coverage of Burma's unrest.

The new economic direction had not yet been announced publicly, but we understood that the sudden proposal for market reforms signaled another attempt to reverse the country's deterioration. No one expected *New Light of Burma* readers to believe the government's latest promises, but we did agree that offering some hope of economic improvement might calm the dangerous mood of discontent and the street demonstrations that surged in several provincial cities.

On July 23 we learned that Ne Win would make a speech at an emergency meeting of the Party Congress to more than a thousand delegates, and our editorial staff reported for standby duty while workers were called in on their day off. With only domestic news to appear in the newspaper that day, I was dismissed early and watched the televised speech at home. Ne Win sounded regretful at first, and his voice faltered so much that a BSPP secretarial board member read part of his speech. I listened intently, feeling overwhelmed by sadness for the state of my country and even some pity for Ne Win who seemed to acknowledge the extent of his unpopularity.

He said the regime had taken careful steps to prevent further bloodshed after the tragic incidents in Taunggyi and Prome, and the government had tried to restore law and order. Now he would resign from the party chairmanship because of his advanced age, aware that the bloodshed in March and June showed a lack of trust and confidence in the government. A national referendum would give people the choice between a single party and a multiparty system, he said, the first time we had ever heard official mention of a multiparty system. My family members listened in silence until Ne Win's tone shifted. With a flash of anger, he issued a final, unmistakable threat, saying that soldiers, if ordered, would aim straight ahead, not shoot into the air, and anyone inclined to anarchy should heed his warning, because facing the troops from then on would be no laughing matter. The mood in our living room instantly tensed.

Ne Win's resignation from office and the announced plan for a referendum raised some hope that the regime might actually change. But just three days later we learned that Brig. Gen. Sein Lwin, who oversaw the bloody crushing of demonstrators in March, had been named Ne Win's successor. One NPC driver recalled hearing Sein Lwin's voice on a police radio during the March demonstrations authorizing riot squads to "beat the heads" of the demonstrators. People assumed Sein Lwin had also been involved in suppressing the U Thant affair in 1974 and that he had likely given the order to fire on unarmed Rangoon University students in 1962.

Sein Lwin seemed to live up to his reputation when he proclaimed martial law on August 3 after a demonstration that drew some ten thousand participants. The Burmese term for a curfew order, *nay win mi njein*, literally means "as soon as sunset, switch off the light," and by then we were familiar with that regulation. Once again, anyone who violated the curfew could be arrested or shot, so the butchers and fishwives at Scott Market, with no way to preserve perishable goods, rushed to sell their meat and fish at huge discounts in the late afternoon. Because of the curfew order I could no longer wander through markets and bookstalls after work but had to return home immediately. I spent the evening hours inside, listening to the radio or chatting or cooking food.

Despite the martial law restrictions, protests continued, and in the hours not covered by curfew, smaller crowds still marched downtown and congregated around City Hall, distributing leaflets, making impromptu speeches, and calling for Sein Lwin's removal. From the windows of our typesetting room on August 4, I could see the five-lane junction where demonstrators would converge. Before the columns came into view, bicyclists had passed word of their approach, and I watched marchers with flags and banners join groups arriving from different directions, led by high school and middle school students in worn white shirts and frayed green *longyis*, their clothing a poignant reminder of the country's poverty. Students even rode on car roofs, somehow daring to issue a challenge, clearly knowing they might be killed.

I felt shamed. Adults did not dare join them, and I had none of their courage. Unlike in 1974 during the U Thant affair, I hesitated to enter the gates of Rangoon University. I wanted to understand the younger generation's thinking, but a visit to the campus would make Military Intelligence assume I had some connection with the activists and the students think I was an informer. Every day more students and monks urged participation in a nationwide strike to begin on Monday, August 8, 1988. The alignment of numbers made that date auspicious. The strike would begin with a walkout by dockworkers at eight minutes past eight o'clock in the morning on 8-8-88.

During those tumultuous days, Burma's news organs provided no coverage of the popular unrest so the foreign media gained enormous influence. Late in July, Christopher Gunness, covering Burma's chaotic events from Dhaka for BBC's Burmese program, managed to reach Rangoon on a tourist visa and announced the 8-8-88 strike date to the whole country on BBC news. He seemed implicitly to encourage people to take part, and the respect for Christopher Gunness was so widespread that some of us at the government press jokingly addressed each other as Ye Gunness and Aung Gunness, playing on the names of medical student leader Ye Min and our national hero Aung San. Not only did the British journalist make reference to the brutal suppression of the Phone Maw affair, but he also aired a taped interview with a female student, Aye Nyein Thu, who claimed that girls had been raped in prison after the March protests. That broadcast heightened people's anger.

On the morning of August 8, thousands of people surged through downtown Rangoon to support the general strike. With scarlet bands tied around their arms and heads, they carried the now familiar symbols of resistance— banners announcing slogans, old Burmese national flags, and posters with the portrait of Aung San. Their clenched fists along with their cheers and slogans calling for democracy proclaimed the spirit of defiance. Standing a short distance from the top of York Road, I could see the Sule Pagoda and watched the crowd of marchers with tense emotion. Inspired by their determination, I also feared the consequences of their challenge.

Unable to travel by bus when streets were blocked by demonstrators, I walked for forty-five minutes to reach the press compound, amazed by the extent of popular support. Crowds of onlookers thronged the sidewalks, and tens of thousands of demonstrators moved through the streets, clearly elated. At the press we learned that the strike had succeeded in shutting down both industry and transportation in many parts of the country. Somehow the day passed without retaliation.

Just after 10:00 that evening, I heard shooting. I rushed first to check on May May, giving her water to drink, then joined my brothers upstairs. From our back window we could see the street alongside Scott Market. The gunfire had come from the direction of Sule Pagoda, just a short distance away. Within ten minutes a few people reached the market in panic, but we knew most would flee in the opposite direction rather than head toward the War Office. I watched silently, gripped with fear, hearing the rumble of military vehicles pass in front of our house followed by bursts of machine-gun fire. I had never imagined such sounds in downtown Rangoon. May May was right, our city had become a battleground.

None of us slept that night, and more shooting broke the stillness of the early morning hours. With no public transportation, I gave in to May May's pleading and stayed away from the office. Sitting in my usual teashop at the top of York Road, I shared rumors and opinions with friends. The owner's son let me listen to the radio so I wouldn't miss the BBC news reports, and as the hours passed, I heard that soldiers in military vehicles had fired indiscriminately into crowds near the Sule Pagoda, with many casualties.

I had no idea how to help the wounded or the families of the dead, but according to Buddhist tradition we make an offering on the seventh day. As a gesture of support, I joined with a neighbor to collect donations from friends and acquaintances. People contributed readily, and on the sixth day after the killings, we went to a monastery and told the chief abbot we wanted to make an offering on behalf of the donors for those who died in the shooting. The monk accepted our donation in keeping with Buddhist belief that if no one makes an offering on behalf of a dead person, especially someone who dies through violence, he or she will not be freed from the endless cycle of rebirth. I saw no other way to express my sympathy and anger.

Outrage exploded after the August 8 killings, and students started boldly pulling off the scarves tied as masks around their faces, giving up their anonymity. Their speeches became more impassioned as they called for government staff to join the general strike and march alongside them. Meanwhile military vehicles patrolled in a show of force, taking direct aim at the few determined lines of demonstrators or anyone still carrying banners, flags, or Aung San portraits. Survivors gave chilling accounts of the bayoneting of unarmed citizens. At Rangoon General Hospital, demonstrators and sympathetic onlookers mixed with relatives and friends trying to identify the dead and wounded. One person told me that military vehicles had deposited a mass of wounded bodies outside the hospital, some already dead.

A neighbor said she saw young students dressed in their green *longyis* among those killed.

We also heard reports of violence outside Rangoon. Some three hundred people accused of trying to take over a police station were shot on August 9 in Sagaing, once the royal capital of Upper Burma and a quiet town dotted with monasteries and pagodas in the hills along the Irrawaddy River. People had also been killed in Bassein and other towns in the Delta area. Whenever the BBC's Burmese program reported which towns were taking part in demonstrations, people applauded.

Traditional notions of duty and discipline dissolved as passions ignited by the military's brutality combined with long-simmering personal resentments against the BSPP, sparking crude violence. Someone had only to point at a man he disliked and shout, "Look, that man is *ma-sa-la*," meaning a supporter of the BSPP, and others would rush to surround him. On August 9, soldiers knelt in formation and fired point blank into a North Okkalapa crowd before horrified witnesses, killing several, including a teenage girl carrying a portrait of Aung San. In the torrent of rage unleashed in that working-class suburb the next day, a mob beheaded a policeman. The densely populated satellite town served as a breeding ground for resentment and fertile soil for political agitation. The beheading drew cheers from local residents.

The military was said to be carting bodies away for disposal, their identities unknown, some of them not yet dead, and people described smoke spewing from Rangoon's main crematorium. When army trucks drove past the hospital early in the afternoon of August 10, my brother witnessed soldiers in one vehicle waving to the crowds just before those in the next truck opened fire. Victims' relatives gathered inside the hospital courtyard, as well as several doctors and nurses crossing Bo Gyoke Road, suddenly became targets. A number of people were killed and wounded. My brother, watching the carnage, ducked behind a bush and escaped injury, but the man beside him was shot in the leg. News of the army's latest brutality spread quickly, and people's anger turned wild.

When News Agency Burma released an announcement on August 12 that Sein Lwin had resigned, to be replaced by Dr. Maung Maung, a lawyer and writer educated in the West, some people rejoiced. Most found this attempt to calm popular anger unconvincing. Dr. Maung Maung had published a book in 1968 praising Ne Win, and later he was assigned to draft the 1974 Constitution. The leadership change seemed only the thinnest pretense of civilian rule.

CHAPTER THIRTEEN

~

Bullets at the Pagoda

Throughout the tumultuous weeks of July and August 1988, newspapers, television newscasts, and radio broadcasts repeated the junta's message that troops had tried to restore order. Some of those prescribed articles came from the Information Ministry and the BSPP, but perhaps 90 percent originated with Military Intelligence and the research section of the War Office. The goal was to cast the motives and tactics of protesters in doubt, but the result was growing anger at the complicity of the government press. In that charged atmosphere some NPC workers dared not return home to their tightly knit working-class communities where neighbors accused them of supporting the articles condemning the protests.

Viewers could tell immediately when a televised interview had been staged. One chief reporter at *New Light of Burma* was assigned to elicit an apology on camera for an arrested community leader's alleged antigovernment actions. The reporter had to rehearse for three days to master the questions and answers provided by Military Intelligence. Such propaganda efforts produced a reverse impact, and Burma's citizens from all walks of life spoke condemningly of "Sein Lwin's eighteen days." Dr. Maung Maung's appointment had little effect on public outrage.

Rangoon General Hospital became a public forum. Film stars, movie directors, writers, lawyers, private tuition teachers, and university graduates gathered to make speeches denouncing the attacks against nurses and doctors and criticizing the BSPP. Sometimes they engaged in witty repartee, but we also heard crude language alluding to Ne Win's personal life, especially his four alleged marriages. At home, at friends' houses, and at the government press, we read leaflets written by various newly formed organizations of students, monks, and professionals. Organizations like the Bar Council and the Medical Association continued to support protest activities after the removal of Sein Lwin, and rallies persisted with demonstrators thronging the streets in Burma's cities, satellite towns, and villages.

In another attempt to end the unrest, the regime appointed a commission on August 19 to investigate people's opinions about current political and economic conditions, then submit reports to the People's Assembly by the end of September. The commission's office was just a ten-minute walk from my house, and I saw tens of thousands of people march there to protest. In response to such huge demonstrations, the commission's leader, Chairman of the People's Justice Council U Tin Aung Hein, an ex-colonel and an outspoken man with a gray mustache who enjoyed considerable respect from the public, simply shut down the office after two days. According to rumor, he declared that the masses had made clear their dislike for the BSPP so there was no need for a commission to investigate.

Sunday August 21 was my day off. All morning I walked through the downtown streets, reading statements posted on walls and meeting with friends in teashops to exchange news. A car from the NPC was parked outside my gate when I returned home, and the driver handed me a note with instructions to contact the news director immediately. He also alerted me that I had been assigned a television interview to discredit the rape interview broadcast by the BBC in July. I told the driver I could not agree, but we both knew I also could not ignore the summons.

On Monday morning I was still debating how to respond to the summons when I headed out to the streets, determined that I would not accept the assignment but also not wanting to quit or cause problems for my chief editor. Over eight years working at *New Light of Burma*, I had come to feel part of a family at the NPC and devoted to my work as a journalist despite the controlled nature of our reporting. The officer in charge of administrative work at my newspaper was waiting at my front gate, and courtesy required that I invite him inside.

He seemed uncomfortable in our sitting room when he told me my head was too strong. I replied that even so, I could not hit my head against a concrete wall. He laughed awkwardly as my mother and grandaunt observed. Tomorrow we would have to buy our own newspaper, I told them quietly as I wrote a short letter of resignation. The administrative officer urged me to request temporary leave instead, so I agreed, uncertain what consequences my refusal of an assignment would bring. When a nationwide general strike was announced that day, I knew my interview assignment would not be the only thing to concern NPC leaders.

The next morning I reported as usual to my office, but not half an hour passed before the news director phoned to say he felt sorry I had refused the assignment, so I replied politely that I also felt sorry. He said he relied on me as a colleague, and I returned the compliment. Then he assured me we were like family members and he had always enjoyed discussing films with me. We continued trading courteous words, my answers almost rhythmic, until finally I spoke my mind. If he had assigned me instead to cover the demonstrations and report how many people had taken part, and where, when, and why, or how they were protesting, or what they were demanding, or how many had died in the shootings, I would even dare to walk amidst the bullets. He hung up the phone. I could never have said such things to his face.

Walking home on August 23, I saw the first indication that government personnel would participate in the general strike. A banner hung outside the Telecommunications Office declaring that its staff had taken part in demonstrations. That evening BBC news announced that telecommunication workers would join the work stoppage, and the next morning workers at *New Light of Burma* debated whether to follow the lead of typesetters at *The Mirror*, who had refused to print official articles denouncing the ongoing mass demonstrations. After several hours, the main NPC strike committee, a group of workers and desk editors who knew they could be arrested with serious consequences for their families, announced their decision to join the strike. I felt collective relief among my colleagues, mixed with apprehension.

Responding to the crescendo of events, Dr. Maung Maung made a public speech on August 24, carried live on radio and television, announcing that martial law would be lifted and a special BSPP congress convened to prepare for Ne Win's promised referendum on one-party rule. Few believed the Western-trained lawyer's elegant words and assurances, but exuberant crowds still took to the streets in celebration. That afternoon, musicians performed from open trucks to cheering audiences, famous singers serenaded demonstrators with lyrics about democracy, and cymbals clanged as if they were ringing in the Water Festival. Monks and ordinary workers shouted, "We want democracy," as if years of suffering and repression might soon come to an end. The day's developments fed people's yearnings, and many acted as if victory had already been achieved. That afternoon I marched for the first time. Watching the jubilant demonstrators, I felt enormous love for my people but also pity and fear. Power was not yet in their hands.

No newspapers appeared on August 25, but everyone reported to the press compound for the sit-in strike. Later that morning I marched with a group of artist friends, then joined my *New Light of Burma* colleagues to listen to a speech by Aung Gyi at the Padonma grounds, close to my high school. Ex-Brig. Gen. Aung Gyi had just been released from confinement. Ne Win's closest comrade since the 1940s and long a high-ranking officer, he had been arrested during Sein Lwin's eighteen-day rule after writing a series of open letters to Ne Win criticizing the junta. When he was jailed, not everyone believed his opposition was authentic, but May May said he was bearing the consequences of his past misdeeds, mindful that Aung Gyi had been second in charge of the caretaker government when Pe Pe was arrested in 1958. Thirty years later Aung Gyi was a successful businessman with a prospering chain of bakeries and teashops and his own political ambitions.

After martial law was revoked and a referendum promised, Aung Gyi was not the only political leader hoping to influence the direction of Burma's future. News spread quickly that General Aung San's daughter would make a speech at Shwedagon Pagoda on August 26. Rather than joining anyone from the press for that gathering, I marched again with artists and cartoonists under a banner that identified our group. Never had I seen such a huge wave of people surging ahead, and I wondered how many Rangoonians had stayed at home. The crowd, perhaps five hundred thousand strong, pressed inside the Shwedagon compound, and our group could not get near the foot of the pagoda where the only daughter of our national hero would speak.

Aung San Suu Kyi, then forty-three, had married British scholar and Tibet specialist Michael Aris in 1972 and raised two sons abroad. Over the years she received sharp criticism from conservative Burmese for her foreign marriage, but the serious illness of her mother, a distinguished diplomat and Burma's former ambassador to India, brought her back from Britain on April 1. Nearly five months later, with the country in crisis, the masses did not care that her husband was British. Yearning for a benevolent leader, they trusted in Aung San's blood.

For several hours I waited in that expectant crowd as her car inched forward and supporters arranged her security. I met many friends, some eager to hear Aung San Suu Kyi's words, some just wanting to see Aung San's daughter, others appearing as a protest against the junta. When finally she began to speak, waves of applause drowned out her words despite the many loudspeakers. Only the next day when her full speech appeared in one of the privately printed bulletins that sprouted after the general strike did I learn what she said.

Praising the students' willingness to sacrifice their lives, Aung San Suu Kyi asked for a moment of silence, both to show respect and to share the merit of their deeds. She explained that she was accepting a political role only because of the national crisis, which she called the country's second struggle for independence. Pledging to follow in her father's footsteps and struggle for democracy and freedom, she insisted that all demonstrations proceed peacefully, with tolerance overcoming differences. In her final resonant words, she called for dismantling the one-party system and moving quickly to free and fair elections. What impressed me most was the way her rousing calls for change accompanied urgent requests for discipline and unity as the best way to demonstrate the entire population's desire for multiparty democracy.

The spirit of peaceful dissent seemed contagious. Aung San Suu Kyi's invocation of Burma's "second struggle for independence" filled people with hope and resolve, and that day thousands of government workers joined the marches with banners announcing the names of state ministries and departments. Police and customs staff marched in uniform, and even some BSPP staff members dared join the protests. Peasants arrived in trucks from villages along the Rangoon-Pegu Road. Groups of gay men joined together in a throng of beauty parlor workers. Housewives marched with their associations, carrying pots and pans, baskets and spoons, calling attention to their economic plight. Seeing the exultant, determined crowds, I couldn't help worrying that the government would easily find an excuse for military intervention.

The next day the NPC strike committee agreed to print some information from News Agency Burma, whose workers had also joined the strike, provided that half the articles appearing in *New Light of Burma* and other newspapers were selected independently by the editors. Dr. Maung Maung's news still appeared at the top of the front page on August 28, but below that lead story and on the inside pages readers found uncensored reports sent by different strike committees and trade unions. Even partial press freedom brought enthusiastic response.

I was reassigned from the city section back to foreign news, and with the marking system suddenly abolished, I could report on previously forbidden topics like the tensions between Turks and Kurds or an incident in Iraq when police opened fire against separatists using plastic bullets. U Naing Aung wrote short, bold headlines, even borrowing a question from demonstrators: "What do you want? . . . DEMOCRACY!" Readers praised those post-strike issues, saying our country had real newspapers at last.

With no public transportation, typesetters walked to the office, and some press workers stopped their supplementary jobs and spent hours gathering statements from independent organizations. Editorial writers functioned also as local reporters, collecting information on breaking events, while photojournalists spread across the city, eager for uncensored images to appear in print.

The government seemed to have collapsed in those heady days of late August, and the military stopped intervening, just watching the crowds. People ignored trucks filled with troops, rejoicing in their new freedom and sense of victory, but I still worried. Starting on August 26, the government had released some nine thousand prisoners from jails across the country, and the crime rate was rising. News that five thousand convicts had been released from Insein Prison alone led to rumors about suspicious cases of arson and poisoned water supplies. With looting and vigilante violence spreading, fear grew at the idea of having criminals loose in society, perhaps people desperate for money and food. Formal law enforcement seemed suspended, and many of us suspected the government's motives.

Townships and neighborhoods established their own security forces with residents assigned sentry duty, and even monks in cinnamon robes took their turn. I passed many checkpoints on my way home every evening, set up by ad hoc committees trying to maintain security. Meanwhile soldiers watched from their trucks, sometimes accepting food and water from well-meaning crowds, sometimes standing like statues. Military efforts to heighten the anarchy seemed unmistakable, yet no one could predict how events would unfold.

At my newspaper office on September 8, I learned that a large crowd had gathered at the top of York Road outside the Dagon township People's Council office, now occupied by the township's strike committee. Next we received a shocking report that three people accused as informers had been beheaded. The chief reporter asked me to cover that event because it was near my home. Cautious about mingling in such a huge crowd, I watched the mob from two blocks away while a neighbor closer to the scene relayed information to me by phone. I filed a preliminary report, and once the crowd dispersed, interviewed witnesses to write the full story.

Rumors about poisoned drinking water had already circulated in the city. Demonstrators were suspicious of anyone offering water to quench their thirst, so word spread quickly when five people were allegedly caught poisoning a water tank at the Dagon township children's hospital. Witnesses told me that local citizens held the culprits while many people rushed to surround the strike office. Angry voices in the crowd then demanded the suspects be handed over, and somehow the alleged poisoners were seized by the mob. Three were killed, then beheaded, including one woman, their heads publicly displayed, and the corpses set afire in full view of the crowd. Approaching the scene several hours later, I nearly vomited from the stench, but it was difficult to tell what had actually happened.

I tried to piece together the story at the Dagon township strike committee office. Five suspects had been caught red-handed with small vials of chemicals and *jingles*, slingshot arrows, and two of the five had somehow escaped the savagery, a pregnant woman and an older man. He had allegedly admitted poisoning the hospital's water supply but claimed he was carrying out instructions from someone who had paid him ninety kyats, called Bo Thanmani, a name that meant Lt. Steel. In the township office I saw what had allegedly been seized as weapons but noticed they were not bicycle or umbrella spokes, accessible to ordinary citizens, but 4-inch lengths of steel. And they had not been sharpened. We all knew that standard steel rods could be obtained only through the Ministry of Industry, responsible for the manufacture of hardware and small arms.

Rumors had already circulated that the military planned the water poisoning incident to escalate the cycle of violence and display Rangoon's lawlessness when my report of the beheadings appeared the next day, both in *New Light of Burma* and *The Mirror*, along with my appeals to readers to exercise restraint. Later I read the English-language *Working People's Daily* account of those events, which named the persons involved but differed from my account in several details: "Members of the Sangha [monks] and students allegedly caught one Maung Hla Kyaing, who was poisoning drinking water pots near the Central Women's Hospital in Ahlone Township. . . . Of the arrested persons three were killed by the working people." I knew it was impossible to determine exactly what triggered the mob violence, just as it was also impossible to imagine where the unleashed passion and vengeance would lead.

People seemed to confuse anarchy with freedom. Factories were broken into and stolen goods resold. Luxury items available only from warehouses controlled by the military elite appeared in the streets of downtown Rangoon. I saw unbelievably low prices for food, milk powder, medicines, imported consumer goods, and even corrugated iron sheets, and I also watched the buying and selling of imported products previously available only at a high price on the black market. State-run BBS radio began broadcasting increasingly lurid reports of the growing anarchy, and BBS television news announced that the Institute of Medicine's laboratory had been broken into and smashed. When one private newsletter printed a photograph of a soldier opening a warehouse, some people felt certain the military was intentionally increasing the lawlessness.

As street violence spread, local BSPP party and council members dared not appear in public. Rich people, not only military officers but also civilian businessmen, feared they were in danger, and soon Rangoon students called for a hunger strike to protest the lawlessness. Meanwhile at *New Light of Burma* we had already heard leaked reports of a secret meeting held almost two weeks earlier on August 23 at Ne Win's residence, which suggested that junta leaders had indeed developed a plan to resume control, despite the façade of civilian rule.

I repeatedly asked people if they noticed that soldiers had failed to stop the crowd from beheading the three accused persons in my township on September 8. The War Office was less than five minutes away from the Dagon People's Council office, and a military truck full of soldiers had been stationed very near the scene. Firing just one round of blank cartridges might have prevented that outburst of crude violence. I knew it was significant that soldiers had not intervened, but those caught up in the protests disregarded such warning signs. Meanwhile newspapers carried stories about political figures who for years had remained far from public view, like ex-Prime Minister U Nu, then in his eighties, ex-Gen. Tin Oo, and Mann Win Maung, Burma's president from 1960 to 1962. All made public statements, and people waited eagerly for those former leaders to forge a coalition, but instead splits within the opposition became evident. With people thirsting to set up their own organizations, coalitions seemed impossible to sustain.

Student unions and monk associations emerged along with groups representing high schools, townships, lawyers, private tuition teachers, housewives, and artists. In late August, the General Strike Committee had tried to form a united group incorporating all constituents from across the country but found it difficult to meet together in one place with transportation almost completely stopped and communication sometimes impossible. The All Burma Federation of Student Unions joined briefly with monks' unions throughout the country to occupy township offices and take charge of local administration, but that umbrella group had also fragmented.

With censorship removed, *New Light of Burma* received a stream of information and position statements from newly formed organizations and privately published newsletters. Independent groups telephoned to describe their activities, press conferences, and planned demonstrations, or to announce a scheduled meeting place and time. Often my newspaper received information that reflected unfavorably on the government, like the collective burning of party membership cards by a group of BSPP members and the protests by diplomatic staff at Burma's embassies abroad. Never before had we covered such stories.

The political shift began on September 11, when Dr. Maung Maung delivered a speech saying the time had come to restore law and order and that people who had contributed to the state of anarchy would soon run far away. His warning suggested a reassertion of military power. Even though he also announced the establishment of a new election commission to oversee the national referendum, he rejected demands for an interim government. Those with astute political minds concluded that the essence of Dr. Maung Maung's remarks differed little from the thrust of Ne Win's resignation speech in July, except the tone was softer. Once again events unfolded quickly.

Two days later, U Nu, Aung Gyi, Tin Oo, and Aung San Suu Kyi met jointly with the new election commission to condemn the continued exclusion from power of the people's most trusted leaders and to press for an interim government. *New Light of Burma* and other newspapers reported the news as before, but I sensed a change when I walked through the streets and noticed the deputy prime minister's car with its usual escort heading toward downtown Rangoon. Students, monks, and nuns marching in the same direction shouted, "Down with dictatorship," blocking the car and forcing him to turn back. I was so close that I could see his face as he passed. Despite the chaotic situation in the streets, he was smiling. Behind that smile, I thought, lay some plan.

By then millions of people had taken to the streets for almost three months to protest the military regime and call for democracy's return to Burma. We began to hear reports of troop movements, and I watched army trucks moving toward the downtown area with their canvas flaps tied down, raising the possibility they contained arms. Military vehicles carrying rice bags, furniture, and other provisions passed through the entrance gate of City Hall, signaling that soldiers were settling into that compound. Tanks and military trucks stood just inside its exit gate poised to move, and rumors claimed that soldiers were withdrawing cash from the Union Bank.

Meanwhile a writer and translator friend had asked for my help with an independent news magazine about to begin publishing. I had refused earlier requests to participate in private publishing efforts, but as the political situation grew more alarming, I wanted to contribute. When I agreed, my schedule grew busy. At the magazine office in the morning, I chose the news items I thought suitable, edited them, and handed them to the typesetters. If there was breaking news to cover, I went out to report and returned to the magazine office to write up stories about events or strike organizations. At midday I arrived at my newspaper office, where workers and editors also reported independently on strike events, then late in the afternoon I returned to the news magazine office. Often the situation had changed so fast the articles I edited in the morning were already outdated and needed revision.

The news magazine included a section of letters to the editor. Trying to pour a bucket of peaceful water on the raging fires of anger and hatred, I wrote many of them myself. Pretending to be a newspaper reader, I urged people to act with discipline, avoid unlawful acts, refrain from personal attacks, and remain calm. Always I stressed why we urgently needed peaceful demonstrations and an end to violence, but I knew no one could control the crowds. They lacked any experience with democratic practice despite their fervent goals. On September 16, I learned about the first arrests.

The next day a middle-class neighborhood of state-owned apartment buildings, named after Aung San's wartime AFPFL coalition, sponsored one of many public rallies. The event drew large crowds. Adjacent to the housing estate stood an area of shanties occupied by squatters who had fled their villages during the civil war and who worked as hawkers or odd-job laborers. Throughout Rangoon, those marginal city dwellers were often the first to take part in demonstrations. The weakest link in our society, they were the poorest, the least likely to find employment, the first to suffer from the economic crisis, and thus a ready source of opposition. At the rally on September 17, loudspeakers pointed toward the nearby War Office, displaying an undiminished boldness and spirit of provocation. One of the speakers was a popular novelist who sharply criticized Ne Win.

At the news magazine office that day, information arrived steadily by phone and messenger, but I could not verify its reliability or distinguish actual events from disinformation and rumor. I heard that activists and monks had climbed to the top floor of the Trade Ministry building in the heart of Rangoon to seize weapons and uniforms from security guards, and I couldn't imagine how my father would have responded had he been alive. The news magazine's chief editor authorized coverage of that event after we received one photograph showing a man climbing into the Trade Ministry building from an adjacent wall, and another showing a monk carrying guns, presumably seized from the ministry's security force. The next day we published both photographs and only later learned the photographs did not tell the larger story. In fact, soldiers had fired into a crowd of some fifty thousand demonstrators outside the Trade Ministry, and only then did Tin Oo and Aung Gyi condone student leaders' and monks' seizure of the security guards' weapons. At the time I had no way to tell that the military had planned both the incident and the photographs to justify its seizure of power.

That night I heard shooting at about 9:00 p.m. and ran to the top of York Road where I could see Sule Pagoda Road. Others I met in the street said not to go downtown as troops had opened fire on demonstrators, including students sitting peacefully outside the pagoda on a hunger strike. Back at home my brothers accused me of adopting the BSPP's tone when I remarked sadly that the crackdown was inevitable. They were right that I had never fully shared the popular euphoria. And I had said that the military would reassert its power.

By morning, the sounds of gunfire had ended so I ventured out into the streets, surprised to see people moving about the city as if the previous night's shootings had never occurred. In the park across from City Hall, the regular cluster of hunger strikers gathered to express their nonviolent opposition. During weeks of protest, the vigil had drawn donations of support, but it seemed especially courageous that morning when bullets had left fresh scars on the pillars flanking the entrance to Sule Pagoda.

~

CHAPTER FOURTEEN

Reprisals

At 4:00 p.m. on September 18, the announcer on official BBS radio read a prepared statement saying that General Saw Maung had taken power. Once again the army claimed it was assuming control to establish peace and tranquility and prevent the disintegration of the union. The English name for the new junta was the State Law and Order Restoration Council (SLORC), but in Burmese the title mentioned nothing about "law" but only "order," conveying the blunt fact of military rule. Expecting a curfew, I walked home from the news magazine office, watching vehicles packed with soldiers move slowly through the streets.

We heard the statement issued by the new military group repeatedly on the radio in the afternoon and again on BBS television when programming started at 7:00 p.m. Many things were prohibited, including "gathering, walking, marching in processions, chanting slogans, delivering speeches, agitating and creating disturbances on the street." Trained by the BSPP at both a Lanzin Youth Organization summer camp and the cadre school for ethnic minorities I once visited as a literacy volunteer, the television announcer never varied the flatness of his tone.

The SLORC leader, known for his loyalty to Ne Win, had formerly served as army chief of staff and also as Defense Minister during Sein Lwin's eighteen-day rule. When an 8 p.m. to 4 a.m. curfew was announced, my mother tried to joke, saying at least Saw Maung would bring all her children home early for once. I could not imagine the consequences of abolishing all administrative organs of the state. The only thing I knew for certain was that the brief flowering of an independent press was over.

The city fell silent when the curfew started. We didn't realize the silence would be brief. Just after 10:00 p.m. heavy vehicles passed in front of our house, and perhaps ten minutes later we heard shooting from the direction of City Hall. Ko Gyi's voice was tight with emotion when he said our grandmother was fortunate not to have lived to hear such sounds.

The next morning my youngest brother spoke for long periods on the telephone, then decided he would join the groups pledging to continue the protests. The danger was so acute that even I didn't want him to leave the house. Urging him to take care, I tossed him the camouflage-patterned baseball cap I had worn throughout the weeks of demonstration as protection from sun and rain. I thought irrationally that when my mother noticed he was gone, I could tell her my hat would shield him from the scorching midday sun. After that, I tensed at each burst of shooting.

At noon Ko Tue appeared at the door drenched with sweat, his face red, my cap still tucked into his *longyi*. Together with hundreds of students and recent graduates, he had marched toward the Secretariat building, running when troops opened fire. He was lucky. One of my cousins fell when a bullet grazed his leg, and an artist friend who waved his hands trying to stop students on a collision course with advancing troops felt a bullet pierce clean through his palm. Those were minor wounds. When soldiers started shooting at close range, many students in their sandals and *longyis* were killed.

I spent September 19, my thirty-eighth birthday, watching military vehicles ferry soldiers with fixed bayonets through the streets and listening to sharp bursts of weapons fire. That day no friends came to offer good wishes, we had no family gathering, and May May even forgot to send an offering to the monastery. I wrote just two words, "unhappy birthday," in the diary I had kept since seventh grade. Knowing I would pour out my anguish and denounce the murderers if I started writing, I feared to use my pen. Once written, words could not be denied, and people had been arrested for lesser offenses.

A methodical plan for military control subdued all remaining demonstrators with brutal efficiency. Troops used overwhelming force to crush any vestige of popular resistance, shutting down security posts and destroying makeshift barricades thrown up to slow their advance. They fired at anyone in the streets and sporadically used private houses and public buildings as targets, especially in outlying townships that housed poorly paid workers, like North Okkalapa where antigovernment sentiment was especially strong. Within days the city was transformed. Instead of watching people marching, singing, and waving banners in the streets, we saw armed soldiers and military vehicles. Official political slogans and posters appeared overnight on walls and billboards. One message, "Only the army is mother and father to the people," bluntly reversed General Aung San's famous statement, "The people are mother and father to the army."

The SLORC announced when it seized power that general elections would be held once law and order returned, but in the interim it nullified the 1974 Constitution, imposing many restrictions. No more than five people were allowed to gather in one place, so I took care to meet with friends one by one, exchanging information quietly, always alert for informers, never speaking freely. All weapons were to be surrendered at township police stations, including homemade daggers and guns held by licensed users, but I had no weapons. Only the announcement that all government staff must report to work on September 26 or face dismissal affected me directly. Once the military declared unlimited power, I had no idea what would happen to all of us at the NPC who had joined in strike activities.

Lacking any reliable domestic news source, people struggled with uncertainty and fear. Rumors spread quickly about the extent of the killing and about suspect lists and photographs in the military's hands. Reprisals were sudden and swift, and those suspected of antigovernment activity were found shot in the streets. Students simply disappeared. My news magazine editor saw soldiers on the Rangoon-Insein Road shoot a twelve-year-old schoolboy in a green and white school uniform even after he covered his hand, a gesture that everyone knew meant "please don't kill me." Meanwhile the BBC reported that foreign journalists like *Newsweek*'s Melinda Liu had published eyewitness accounts of the bloodshed and described troops shooting point blank into crowds. The foreign press was quoting survivors and diplomats to estimate the dead in Rangoon alone at one thousand.

We had no idea how many were dead or the number of students caught and jailed, but we heard that thousands had disappeared across Burma's borders, taking sanctuary in Thailand and India. Those who sought refuge with insurgency groups became rebels overnight, risking hunger and malaria in the jungle and assuring a dangerous future. At home I watched my youngest brother studying a map, aware that his girlfriend had already left for the Thai border. Friends expected them to marry, and I could not imagine the difficulty of his decision. Choosing my words carefully, I suggested that going to the jungle would not be easy for a boy pampered by his family. He ignored my comment, but as the days passed, I no longer saw him looking at his map. He knew he was May May's favorite. Meanwhile I faced my own decision.

Busy finding and punishing students, monks, military personnel, and civil service employees who had participated in demonstrations, the junta extended by a week the final date for government workers to report to their jobs. Staying away meant certainly being fired, possibly being arrested, and most of my press colleagues had families to support. On Monday, October 3, still uncertain, still debating, I showed up at my newspaper office at noon. I was the last to arrive. The NPC would print only one newspaper in two versions, I learned, *Working People's Daily* in Burmese and *Working People's Daily* in English. *New Light of Burma* would no longer publish. Worried about the contents of my desk, I wanted to check what I had left behind, but an army unit occupied the upstairs floor and refused to give me access to the newsroom.

Following instructions, workers as well as editorial staff signed in every morning, then left the building. I spent my afternoons in a teashop. The NPC was apparently busy identifying activists within its ranks, combing through photographs looking for press workers wearing red headbands, or waving their arms, or standing with their mouths open, a sign they had shouted slogans. Just a single photograph provided evidence of complicity, and the military apparently had many reels of videotape to review, as we heard that a prominent film director had turned over a hundred reels of video film to the SLORC. Those placed on a blacklist were summarily dismissed. Five from each newspaper were also placed on a brownlist, indicating their untrustworthiness. That served as a means of intimidation.

The SLORC's purge of anyone who had played a significant role in the demonstrations threatened all those at NPC who participated in the general strike. My former city editor, U Ko Ko, recently transferred to *The Mirror* in a staff shake-up, was under arrest for publishing a story about Ne Win's Swiss bank account. U Naing Aung, the first editorial staff member from *New Light of Burma* to join the main strike committee, was among the first to be sacked. He had five children but had to vacate his apartment in the NPC staff building immediately on October 13. The chief editor of the *Botataung* newspaper and nearly all desk editors at *Working People's Daily* were dismissed. My chief editor was under great pressure and tried to protect his staff, appealing to the leaders that having one of his editors fired was enough, but he could do no more. I had not participated prominently enough to be blacklisted, but my name appeared on the brownlist. That was a warning, since brown could change to black at any time. The label also denied me any chance for promotion, training, or foreign travel.

All traces of press freedom disappeared. Workers said that on the night of September 18, the military had burned every copy of *New Light of Burma* printed during the twenty-two days of independent reporting. They were certain that every document, photograph, photographic plate, film, and manuscript had been destroyed, but later when the government published its own accounts of the uprising we saw pictures that must have been saved. May

May conducted her own purge at home. She told a maid while I was at work to search for any papers and documents my brothers and I had collected during the demonstrations and burn everything. I was outraged to discover my papers destroyed, but she wanted to protect us by removing any evidence of antigovernment sympathies.

Once the SLORC reiterated that elections would be held as soon as law and order was restored, people seized on Saw Maung's earlier announcement that political parties could register with the Election Commission in preparation for a future multiparty referendum. The National League for Democracy (NLD), led by Aung San Suu Kyi and Aung Gyi, issued a press release announcing its formation on September 24.

Then the BSPP declared its rebirth as the National Unity Party (NUP), even though the name change hardly disguised the same policies and personnel. Within weeks, more than two hundred organizations had registered under provisions of a new Political Parties Registration Law. The proliferation of opposition groups expressed people's yearning for independent organizations, outlawed for twenty-six years, and also their eagerness to take advantage of the law's provision that members of registered parties could meet to discuss politics.

Ethnic minorities, ex-politicians, religious groups including Muslims and Hindus, lawyers, private tuition teachers, all registered themselves as political parties. The NLD remained the strongest, even after Aung Gyi dissociated himself on December 3 and set up the Union National Democracy Party (UNDP), claiming that Aung San Suu Kyi had surrounded herself with CPB supporters and others from the political left. Aung Gyi drew strength away from the NLD, but his UNDP still had fewer members than the military-backed NUP, which remained the second largest party. U Nu's League for Democracy and Peace, though smaller, also drew popular support.

Three weeks later, the NPC had still not dismissed me. A few people kept their distance, concerned that I had ties to the junta or just fearful that associating with someone on the brownlist might bring difficulty. If someone asked why I wasn't fired, I said I had the same question, but if the NPC dismissed a person like me for taking part in the demonstrations, attending the strike committee meetings, and covering the news, it would have to fire almost everyone on staff. Perhaps I retained my job because I had not made public statements, but even after the NPC was reborn as the News and Periodicals Enterprise (NPE), I was one of only three editorial staff members at *New Light of Burma* still denied work. Our chief editor had been sent to *Working People's Daily*-English and our deputy chief editor to *Working People's Daily*-Burmese.

One morning in October I received a letter from the Judicial Office, Rangoon Division. As a reporter from the government press who covered the beheadings in Dagon township on September 8, I was summoned to the courthouse as a witness. The case had received continuing publicity after a woman named Ma Chu and two men were charged with murder. Allegedly she had been identified on videotape participating in the mob killing of the three people suspected of poisoning the water supply at the Children's Hospital. I did not know the source of the grainy videotape or whether it actually showed her holding a dagger, but the image was described on television as firm evidence. I was called to testify in the related case of the two alleged poisoners who escaped beheading by the mob.

It was easy to guess the SLORC's agenda at the trial. Many people assumed that Military Intelligence (MI) was responsible for the poisoning incident and had first bribed the perpetrators, then incited the crowd. That meant the junta would need to protect the man and woman accused of poisoning the water tank so they would not reveal any MI involvement. But almost certainly the court would punish Ma Chu severely to confirm the extreme lawlessness and threat to public safety during the weeks before the military reasserted its power. Probably the judge would want to get from me a statement that I did not know and had not seen the two defendants, or perhaps that I had not seen them put poison in the water tank.

On the day of the trial, I stood among family members of the accused who waited for the jail van to arrive. Once at the courthouse, prisoners remained in a holding cell where they could eat a meal before the court convened. I watched them sitting on the dirty floor of that crowded cell trying to eat in handcuffs. They chewed quids of betel, smoked cheroots, and drank tea nervously as two hours passed before a judicial officer announced a postponement. Angry to have wasted my time, I thanked myself for never taking on the work of a lawyer, as I could not stand the noise, the crowds, or the misery in the courtroom. Nor could I accept the common practice of bribing a judge, reflected in the Burmese saying, "Wherever there is money, justice follows."

On the appointed day for the postponed proceedings a week later, I waited impatiently for another two hours in the courthouse. The woman accused of poisoning the water supply moved freely around the courtroom and put on a fawning look when she offered me tea or coffee, apparently informed that I was an important witness. Someone said she had received bail while the older man supposed to be her accomplice sat quietly on the floor in handcuffs, his bald head drooping, appearing disconsolate. Once the trial began, I was the first to testify.

Some twenty-five newly appointed judicial officers sat flanking the witness stand as I stood before the court with a woman legal officer, a stenographer, and a typist all waiting for me to speak. The judge asked whether I knew the two accused of the poisoning, whether I had met them before, and where I was when the event took place. I answered briefly while the lawyer dictated and the typist typed. Then the judge stated that as a skilled journalist, I had reported the events, but I replied that I was not a strong witness as I had written the news only through hearsay. "Hearsay isn't evidence," I stated, then turned and left the witness stand without looking back, silently thanking the judge for not asking me to reveal my sources.

People stepped aside as I walked through the overflowing courtroom and passed the crowd of people listening outside. The accused woman ran after me holding her baby and said thank you, but I never slowed my step. As I expected, the court treated Ma Chu harshly, imposing the death penalty, but later it was commuted to a life sentence, and she was released after serving eleven years.

In November 1988, the few staff members from *New Light of Burma* still without work were assigned to prepare propaganda booklets featuring selected articles from *Working People's Daily*. I became essentially a proofreader. If I needed to check a reference book in the newsroom, the fifteen soldiers still camped there stared as if I were an intruder. Guns and ammunition lay stacked on the floor, regulation mosquito netting draped the desks, and green uniforms buried the chairs. Our desk locks had all been broken. Holding my useless key, I knew I could never belong there again.

The NPE had become a bivouac site, and soldiers over the next months felled most of the trees that once shaded the compound to feed their cooking fires. One day I noticed their rough rice and crude curry of mixed vegetables and felt pity. But I knew they would resume killing their fellow citizens whenever ordered.

The military presence was evident in many parts of the city. Barbed wire barricades along Prome Road forced cars to drive a zigzag route, and Shwedagon Pagoda Road was closed from 6:00 p.m. until early morning. No private or civilian cars could pass the War Office at night. Meanwhile we heard nonstop military music on the radio and saw the same footage of marching troops replayed on the television news. Rumors circulated about who had been jailed and who had joined the NLD. Arrests happened slowly but systematically.

My literacy campaign friend Nyo Maung, jailed earlier in the U Thant affair, was seized in November. When I went to meet him at the Rangoon Division Judicial Office on the day of his trial, he showed me his wrists tied together with a dirty rope. This time his bracelet was not made of steel, he joked, recalling the handcuffs he waved when he left the courthouse in 1975. Fourteen years later, he said, the handcuffs had worn out. I thought the supply was simply exhausted after so many arrests.

Accounts of torture raised the level of fear. Beating and kicking were common and sometimes inflicted deafness or chronic injury, but a cigarette burn was a petty thing. Electrodes were frequently applied to sensitive body parts, or water dripped on the head until it felt like a pounding hammer. Meanwhile the SLORC offered amnesty to anyone who returned from the jungle before November 18, and many who had fled to the borders and joined insurgency groups accepted. Press conferences featured groups of returned students offering prepared replies to official questions. Soon the deadline was extended to the end of the year.

Three weeks after I started collecting articles for propaganda booklets, the acting chief editor of *The Guardian* asked me to take charge of publishing its monthly magazine. Publishing an official magazine in English seemed barely preferable to preparing official propaganda articles in Burmese, so I agreed. Before starting that work, I was assigned to a short refresher course on news translating designed for NPE English-language staff. Apparently the regulation denying training to those named on the brownlist was malleable. Placed in charge of the magazine's editorial department at the end of November, I sat at a desk on a stuffy mezzanine with no windows and the lights switched on all day. The army unit, reduced to ten soldiers, still camped upstairs in our newsroom.

Each month I delivered copy to the typing section, read proof, assigned illustrators, drew small sketches, prepared required forms, checked every detail before going to print, then rechecked the final layout prepared at the *Working People's Daily* press. I had no fellow editors so the workers became my teashop companions. I hated everything about the job. Sometimes the magazine included a cultural article written by a well-known scholar or occasionally the translation of an established writer's story. Those, plus the English lessons, were the only readable sections. *The Guardian's* lively Sunday supplement published in my childhood was a distant memory.

Whenever the magazine did not keep me fully occupied, I had other disagreeable tasks, like arranging for the publication of propaganda articles already printed in both versions of *Working People's Daily*, usually speeches by junta leaders soon to be published in English booklets. I hated working in that small dark space without fresh air, but most of all I hated preparing those booklets. I began suffering from migraines and nothing relieved the pain, not aspirin or giving voice to my feelings in verse. I carried pills in my shoulder bag to take when I started feeling dizzy, but still the headaches took over. After one compulsory staff meeting I wrote a poem called "Solitary Flight."

> long days
> have I spent
> far from the flock
> a bird
> alone
>
> always
> the storms
> I sing
> the winds
> I ride
>
> strangers pass
> while I wait
> still
> a bird
> alone

I thought repeatedly about leaving the government press and joining the NLD, but always I hesitated. Something held me back, perhaps the memory of childhood visits to my father in jail or many years of listening to my mother's caution. I also clung to the thought that independent-minded journalists in Burma, long respected as writers, might still exert an influence. Twice I visited the NLD information office to meet editors sacked from their previous jobs, knowing those visits violated NPE instructions and also aware that members of the NLD might suspect me. Some people told me directly that they hated my role in the NPE publications, but others said my insider's role was useful, I could offer support to independent voices, and even modest recognition as a journalist was rare for a woman.

Many students as well as government staff dismissed from their jobs did join the NLD. My friend Wah Wah was so busy working as an aide to Aung San Suu Kyi that she had no time to meet me. My other closest friend, Moe Moe, had no experience with politics and felt certain that General Aung San's daughter would somehow come to power. But I could not share her confidence or shake my skepticism and had little hope that the election promised in 1990 would bring an end to military rule.

In the aftermath of the junta's crackdown, arrest was an ever-present threat. The most prominent student in custody was Min Ko Naing, the leader of the

All Burma Federation of Student Unions founded in 1988. His adopted name meant "conqueror of kings," and he had stood as a fearless presence throughout the weeks of demonstrations. In March 1989, after months in hiding, he was dragged away by men wearing civilian clothes, then kicked, beaten, and brutally tortured, alleged to have helped organize a one-year anniversary commemoration of the suppression of students during the Phone Maw affair. Despite protests from international human rights groups, Min Ko Naing was sent to a remote prison in Arakan State, charged with instigating disturbances and illegally participating in gatherings of more than five people.

During those months Aung San Suu Kyi continued making speeches around the country, urging democracy, criticizing the repression, denouncing the SLORC until, in a sweep of opposition members on July 20, she was placed under house arrest. For twelve days she accepted only water. After an official conceded that her NLD associates held in Insein Prison would not be physically abused and would be given the opportunity for a trial, she accepted food. The pledge proved unreliable.

The former chief editor of the *Hanthawaddy* newspaper, U Win Tin, had been the first NLD executive committee member detained. Accused in June of talking by telephone to the father of a fugitive student, he was sentenced to three years. Shortly before his prison term expired, he was sentenced to an additional eleven years, and after the SLORC amended the Publishers Registration Law in 1995 to allow consecutive sentencing, he received a further seven years, extending his initial jail term until 2008.

By the time the monsoon season arrived in 1989, I could no longer count how many friends were in prison, including Wah Wah, Aung San Suu Kyi's close aide, also arrested on July 20. An artist I frequently met along Sule Pagoda Road who drew posters and illustrations for the NLD's information section had been seized. A friend who sold used books but had no affiliation with the NLD was taken in for alleged CPB connections after delivering a letter for a politically connected friend. When a person targeted for interrogation or arrest could not be found, his parents would be taken in, which usually forced the suspect to show up and face his accusers. The SLORC's methods were effective, and informers shadowed people's footsteps. When a week passed without seeing one of my friends, I began to worry.

Meanwhile attempts to bolster a sense of national pride brought a surge of gestures to enhance "Myanmarization." Most glaring was the SLORC's decision to eliminate colonial place names, which some viewed as another way to discredit Aung San Suu Kyi, who had a British husband. We heard the announcement that Burma would henceforth be called Myanmar on May 27, 1989, and noticed again that the junta always issued orders on a date whose numbers auspiciously divided by nine. Then on June 18, a number also divisible by nine, our street names changed. York Road was the first, becoming U Pho Hlaing Road to commemorate Yaw Min Gyi U Pho Hlaing, a higher officer in the Burmese monarchy. Soon York Road changed again to Yaw Atwin Wun U Pho Hlaing Road, perhaps because a dispute arose over the minister's correct rank. Finally the minister's name was omitted and York Road had a third change to become Yaw Min Gyi Road.

Actually I admired Yaw Min Gyi U Pho Hlaing (1829–1883), who encouraged Burmese scholars to acquire foreign learning yet preserve Burmese traditions and also introduced the idea of a bicameral parliament. Because of his outspokenness on foreign policy and his belief in the importance of democratic institutions, he was dismissed four different times, but the king always reinstated him.

Soon Rangoon became Yangon, the Irrawaddy River became the Ayeyawaddy, Pagan changed to Bagan, Pegu to Bago, Sandoway to Thandwe. The changes were confusing, and the postal service faced many problems. One letter sent to me through the Rangoon General Post Office arrived with multiple postmarks after making a long journey to two other townships with streets named U Pho Hlaing Road before finally reaching my gate.

As the first anniversary of the 8-8-88 affair approached, official media blamed the democracy uprising on a CPB conspiracy and accused the NLD of being manipulated by underground Communists. News articles and policy statements repeatedly mentioned this alleged underground movement, using the English initials "UG." Soon after Military Intelligence chief Brig. Gen. Khin Nyunt held a six-hour press conference in August 1989 to highlight the regime's effort to affix blame on a CPB conspiracy, I received a new assignment. I had to prepare for publication a booklet in English titled "Widespread Conspiracy by Burma Communist Party and by Underground Elements to Destabilize and Take Over State Power," complete with photographs and supporting documents. By the time I finished editing and proofreading, I could recite almost the entire tract from memory.

When another round of accusations appeared in the newspapers in September, I had to arrange publication for a second booklet, "The Conspiracy of Treasonous Minions within the Union of Myanmar and Traitorous Cohorts Abroad." Included among the traitorous cohort were Burmese exiles, foreign embassies, foreign journalists, and even U.S. senator Daniel Patrick Moynihan. A third publication I prepared during the SLORC's intensifying propaganda campaign was "Skyful of Lies: Their Broadcasts and Rebuttals to Disinformation." At one point I was engaged in publishing seven different propaganda booklets. I could not imagine who would read such tortuous explanations and absurd accusations in English, but newsagents in shops and street stalls were required to stock them.

Coinciding with the heightened propaganda campaign came efforts to boost international respectability, restore public confidence, and return the country to normal life. Primary schools had reopened in June and middle schools in mid-August. On September 25, 1989, instruction resumed at Burma's high schools, and business opportunities increased, especially for members of the military, former officials, and ex-BSPP ministers. Crucial to the restoration of normalcy was a further widening of the door to commerce.

CHAPTER FIFTEEN

~

Turning to Ash

Economic opportunity grew alongside repression. When the SLORC started removing unsightly neighborhoods in Rangoon, developers discovered lucrative opportunities while those forcibly evicted faced new hardship. Once a resettlement notice arrived, squatters had to demolish their own dwellings if they wanted to salvage anything useful. Soldiers would force reluctant residents to leave at gunpoint, so most stacked their bamboo mats and roofing thatch obediently alongside a few baskets and wooden boxes containing bedding, clothing, dishes, and cooking pots. On the specified date, those meager possessions were loaded onto army trucks, and I often saw military vehicles stacked with civilian belongings passing along the Rangoon-Pegu Road.

When they reached a resettlement site, soldiers carelessly tossed down essential items as if handling rubbish. Often there was not even a plan for water, toilets, electricity, transportation, primary school, market, post office, or clinic, as the infrastructure for a proposed new town took several years to develop. In the interim many people would die, whether from dysentery or snake bites or lightning strikes.

Because low-income areas had proved seedbeds of opposition during the protests, the displacement of city dwellers in 1989 was motivated not only by plans for urban renewal but also by revenge. Merchants at the sprawling Theingyi Bazaar, where Rangoonians said you could buy anything from a needle to an elephant, had offered food and cash to demonstrators during the general strike. A year later the shop owners were all evicted, their source of income denied. Much later the bazaar became a six-story building.

The construction boom in Rangoon created many opportunities for sharp-eyed developers who searched for contacts. Usually they found ways to get the approval required to replace low structures, whether shops or residential housing, with buildings of multiple stories. A single developer initiated the construction fad in the early 1980s, identifying ownerless dwellings that squatters had occupied, then dealing with authorized persons, assembling shareholders, and launching new construction. The junta granted building permits to military officers or ex-BSPP members with whom it wove a network of mutual support based on common interest, displacing people whenever it desired to sell a property.

Development schemes, like a string of construction projects along York Road, destroyed many of the city's older residential neighborhoods. Soon my own family became part of the trend. Burdened by payments on the property she had purchased with my grandaunt, May May agreed to sell part of our land to a developer. Half of our white-washed stucco home disappeared along with our front garden, and after many pieces of paper passed through many hands, a four-story apartment building opened late in 1988.

Reflecting on the altered cityscape, I wrote a short story using a walk between my house and the junction with Sule Pagoda Road to convey a message. Observing the commercialized atmosphere of York Road, the narrator comments first on the neon signs illuminating unfamiliar faces. Noticing that some passers-by now speak Chinese, he also describes the teenage sex sellers lurking in the shadows waiting for customers, smelling of cheap perfume. Then he recalls having once watched people pour from a nearby soccer stadium after a match, which forced a lone pedestrian to give way to the crowd. Reaching home, he comments sadly that something essential has been forever lost, just as water flowing past in a river can never return. The Press Scrutiny Board's report objected that the final paragraph contained a hidden message, but the editor submitted an innocuous explanation, which cleared my story for publication in 1990.

Once the SLORC took power, private magazine editors used different strategies to deal with tightened censorship. Required to submit all manuscript copy for approval, they chose submissions carefully, not wanting to waste time or money. Words, sentences, or paragraphs judged offensive had to be inked over and sometimes whole pages ripped out. Editors sometimes placed an ambiguous poem immediately after one with a patriotic theme by an authorized poet, or positioned a sensitive poem and a risky cartoon back-to-back so only one page would be lost if an entry had to be removed. Readers understood when they came upon blank spaces.

After the first anniversary of the 1988 demonstrations, lucrative business deals increased, and Burma's potential market, along with its raw materials, beckoned to investors. Agreements signed with foreign companies offered new incentives, bringing food products, clothing, and small appliances not seen for two decades into local shops. In September we read about negotiations to produce and sell Pepsi Cola. Then the oil fields opened to foreign exploration, and many arrangements with European, Japanese, and North American companies followed. The marketing of timber, minerals, gems, and other natural resources brought needed revenue to the junta and rewards to senior military officers who found generous sources of income.

Still the repression continued. U Nu was placed under house arrest in December, and a friend who was the editor of a private magazine was seized early in 1990, accused of involvement in secretly distributing anonymous poems in a pamphlet titled "What Is Happening Now." Those irreverent verses satirizing the country's present situation and mocking the same lengthy speeches by Saw Maung that I had to prepare for publication in English spread quickly in Rangoon. People laughed at the sardonic lines.

Meanwhile the SLORC faced new international pressure in February 1990 when the United Nations' Human Rights Commission, headed by Sadako Ogata, appointed a special rapporteur to investigate Burma's human rights abuses. The government's ongoing propaganda campaign quickly took an anti-Japanese turn as newspapers provocatively recalled the years of wartime occupation, offering pointed reminders of how the Japanese had oppressed and tortured the Burmese people. When I attended a required monthly staff meeting, I was startled to hear the managing director ask if my father, Bo Ba Tin, had been tortured by the Japanese. I nodded, and he requested that I describe those events at a press conference. Barely controlling my anger, I refused, giving the excuse that I would try to find the article my father had written about his arrest. I knew I would never provide it.

Desperate for a break from the propaganda, I asked for a week's leave, planning a trip to the Delta, choosing the dates carefully so I could return before the novitiation of my friend Moe Moe's sons and the ear-piercing ceremony for her daughter. With two friends, I first visited one of my brothers teaching Burmese at Bassein College, then took an overnight boat trip to attend a festival at the famous Maw-tin-soon Pagoda, surrounded by water at the mouth of the sea.

Returning to my office on March 12, a Monday, I faced an overload of work assignments on my first day back. Unable to squeeze into the crowded city bus after leaving the office, I decided to wait a day to visit Moe Moe and instead roamed the streets. The next morning, reflecting on the second anniversary of the Phone Maw affair, I reached my office to find urgent telephone messages informing me that Moe Moe had passed away a few hours before. My first reaction was disbelief.

Thinking she could not have left me without saying good-bye, I reached her apartment just in time to pull the blanket around my dearest friend's body before the mortuary crew took her away. News of her heart attack at age forty-six spread quickly. Writers, artists, poets, and publishers gathered at her home. Dazed with grief, I sat in silence.

A huge portrait of Moe Moe painted by artist friends stood above her open coffin on the day of her funeral, but I saw only her beautiful face, finally at peace. Just before her cremation, I laid a cluster of her favorite red anthurium blossoms on her chest amid a cascade of flowers, along with a simple note, "At last the triangle has broken." Perhaps a thousand people attended her funeral, and I carried a wreath at the head of the procession. At the gravesite several writers and artists spoke, leaving commemorative lines to be buried with her ashes. I remember only the words of poet Tin Moe, "Life is short for those who love but long for those who hate."

A prominent writer and private magazine editor, Moe Moe had written many books and short stories, receiving several literary prizes. She had also long concealed the infidelity of her husband, but our world was small. When her personal circumstances became known, she moved into a cramped apartment with their three teenage children. Usually the mother makes all preparations for the novitiation of her sons, just as May May had for my brothers, inviting friends and relatives, arranging details of clothing and offerings. But Moe Moe had no financial resources and no parents or siblings to help, so her husband's family took charge of the ceremony. Before I left on my trip, she seemed not just apprehensive but frail, so much did she dread having to face her husband and the guests, displaced from her family role on such an important occasion.

Women close to me had dealt differently over the years with marital unhappiness. My grandaunt on York Road simply ignored her husband's second family and lived with him until he died, while my favorite grandaunt, who moved in with my family on Ma Kyee Kyee Road, and tried to endure the stigma of separation until her early death in 1958. My other closest friend, Wah Wah, sued for divorce immediately when her husband took a mistress, but she had no children. Also, she could claim as her personal property her income as a painter, writer, English tutor for Burmese, and art teacher for foreigners. Moe Moe had no such financial option, since her husband was her publisher and could claim her writing fees as his own. Just thinking about whatever ancestor introduced the notion that "Even if a woman has ten brothers she is nothing without a husband" always made me feel outraged and insulted.

After Moe Moe's death, numb to all feeling, I barely fulfilled my obligations at work, thinking always of my friend's boundless understanding and caring heart. When her magazine asked me to contribute to a commemorative issue, I poured my emotions into a poem and at last felt somewhat eased. I titled the poem "Yearning."

> a thornless rose
> has fallen
> she who dared to be luxuriant
> does she dare to disappear
> she who dared to bloom abundantly
> does she dare to disperse
> I cannot bear
>
> her fame reaches far
> her beauty unmatched
> the essence of rose
> her pride can flare
> sometimes overflow
> but no thorns will prick
> this I know
>
> while still vibrant
> her petals fall
> yet even in death
> her radiance lasts
> her splendor endures
> I yearn for her

Moe Moe did not realize her dream of voting for Aung San Suu Kyi when the long-promised general election arrived, but I thought of her as I cast my ballot in May 1990. Unlike the 1974 referendum when my family delayed voting, we woke early that Sunday morning to reach the polling site in the township high school, formerly the Methodist English High School. The room was silent. Even neighbors didn't speak, sensing a mood of caution.

To vote for a slate of township candidates for the People's Assembly, you pressed a stamp beside the appropriate symbol on the ballot. With five or six political parties listed, the ballot was confusing so the staff allowed me to assist May May inside the voting booth. Beside the farmer's broad-brimmed bamboo hat, the logo of the NLD, I stamped an X, happy that I could cast two ballots that day for the NLD. In the evening my family never left the television.

Confident of its victory, the regime had authorized an unprecedented granting of last-minute visas to foreign journalists gathered in Bangkok waiting to report on the election. Television cameras followed the SLORC chairman and other junta members as they approached the polling booths with their families, recording even the moment when Saw Maung's glasses fell off in a crush of foreign journalists. As we waited for the tally, I thought about the last general election when I was ten and my father was locked away in Insein Prison. I had hoped fervently that U Nu's Clean Party would win, and thirty years later I longed even more for political change. Loud cheers came from my neighbors' houses when the news announcer declared the first township results as a victory for the NLD.

Our Dagon township was important to the election results because it included not only the War Office, which would certainly support the NUP, but also a high-ranking military officers' compound and two large housing estates where residents were either BSPP members or high-ranking government officers. Our township was the last to be called. At midnight a car passed outside with someone shouting, "NLD wins in Dagon."

The junta's certainty that its opponents would meet defeat proved misplaced, and news spread quickly that the NLD had received 60 percent of the popular vote while the SLORC-backed NUP won only 21 percent. The NLD also secured 80 percent of the seats in the National Assembly, and no one from the NUP was elected in Rangoon Division. Not only in Dagon township was the NLD victorious but even on the remote Co Co Islands, where the NUP candidate was the son-in-law of another of my grandaunts. Political loyalties divided many families, including my own.

When the SLORC delayed implementing the election results, we waited impatiently for the NLD to take power. But on June 19 Saw Maung announced that power would not be transferred until a new constitution was drafted, and another month passed with no progress. The NLD called for a dialogue between the SLORC and the opposition parties, but by then the second anniversary of the 8-8-88 affair approached. Troops and military trucks were conspicuous in many parts of Rangoon. On July 29, I saw soldiers patrolling the streets, concentrated near Gandhi Hall where the newly elected NLD candidates met to adopt a resolution calling for "frank and sincere discussions with good faith and with the object of national reconciliation."

On August 8, 1990, thousands of monks marched through the streets of Mandalay, home to hundreds of monasteries and some eighty thousand monks. They walked quietly, as if pursuing their morning alms round, and many people donated food. Then some students raised a peacock flag, and soldiers opened fire. The news spread quickly around the country even as official broadcasts claimed that students and monks in Mandalay had attacked security forces and one monk had been injured. The BBC's report stated clearly that troops had fired on demonstrators, killing two monks and two students. Soon a junta spokesman denied that anyone had been killed.

As the SLORC continued to accuse the NLD of inciting unrest around the country, monks denied requests for religious ceremonies from members of the military and refused alms or offerings given by military families. When monks gathered again in Mandalay on August 27, the protest spread to Rangoon, and many hundreds of monks joined in solidarity. In both cities pagodas were closed, monks were arrested and forcibly derobed, and even young novices were taken into custody.

When U Kyi Maung, who led the NLD party during the election period, was arrested in early September and sentenced to twenty years, people understood that the SLORC intended to ignore permanently the election results. During the last week of that month, sixty-five NLD candidates were detained. Almost every day I learned of more arrests, and after the official BBS television reported on October 22 that monks in Mandalay and Rangoon had again been arrested, I felt exhausted. The television footage showed trucks filled with soldiers, red scarves tied around their necks, entering monastery compounds. I could see no path ahead for my country.

That day I wrote a poem about a cinder turning to ash. A Burmese saying describes someone with hidden strength or ability as an ash-covered cinder ready to reignite, but I wrote about how an ash buried too long stays cold forever. The magazine's camera-ready copy had already been prepared when my poem was censored. Another magazine editor tried to publish it with the same result. The censoring board's report said my words called for revolution.

> unhappy
> in this world
> for a long time
>
> people may say
> an ash-covered spark
> will flare again
>
> but long buried embers
> turn to cinders
> as time passes

tomorrow is not
a fairytale
and waiting
to live brings
sharpening pain

before blood dries
one longs
for happiness

On November 16, a Friday night, my friend Nita, three years my senior at St. Philo's and always quiet in school, was arrested. A writer about popular culture and women's news, she also taught English, and three years earlier I had accompanied her when she interviewed successfully for the position of Information Officer at the British Embassy. That evening in 1990 I visited her home and, taking a risk, left a list with names of the government press columnists who were writing the most sharply worded denunciations of the NLD. An NPE chief editor had asked if I met with Nita, and I understood his warning that her ground-floor apartment was watched, most likely from the Burmese restaurant across the street, and that my visit had been noted. But I didn't know she had been arrested just hours after I left. MI searched her home but somehow didn't notice on a cluttered table a paper with my handwriting listing the news columnists.

Month after month, I wrestled with indecision about whether to join the NLD and face the likelihood of arrest. My headaches descended often, and my hair had streaks of gray. Meanwhile my responsibilities at *The Guardian* magazine grew heavier. Ignoring the brownlist, the managing director assigned me to attend basic computer training after NPE headquarters announced in 1991 that it would computerize its system. Then he asked me as a personal favor to assist with the publication of his collected poems in Burmese and English, saying he needed an editor who understood poetry and knew English. I had no way to refuse. During those months, I numbed myself with work.

I also contributed regularly to a private education magazine and helped translate a pamphlet about iodized salt for UNICEF Burma's program to prevent iodine deficiency. Then my former editors at *New Light of Burma*, U Ko Ko and U Naing Aung, launched a new magazine whose owner and financial backer was a *thakin*. They accepted articles only from veteran journalists and former politicians, and until I joined had invited just one woman. I had refused such offers before, but this time decided to join. First they asked me to translate foreign news stories, then to write monthly art reviews. With the economic opening drawing more foreigners to Burma with money to spend, the art market was expanding. Reviews of painting exhibits had almost disappeared after veteran art critic U Win Tin's arrest in 1989, and I said I could not replace him, but I would write something about the growing art scene.

In the past the only foreign customers for Burma's paintings and folk art were diplomats and UN or NGO staff. With new buyers, gallery owners marketed more local artists' work, setting prices for paintings that included a 20 percent commission. Tourists who appreciated paintings visited the Golden Valley Art Center and the Treasure Art Gallery located near the expensive homes and gardens in Golden Valley or near Windermere Road. Tourists who simply wanted souvenirs bought the more clichéd artwork available at several stalls in Scott Market.

Though somewhat freer than writers, artists had to submit their paintings and titles ten days in advance of an exhibition's opening. Without approval, no artwork could be shown at an advertised exhibition, and the only way to avoid the censorship board was for a gallery to announce a special sale. U Ko Ko liked to feature artwork on the cover of his new magazine, so my articles often became lead stories. Relying on my art school training and past experience writing reviews, I expressed whatever I felt about a particular painting. Gradually readers forgot my environmental writing and knew me better for my comments about art.

As part of a continuing effort in 1991 to eradicate the influence of the NLD, the SLORC announced a mandatory examination for the civil service. Another tool of intimidation, the test evaluated the loyalty of the bureaucracy in thirty-three yes-or-no questions. One asked, "Do you know that violating civil service regulations can lead to dismissal?" while another asked, "Is it appropriate to elect as head of state someone married to a foreigner?" The expected answers were obvious. I truthfully marked "yes" for the first question but, angry at having to take the test, wrote "no" for the second question and several others, since in mathematics two negatives make a positive. My gesture was meaningless, but I was ready to provoke my dismissal.

In September when the Nobel Committee awarded the international peace prize to Aung San Suu Kyi, people in Burma rejoiced, but it was the BBC's November 8 rebroadcast of her essay "Freedom from Fear" in Burmese that actually changed my path. She had been awarded the Sakharov Prize for Freedom of Thought in 1990 based on that essay, and I had read its stirring words in English when a copy circulated secretly. In Burmese the ideas gained new urgency. Like the captive spirits she described, I knew that I too was being held like water in the cupped hands of the ruling powers. Aung San Suu Kyi's message that even tiny splinters of glass with their sharp glinting power can defend against hands that crush seemed directed at me. I vowed that day to free myself from passivity and the grip of fear.

No longer caring how I would earn an income or what I would do in the future, I wrote two copies of a resignation letter and handed them the next day to both the NPE's deputy director of administration and to *The Guardian*'s general manager. We had worked closely, and he asked me please to be patient. I replied that I could not accept any more propaganda assignments, or comply any longer with meaningless regulations, or take charge of the computer center, or continue as a representative of the Information Ministry. Besides I had to take care of my health, I no longer wanted to have migraines, and I had sworn before a statue of the Buddha not to engage in wrongdoing, so I could not continue to oppose the people. He said nothing, just turned away.

That evening at our usual teashop some of my writer friends supported me while others criticized my decision, having valued my help and my contacts inside official publishing circles. At night I could not sleep and in the morning opened the window beside the bed I shared with my mother to breathe in fresh air from the garden as was my habit. I had not yet told her of my decision when she said sadly that her health was failing, she dared not stay alone each day, and she wanted to ask me to quit my job.

CHAPTER SIXTEEN

~

Relocation

The SLORC had to address many problems after it nullified the 1990 election results, not only internal problems like the collapse of the country's infrastructure, the failure of the education system, and the deplorable level of health care, but also growing international pressure. Financial mismanagement grew more extreme as the regime tried to juggle several different currency exchange rates, support state enterprises that showed low productivity, and subsidize essential commodities like rice, all with disastrous results. The junta reportedly consulted astrologers whenever it formulated policy, but invoking supernatural powers had brought no remedy.

Information on political arrests, prison conditions, forced labor, mandatory resettlement, and the abuse of ethnic minorities seeped abroad despite intimidation by Military Intelligence, restrictions on foreign journalists, and tight controls on domestic news. International agencies listed Burma as one of the world's largest suppliers of illicit opium and heroin, and estimated its internally displaced people, including those forcibly evicted by the military from insurgency areas, at more than one million. In November 1991 the United Nations General Assembly adopted a resolution condemning a range of human rights abuses in Burma and calling for the release of Aung San Suu Kyi and other political prisoners.

Held under house arrest since July 1989, the Lady, as she was known, could not attend the Nobel Peace Prize award ceremony in Oslo on December 10, 1991. When the BBC's Burmese Service reported that the prize would be conferred without the prize winner, several thousand students gathered at Rangoon

University to shout anti-SLORC slogans and demand Aung San Suu Kyi's release along with democratic reforms. Once again troops surrounded the campus, cleared students from dormitories, and closed down the university. Several hundred students were taken away. Other arrests followed.

The renowned poet Tin Moe, whom I knew as a consulting editor to our literacy campaign magazine *The Echo* in the early 1970s, was arrested at home when he returned from the university canteen's teashop where he regularly met with faculty friends. The Press Scrutiny Board had prohibited his work from appearing in print, but Tin Moe continued writing. His poems had appeared in NLD pamphlets that circulated secretly on occasions like Union Day and Resistance Day, and in 1991 he accepted the position of chief editor at the magazine that had just resumed publishing after being closed for printing the poems that mocked Saw Maung's speeches. The magazine was still closely watched, and after the campus protests Tin Moe was sentenced to four years in prison, accused of opposing the state. I imagined him endlessly smoking cheroots, missing his teashop companions, writing poems in his mind, and struggling to fit his round body on a narrow prison pallet to sleep.

Within a month, the university's teachers were assigned to a training course at Phaunggyi, allegedly after the powerful SLORC intelligence chief Khin Nyunt criticized the faculty for failing to manage the students. A mandatory one-month refresher course subjected them to political lectures, military discipline, and propaganda. Other groups of intellectuals received similar assignments, first medical doctors, then state school teachers. I heard that the barracks at Phaunggyi were being outfitted with temporary toilets and shower facilities to accommodate the thousands of new trainees.

Also in response to the December demonstrations, the Press Scrutiny Board issued new instructions in January 1992 that increased pressure on writers. Every publisher, printer, editor, and writer had to fill out a form that required the person's real name, pen name, parents' names, national ID number, address, date of birth, religion, occupation, political party affiliation, and any prior criminal convictions. The primary targets of the new registration rules were opposition party members, especially those affiliated with the NLD, and anyone who had spent time in prison, but I hated complying and I told a seasoned magazine editor that I wanted to stop writing altogether. He advised me not to be foolish. If I disappeared from the pages of magazines, no one would notice my principles, he said, while the regime's intimidation would remain unchanged.

The NPE continued to pay a percentage of my salary for four months, officially considering me on leave of absence. That was the only retirement benefit I received after twelve years of work. Some who stayed for more than a decade received small plots of land in one of the new satellite towns, but I never applied. Finally I received my severance order along with my last pay in March 1992, and withdrew my savings of three thousand *kyats*, less than $30, from the cooperative credit society.

To counter dissatisfaction with the regime's economic mismanagement, news about charitable donations often made media headlines. We read many announcements that well-wishers had donated a certain amount for building or maintaining a pagoda, or for other government-sponsored projects, and we often saw the faces of the donors on our television screens. Usually they were successful businessmen who had established an export-import company or received a construction contract. Generosity is an essential part of Buddhist practice, but business dealers also had a financial motive for their donations, which were often indistinguishable from bribes.

Like many people who gave alms simply out of compassion and kindness, May May offered frequent donations. Every month I took her contributions to a hospital for monks, a home for the elderly, or an orphanage school, but I especially liked offering food at a chronic diseases hospital where patients convalesced for years. The previous evening I would soak rice in cold water and boil a chicken. In the early morning I prepared the rice and cut the chicken into pieces, mixing it with ginger and garlic to flavor the porridge. Ko Lay drove our car while another brother and I balanced the steaming pot on the back seat. I never notified the hospital administration or called attention to our gift but walked straight onto a ward and said we wished to make a donation. The nurses readily accepted our offer, and about forty patients would bring their bowls for us to fill. Back at home, May May shared our gratitude, but there was no ceremony, no photograph, no record, only the happiness on the faces of the patients.

I wanted to share my last small amount of salary with those who were needy and remembered a Baptist pastor I had met in Rangoon. He ministered to a community of resettled lepers outside the city, and I had vowed someday to support his selfless work. To reach the leper village in Min Gone, I took a public bus to Hlegu and from there an even older bus to Phaunggyi. At a junction I waited for an old Toyota pickup truck that travelers hailed as the only local transportation. Covering my nose with a handkerchief against the clouds of dust and exhaust fumes, I clung to the overhead bar to keep my balance and at one stop watched a woman remove a dirty head pad, set down her heavy load, wipe the sweat from her brow, then load her toddy palm juice tray and earthen pot into the truck. I was shocked to see one of my artist friends board the bus behind her, never knowing he had been relocated. He invited me to rest for awhile at their home.

The village of Nga Zu Taung, designated a model resettlement site, had electricity for several hours each day. A few cottage industries produced inexpensive plastic products like hair clips, providing some local women with a daily wage. Most resettled residents could not find a local source of income and left by bus early in the morning for Rangoon to work at odd jobs. My friend had lost his position as an illustrator for the BSPP after the general strike in 1988. He earned a small income clearing a nearby tract of land for a private businessman planning to grow cashew trees. Sometimes he also helped his wife peddle toddy palm juice.

At midday the resettlement village seemed deserted. What caught my eye in the newly built bazaar, its stalls mostly idle, were the glaring red billboards that warned, "Crush all internal and external destructive elements as the common enemy." Pointing at the billboards, I joked to my friend that for the moment he had better just crush brush and grass. When his family was relocated in 1991, each household had received a small plot of land but also a requirement to surround the property with a fence. Fencing materials were costly and had exhausted his savings, so he could build only a raised platform with a roof, using the lumber, bamboo, and thatch salvaged from his demolished house in Rangoon.

Six family members lived in about eighty square feet with no kitchen, no bedroom, no bathroom, cooking and washing dishes on the tamped earth outside. While the eldest daughter helped prepare a modest lunch of coarse rice, some hastily purchased vegetables, and green tea, my friend explained how he had sent her a few years earlier to provide assistance and companionship to his unmarried grandaunts living in the Delta area. When the regime required that one person from each household participate in community military training, the teenage girl had to attend. Pursued by a married instructor during that training session, she gave birth to a child. My friend was supporting his daughter and her baby along with his two younger children in the resettlement village.

Leaving Nga Zu Taung, I noticed large plots of fenced land on both sides of the road, empty except for a few signboards advertising a business or trading company. Clearly, more schemes like that of the cashew tree planter would follow, as developers expected this would someday become a new suburban area outside Rangoon. I saw only scrub brush growing on that dry, inhospitable land.

Development projects in the countryside were rarely successful unless backed by the military's commercial interests. Many hastily conceived business plans resulted in failure, like one export venture launched by three former Foreign Affairs Ministry employees dismissed after the 1988 military coup. Planning to grow fields of watermelons on both sides of a narrow road not far from Nga Zu Taung, they signed a contract to rent the land, then bought seeds, hired villagers to work the fields, and signed another contract with a foreign company specifying a delivery date. But the cost of gasoline was high, and the access road accommodated only a small truck, so they had to rely on human labor for transport, which raised costs. Bureaucratic procedures took unexpected time, and without military backing, the endeavor failed. The developers missed the delivery date and not a single watermelon was exported. They sold some of their crop to the local people at a greatly reduced price, then tried just to give the ripe watermelons away.

I had kept in contact with several of the civilian women working as trainers at Phaunggyi and spent that night in one of the re-outfitted barracks, then caught another bus to reach Min Gone. The Baptist church was just an open bamboo structure on wooden stilts where resettled lepers gathered on Sundays to pray. The assistant pastor explained that Baptists were prohibited by their religion from distilling liquor as a source of income like the lepers at Htauk Kyant, so his community depended entirely on donations. I offered my final NPE earnings and stayed to share a simple lunch. Before leaving Min Gone, I noticed a man working in a backyard liquor distillery.

This villager, relocated from Htauk Kyant, was a Buddhist and thus not affected by the Baptists' restrictions. Like my artist friend in Nga Zu Taung, he lived in a fenced-in house built from salvaged lumber and thatch, but the income from his simple distillery allowed him to make improvements. He said his leprosy had been cured by a local government clinic providing free medicine to lepers who resettled and registered. I watched him fill a bucket from a marshy pool near his house where water seeped from the ground, then pour the water into a large pot of fermented rice on an earthen stove. A length of plastic tubing funneled drops of distilled rice liquor to the jar below. Fearing arrest if he carried the illegal moonshine to Rangoon by bus or hired car, he sold his liquor to collectors, supposedly licensed, who transported his home brew to the city in a battered truck.

The liquor distiller was fortunate to receive treatment in a government clinic, as relocated people had limited access to health care. Even in Rangoon, ordinary civilians suffered from illnesses that could have easily been cured. The defense hospitals dispensed reliable treatment for privileged patients, but over the years I had watched many relatives and friends without that access suffer needlessly and die prematurely. Public hospitals in the city were overcrowded and underequipped, doctors were underutilized and underpaid, medicines and laboratory equipment were scarce and outdated. In more remote areas where intravenous drug use and HIV/AIDS spread alongside tuberculosis, malaria, dysentery, and malnutrition, medical conditions were far more desperate. Basic information about hygiene and disease prevention was almost unknown.

The requirement that doctors after graduation take the Selection Board for Public Services' examination contributed to the shortage of health professionals. Some of those selected by the board were posted to distant towns and cities, an especially difficult assignment for women, causing many doctors to leave medical practice. Medical school graduates who failed the government exam could work only as general practitioners without hospital affiliation. Some opened small clinics, but others found different jobs, and I knew many people with valuable medical training and experience who worked in business or as real estate brokers in Rangoon. Others had relocated to Thailand, Singapore, or Hong Kong, and a few had managed to reach Britain or the United States.

Meanwhile fraudulent medical workers preyed on the needy in Burma's villages. Sometimes a former hospital worker or an ex-soldier with experience in a medical unit claimed to be a trained doctor. Unable to assess his credentials, local people extended friendship and trust to any self-proclaimed medical worker, relying on the outsider for help and treating him as a relative living among them. Their well-intentioned support contributed inadvertently to the complications and sometimes deaths that resulted from malpractice.

One self-described doctor with no medical training opened a clinic in a midland town claiming he could cure eye diseases. He earned an easy income as local people had no knowledge of how to treat cataracts or glaucoma and typically attributed failing vision to eating spicy foods, or weather conditions, or just to age, relying on home remedies. Blindness was a common affliction even though a twenty-minute operation could remove a cataract. Even if people in a remote village somehow knew about cataract surgery and could afford to pay, the scarcity of trained medical doctors could still condemn them to blindness.

Organizations like WHO, UNDP, UNDCP, and UNICEF delivered humanitarian relief in Burma until 1988, but after the coup the SLORC tried to foster a sense of national pride, heralding self-reliance and promoting Myanmarization. More important in the junta leaders' rejection of assistance from international aid groups was the suspicion they would reveal information about Burma's poverty or support the NLD. Their policy moderated in the early 1990s only because of Burma's dire need.

After I translated the pamphlet for UNICEF Burma on iodized salt, then edited a solar refrigeration manual, I was hired as an external consultant early in 1992. My next project was translating into Burmese a basic health care handbook, *Where There Is No Doctor*. As I translated, proofread, and prepared camera-ready copy, I learned about diseases, symptoms, prevention, and treatment, hoping that the pamphlet's simple health care precautions would help my people. That UNICEF project brought three benefits: knowledge, money, and merit. It was the best job I had found.

When the SLORC abruptly announced a leadership change in April 1992, official media reports claimed that General Than Shwe had assumed power because of Senior General Saw Maung's ill health. But the decision seemed at least partly an effort to counter the junta's negative image after it nullified the election results, caused an international refugee crisis, failed to control opium cultivation, confined Aung San Suu Kyi, prevented her from receiving the Nobel Prize, and arrested and tortured students, writers, and NLD supporters. One of my York Road neighbors whose family was connected to Saw Maung's by marriage told me that the former SLORC leader had not stepped down willingly. She said troops entered his residence, seized weapons from his armed guards, and cut his telephone line, but whatever the circumstances, the junta's former leader benefited. Saw Maung received several plots of land, including a valuable piece of real estate on Inya Road where he constructed two buildings and rented space to foreign companies, generating substantial earnings in foreign currency. People said the SLORC leader exchanged power for land.

In addition to the leadership reshuffle, the junta lifted remaining martial law restrictions, declared that a National Convention to draft a new constitution would include NLD representatives, and announced that an amnesty would release two thousand political prisoners, including students arrested in July 1990. Many people hoped the military government might change direction under the more pragmatic Than Shwe, and even I wondered briefly if the recognition of NLD delegates and granting of amnesty might signal a shift. When several of my arrested friends were released, I felt a surge of relief and gratitude, but hopes for change faded quickly.

The National Convention met first in January 1993, then from February to April, then again from June to September. News about the meetings continued to appear in newspapers and on television, but after hundreds of meetings over many months produced no results, people stopped paying attention. Even if a draft for a new constitution finally did emerge, it would require the approval of military leaders before a referendum could be scheduled, making it impossible for NLD delegates to exert a significant influence. Soon the junta's announcements were viewed as just another strategy to reduce domestic and international criticism.

I had not yet completed the medical manual when UNICEF asked me to oversee the publication in six ethnic minority languages of *Facts for Life*, a basic handbook on hygiene for women and children. Burma incorporates more than sixty indigenous groups and some 240 distinct languages and dialects, but I had little contact with my country's minority people. Aware that my own viewpoints had been shaped by the culture of the Burmese-speaking majority, I saw the new project as another opportunity both to contribute and to learn.

Facts for Life encouraged the most rudimentary health precautions, like washing hands thoroughly before meals, since most Burmese and Indians do not use utensils to eat. Again I would submit camera-ready manuscripts with a hard deadline, and I began searching for Karen, Kachin, Chin, Kayah, Mon, and Shan translators while also arranging for computerized typeface settings. My first step was to visit a former classmate in her crowded downtown apartment where she lived with more than a dozen Chin relatives, forced by economic need to live in the city like an extended village household. Chin State in the country's mountainous and impoverished northwest along the border with India includes many mutually unintelligible linguistic groups, like the Hakka, Tidem, and Falam Chins. UNICEF could publish the book only in the most common Chin language, which has no written script and uses the Roman alphabet, but I hoped it would still be of use. Through my friend's husband, I located a Chin translator.

At the Burma Archives I found a Mon translator, and soon a famous music composer who was also a medical doctor, named Sai Khan Leik, agreed to help with the Shan version. At Rangoon's Gyogone Theology School and also at the Karen Bible School close to my brothers' former St. John Diocesan high school, I found women who recognized the need for basic information about birth spacing and reproductive health and offered to set up a translation group so that *Facts for Life* could appear in two different Karen languages, Po and Sagaw.

A woman newly appointed at UNICEF had learned the Kachin script from her father, then in jail for political crimes, and finally I located someone to translate the manual into one of the major local languages in Kayah State. The best known among its many ethnic groups are the Padaung, exploited by Burma's developing tourism industry. Tourists pay to photograph Padaung women, whose necks are stretched with rows of thick brass rings. According to tradition the rings are introduced when a child is ten, with new rings added until some women wear twenty or more and can no longer support the weight of their heads if the rings are removed.

While I was busy learning about public health issues and minority cultures, a friend who had worked as a consultant for UNICEF, co-authoring with government officials the UN Convention on Children's Rights, was arrested. Formerly a practicing dentist, he had moved to Singapore for graduate study in public policy, part of the flow of medical professionals who shifted direction. In 1994 he came back to Burma to conduct research for his thesis project on the National Convention, but when I learned he was interviewing members of an ethnic minority political party, I urged him to return to Singapore before July 7, the anniversary of the 1962 demonstrations that brought the demolishing of the student union. Any such occasion could easily trigger a renewed crackdown, and someone suspected of even peripheral connection to a possible protest could be arrested in advance of an anniversary.

Aware of the risk, my friend boarded a flight from Rangoon's Mingaladon Airport on July 4, but he never arrived in Singapore. Worried about his safety and concerned that I might be questioned about his activities or his contacts, I again felt fear. Several of his friends were also arrested, and an interim UN report on human rights in Burma connected me to the case. Somehow my name appeared in error among those detained and the UN list included: "Daw San San Tin (a translator who had apparently been working occasionally for UNICEF)." My friend received a fifteen-year term and was later sent to a remote prison in Kachin State in the most northern part of the country near the border with China. I knew that any misstep would land me also in jail.

It was hard to know whether I was being watched, but I became more wary. Assisting the regime brought many benefits to informers, and a teashop owner could secure the permit needed to operate along the sidewalk by providing information. When an unfamiliar man sat close to my table in the downtown teashop where writers gathered, I took care not to mention politics, even though I didn't hesitate to complain loudly about inflation or about some article appearing in the newspaper. Informers focused their attention on any hint of contact with exile groups, with the underground CPB, or with the NLD, but other kinds of criticism carried little risk. Concerned that Military Inelligence might anytime knock at my door, I passed the time consulting for UNICEF, reading, writing, visiting art galleries and book stalls and libraries, watching films, listening to the radio, meeting with friends, sitting at teashops, and worrying about those in jail.

When Khin Nyunt in a 1995 speech denounced the opposition political parties and then a pro-SLORC columnist's article warned that Aung San Suu

Kyi might soon face a prison sentence, I waited for her trial to be announced. Already held under house arrest for six years, the extent authorized by law, she would either have to be tried or released. Instead we heard news of her release on July 10, 1995, and hope flared again that a dialogue between the SLORC and the NLD leader would begin. Huge crowds gathered around her residence at 54 University Avenue every weekend when she spoke to the public, and many of my friends attended each speech. I reluctantly stayed away, worried about MI's photographers, fearing informers and agents, believing I could help no one if I too landed in jail.

Trying to counter her charismatic influence and broad popular appeal, newspaper articles condemned Aung San Suu Kyi as "an actress of democracy" and called her speeches a democracy stunt by the wife of a foreigner who longed for the West. They derided her listeners as tramps and demeaned NLD leaders as men who depended on a woman's *longyi*. Such extreme rhetoric exposed to the world the petty, vindictive character of Burma's leaders. It also dashed any hope of change.

CHAPTER SEVENTEEN

~

Spreading Corruption

Behind the façade of Burma's economic development lurked an entangling web of corruption. The regime's strategy to deflect international condemnation depended both on propaganda initiatives and on commercial alliances, so SLORC-favored businessmen developed partnerships with Korean, Chinese, Singaporean, Indonesian, and Thai companies. We saw Daewoo buses carrying passengers through Rangoon's streets, trucks delivering Pepsi Cola, and the French company Total Oil opening offices in an estate on Prome Road, one of the city's most expensive neighborhoods. In her ongoing house speeches, Aung San Suu Kyi implored foreign companies and international visitors not to replenish the junta's coffers, but military leaders continued to dispense opportunity in many ways.

The Defense Ministry provided 40 percent of the foreign exchange needed by any army officers who wanted to set up their own businesses using the Burmese kyat as currency. The Myanmar Economic Holding Company (MEHC), run by the Defense Procurement Agency with current and retired military officers, was highly capitalized with ten billion kyats. Besides that major holding company, the military operated a number of factories as well as its own bank. The military-owned Myawaddy Bank openly declared that it would ask no questions about how much depositors earned or how much tax they paid on their deposits. Merchants and investors who deposited cash indirectly provided investment capital for the military. Substantial military assets also flowed from officially laundered cash funneled from racketeering, bribes, and other forms of graft. Through the military bank, black money could be turned into white money overnight.

Favor followed many pathways, perhaps by allowing someone investing in the hotel industry to import building materials. In one case a developer imported three times more construction materials than required for his approved hotel project and made a handsome profit by selling the unused materials on the black market. Leaders of ethnic minority groups who agreed to surrender in amnesty arrangements, described as exchanging arms for peace, also contributed to the military's financial deals. Investing the profits they accumulated through opium trading or other illegal enterprises caused their assets to multiply while helping sustain the SLORC's monopoly on a wide range of businesses.

Arrangements between the SLORC and Burma's drug lords were well known. Indicted for heroin trafficking by a federal grand jury in New York in 1989, Khun Sa was one minority leader who laid down his arms in a lucrative arrangement when he surrendered in January 1996. As commander of a well-armed militia in Shan State, he had controlled for two decades much of the territory along the northern Thai-Burma border and dominated the region's opium production and smuggling. After negotiating his surrender terms with the junta, he ran transportation systems throughout Rangoon and invested in several hotel ventures and other businesses there and also in Mandalay and Taunggyi, always in partnership with the regime and a group of foreign investors.

My ninth grade English teacher, who had spent our class time idly chatting about family affairs, lived in an expensive residential neighborhood near Khun Sa's home. Her husband, a former military officer, served as managing director of a gem-processing and jewelry-making company that Khun Sa owned. As in many other cases, such lucrative businesses provided comfortable salaries to the children of military families, cementing ties and assuring support.

Other former insurgency leaders also prospered. Lo Hsing Han had reaped vast sums from the opium trade after joining the Shan State Kokang Army in the early 1960s. Pardoned from a death sentence, he built his Asia World conglomerate into one of the most successful enterprises in the country with diverse interests in banks, factories, hotels, transportation, real estate, jade mines, and road construction, all ventures likely to have links with drug profits. Among Asia World's projects was a highway estimated to cost $33 million that connected Burma's opium cultivating areas with China's border.

No one could easily avoid the spreading influence of Steven Law, Lo Hsing Han's son. Several times I saw him dressed stylishly in a tuxedo at the Traders Hotel on Sule Pagoda Road, an enterprise backed by investment from Malaysian tycoon Robert Kuok but actually run by Steven Law's Kokang group. With his Singaporean wife as his business partner, Law maintained close financial ties to sprawling business holdings in both Singapore and Malaysia. Other prominent entrepreneurs invested in golf courses, motorbike and automobile dealerships, retail outlets, and soft drink and bottled water businesses, all assisted by government partnerships.

When the construction boom slowed after its initial burst in the 1980s, giant construction groups, owned by businessmen and former rebel group leaders with military ties, adapted quickly. Much of Burma's arable land was appropriated for large agricultural conglomerates, with investors in those enterprises exempt from paying taxes or customs duties when they imported raw materials and machinery. One investor received a one-hundred-acre plot in the Delta area to start an agriculture business but still needed manpower to clear the jungle undergrowth. Making a deal with an army officer, he provided money to hire local villagers to do the work, knowing that the officer would pocket the wages and use forced labor to clear the land.

It was common practice for villagers not only to plow, sow, and harvest paddy fields for a regional army without receiving wages, but also to comply with demands that they sell a required quota of chickpeas, the staple food for soldiers, to the military at a reduced price. If weather conditions prevented local farmers from meeting the quota, they faced punishment, perhaps ordered to stand in the scorching sun for extended periods. Military-controlled private industries also required the labor of local residents, and the animal husbandry industry was largely controlled by the army. For a venture in Arakan State that produced cattle feed, one person from every household was conscripted to contribute labor removing the heads from small dried fish.

In the early phase of Burma's development, people who earned illegal profits had tried to remain inconspicuous and spend moderately to avoid income tax, but such precautions were unnecessary after the Myawaddy Bank opened in 1991. Tycoons could spend extravagantly, and the new rich bought buildings, gold, and gems. Wealthy families owned five or six cars and sent their children abroad for education. Wives and daughters showed off elaborate diamond and ruby necklaces at weddings and other social occasions. But even as entrepreneurs who worked with the regime received tax exemptions, ordinary people shouldered a growing tax burden. In the teashops my friends talked angrily about the rampant spread of illicit deals and the junta's continuing allocation of scarce resources to fund a military expansion that extended its control while neglecting the people's welfare.

Another attempt to bolster the faltering economy while reshaping the country's pariah image came when the regime proclaimed 1996 Visit Myanmar Year and launched a publicity campaign to attract international tourists to visit historic temples in Bagan or cruise in canopied tour boats down the

Irrawaddy River. Opposition groups countered official tourist initiatives with reminders that luxury hotels and restored temples had been built with forced labor, and Aung San Suu Kyi implored foreign visitors not to help extend the life of the brutal regime. But still tourists came, providing the regime with much-needed hard currency.

By then more than three years had passed since my journalism career ended. Continuing to volunteer for UNICEF assignments, I oversaw an AIDS survey, then helped translate the television script of an educational AIDS program for distribution in Shan State and Kachin State, where HIV was spreading. But perhaps because of my close ties to the arrested consultant, UNICEF never offered me a permanent staff position. I felt useful helping make available information about AIDS and public health, but I could not continue indefinitely as a part-time consultant and translator. Not wanting either civil service work or political involvement, I considered what job to take next.

When my friend from the literacy campaign, May Su, a medical doctor, asked me to join her in a French medical supply company in April 1996, I had many misgivings. Naïve about commerce and finance, I lacked any business interest but went for an interview, thinking the work might let me contribute to the upgrading of Burma's medical infrastructure. At the same time I would learn how a foreign enterprise was run, expand my understanding of technology, and earn a regular salary in foreign currency.

When I was chosen out of six applicants to become the marketing manager for the French company that distributed medical and laboratory equipment as well as packaging machines, I tried to adapt to an unfamiliar role. My first task was to collect data for a marketing survey, which involved listing all hospitals and clinics in Rangoon, including their locations and the names of contact persons, then inquiring what medical equipment they needed. I visited clinics throughout the city and every Saturday submitted a report with my week's findings. After that initial training period, I was assigned to handle a million-dollar project selling equipment to a government department where the persons responsible for awarding the contract were the husbands of my friends. From then on, I knew the compromises required in the business world would touch me directly.

Even at the NPE I had not escaped the spreading corruption. With only one newspaper and an increasing market orientation, more private companies wanted to advertise than there was column space available. I helped my friends by going to the advertising department and requesting that their copy appear in the newspaper on the same day. Once I searched for a channel to help a friend, feeling ashamed to engage in such practices. My efforts stopped when a former army officer, rumored to have engaged in the illegal jade trade, arrived at the NPE as a deputy chief editor. From his desk in the managing director's office, he wielded power and reaped rewards. Businessmen started paying bribes to list their companies' ads, and higher bribes brought favorable articles about particular companies. His financial dealings were obvious, and people said he was like a heron waiting at the mouth of a dam to catch fish. I felt as if I was swimming in polluted water.

When the French director asked me to inform the wives with whom I had personal relationships that anyone involved in purchasing our machinery would receive a 3 percent commission, I knew that selling medical equipment required the same systemic bribery. I thought about my friend and former editor U Tint Lwin's long struggle with respiratory illness. Because the industrial demand for oxygen was high, patients often faced a shortage. Hospitals in Rangoon obtained their oxygen supply from the government-run factory that also served the dockyards, where oxygen was needed to weld sheet metal. After U Tint Lwin was hospitalized, his relatives tried using sums of cash to assure a regular supply of cylinders, then visited other hospitals and offered more money to buy oxygen in bulk. When they were not successful, U Tint Lwin passed away. For some, even breathing was denied in Burma.

So many deaths could have been prevented, like that of my artist friend in Nga Zu Taung, who died suddenly from dysentery. Did he not know about oral rehydration therapy, I wondered, or did he not go to the local government clinic, or did it not dispense that simple remedy? As a translator I had tried to make health care information available and at the French company I hoped to help distribute updated medical equipment, but remaining apart from the corruption proved impossible.

As if to defy the international criticism that followed the regime's promotion of the Year of the Tourist, 262 NLD delegates were arrested around the country before they could convene in Rangoon in May 1996. The next month the SLORC threatened that anyone who attended Aung San Suu Kyi's weekend public speeches would face twenty years in jail, and in September, barricades appeared outside Aung San Suu Kyi's home. Heavily armed police blocked University Avenue, making the business-minded French company manager complain about jammed traffic when cars and buses had to take a lengthy detour.

By then he had assigned me as marketing manager to take responsibility for trade exhibitions, the first one held in October 1996, sponsored by a

Singaporean company in partnership with the Myanmar Economics Holding Company, the wholly owned military venture founded in 1990. I was working on a sales display when I learned about a brawl that started after local residents drinking in a bar owned by Military Intelligence argued over a cassette with students from the Rangoon Institute of Technology. News of the fracas spread. As more students gathered at the Heldan junction adjacent to the university campus, the demonstration drew a large crowd. The bar fight recalled the incident leading to the Phone Maw affair in 1988, so security forces made many arrests. Soon the SLORC accused the NLD of abetting the incident, saying that students involved in the protest had visited NLD leader U Kyi Maung, already released after his arrest in 1990 but quickly arrested again. The authorities held him at a guest house for questioning but then freed him in what seemed a display of concession. But even though the Home Affairs Ministry reshuffled the police department after one member of the security forces stabbed a student, the arrests continued and the investigation of the bar fight expanded.

Facilitating the commercial efforts of a foreign country turned out to require impossible compromises. In charge of a display of industrial medical equipment at another government-sponsored exhibition in early December, I had to introduce the French manager to visiting junta leaders while media covered the opening ceremony. I recited their ranks without making a mistake, then explained the purpose of the machines as my assistant photographed me speaking to Than Shwe. Suddenly on December 2 the exhibit booths were closed down before the usual hour, and I learned that RIT students had again marched boldly in protest. Demanding not just the release of those detained in October, but also the right to open a student union, they gathered a crowd estimated at two thousand and marched toward the downtown streets, carrying flying peacock flags and pictures of General Aung San, assembling in the early morning at the Shwedagon Pagoda. The next day I heard that two of my friends who followed the marchers in a pickup truck had been arrested. One was the artist who received a bullet through his hand in September 1988, and the other a member of the group that regularly gathered to hear Aung San Suu Kyi's speeches. Both were sentenced to seven years.

More protests followed on December 6 when students again clustered at the Heldan junction, making speeches criticizing the examination system that required them to sit for an exam after four months of instruction rather than at the end of the nine-month academic year. Students from different universities in Rangoon joined together, and professors were summoned to persuade them to disperse, but by 3 a.m. about a hundred persisted in a sit-down strike while others waited on side roads. More arrests came when troops appeared with fire hoses to disperse the demonstrators, shout warnings at onlookers, and throw stones at people watching from their balconies. Once again universities throughout the country were closed, and only the Defense Services Academy in Maymyo continued instruction.

On the night after troops controlled the student demonstrators, I passed through the Thamaing campus and saw soldiers with red neck scarves standing at attention, their weapons ready. The usual barricades were in place, and military trucks waited to dispense more troops if needed. The road was still wet from the fire hoses that had recently dispersed the crowd, but in the midst of that tense security crackdown, foreigners were celebrating. The French company was commemorating its seventy-fifth anniversary at the Inya Lake Hotel where regional branch office managing directors from around Southeast Asia mingled in a courtyard lit with Burmese-style oil lamps. Enjoying traditional music and dancing in the Inya breeze, they seemed unaware of troops deployed in the streets not far away.

After that I argued increasingly with the French company's manager, urging him to recognize that foreign medical equipment prices were too steep and prevented purchase by hospitals and clinics, except when a favorable deal could be struck through the right contacts with big business or regime members. In July 1997 we argued seriously. The government had issued a list of drinking water companies suspended because of unhygienic products, and the manager told me our company would begin promotion to enter that market. When I corrected him on the specific kind of technology required, based on training sessions I had attended, he said I did not need to keep coming to work and accused me of pursuing my own writing on the job.

Even while busy working for the company, I continued to write poems, translate articles, and make regular contributions to two monthly magazines, but rarely during company hours. Only after working half a day on Saturday would I tour gallery shows, then write my art reviews on Sunday. I had even introduced the equipment and machines sold by the French company in a business magazine, telling readers that patients could not rely on the state-run oxygen industry and that an oxygen concentrator was now available. I was not trying to promote the company's product but remembering U Tint Lwin's ordeal.

My misdirected engagement with Burma's private sector lasted just a year and three months, bringing valuable lessons. I hated the personnel conflicts, the corruption, the compromising, the pressure to find strategies to defeat competitors, and the need to behave humbly to both the French managers and the customers. Finally I negotiated a settlement of two months' salary as severance pay and gave silent thanks to May May for not objecting when I lost my regular income and could no longer contribute a large sum to the household expenses. Commercial transactions were not my strength, the twists and turns of business tactics eluded my grasp, and the attitudes of foreign investors provoked my resistance. But in some ways I benefited from being pushed to swim in business waters. I saw how industrial zones worked, witnessed which businesses were run by whom, gathered firsthand information about the market operations of large companies, and understood the links between enterprises and drug traders.

News that the SLORC had dismissed several ministers in November 1997 and reconstituted itself as the SPDC, the State Peace and Development Council, came while I was in Bagan visiting an art exhibition. Superstition suggested the SLORC's lifespan would last only nine years, and even before Gen. Saw Maung's death in July, rumors had circulated that the SLORC was searching for reliable advisers, meaning astrologers and fortune tellers, to offer advice about changing its name. I saw no sign of its lifespan ebbing. Many times we grasped at fleeting hopes, but five years had passed since Than Shwe succeeded Saw Maung with no new direction emerging. My own life brought parallel disappointments. Opportunity in the private sector briefly kindled my hope, then drew me into the mire of Burma's moral decline.

After leaving the French company, my wandering schedule resumed, with no business, no marketing, no bribery, no compromise, and no salary. Without husband or children, I could rely on my family's resources, and my independence was unusual for a Burmese woman, as I had no obligations, no encumbrances, no assets, and no possessions. But I saw no path left to follow, and no hope for a democratic Burma, so I applied in 1998 for a short-term environmental journalism course in Bangkok, then for another program in Wales. Hoping still to resume my work as a writer and journalist, I applied next to a program for visiting scholars at the University of California, Berkeley. Overwhelmed by the resources of that large research university, I took many courses, browsed in libraries and bookstores, learned to navigate the Internet, met Burma's professional and political exiles, and began exploring my country's recent history from afar. Examining its painful odyssey gave me new perspectives, new goals, and new difficulties.

By then my family members followed consistent paths. Ko Gyi had become a successful lawyer, effectively settling civil cases and expanding his client list. Ko Lay never went back to sea but worked in the lottery shop, and my sister Ma Ma remained in Mon State married to a military officer and raising three children until she moved to Rangoon when her husband received a high civil service post. My younger brothers all stayed in Rangoon, one at Rangoon University where he lived in a dormitory as an assistant proctor, another helping in May May's shop with several cousins, a third earning income as a money changer. My youngest brother, Ko Tue, worked for the UNHCR, attached to the Immigration Department as a bilingual translator, traveling often to Arakan State. According to a memorandum of understanding with the SPDC, the Immigration Department took part in a program mandated by UNHCR to issue national identity cards and official documents listing family units before it could accept returning refugees who had fled to Bangladesh.

But during the decade since 1988, my sense of purpose had disappeared. I felt sad for the prisoners, sad for the students not getting proper education, sad for the girls who became prostitutes, sad for the external refugees and internal migrants, the drug dealers, the forced laborers, the child soldiers, and the families like my own divided by political difference. My list of victims and victimizers, all products of the same corrupt and repressive system, was very long. For ten years I had lived fearfully and resentfully while the regime deprived people of their elected officials and all but eliminated the chance to find opportunity with integrity. My temperament had changed, and sometimes I scarcely recognized the woman who spoke bluntly in my voice.

The decision to live abroad offered new freedom while imposing its price. Leaving my tightly-knit family brought loneliness, facing their disapproval brought sorrow, and failing to assist my mother at home brought guilt. And because the junta routinely attacked any journalists expressing opposition views outside the country, branding them traitors influenced by colonialists trying to destroy the nation, I relinquished my audience and in some circles my reputation. Separated from friends, teashops, and the magazine writing that had sustained me, I wandered through unfamiliar streets, adrift between cultures, preserving small links. My woven shoulder bag still bulged with books, and my head remained uncovered in the Bay Area's drenching winter rains. Walking with the raindrops, I reflected on the Buddha's teaching that everything is impermanent and only destiny determines one's path. As always I found consolation in poetry.

> between two bridges
> choosing one
> only time will tell
> wrong or right
>
> consent whispers
> its truth

if impediments
endure stoically

no time for dreams
when flower-lined roads
live only
in fairytales

and practicality needs
calculation
as a matter
of course

the road I have chosen
the path I have walked
meets honesty tenderness
arrogance lies
always confusion

showing the way
of the mundane
world

whatever wherever
I deeply vow
not to lose
trust

~

Selected English Sources

Gerry Abbott, ed. *Inroads into Burma: A Travellers' Anthology*. Oxford, 1997.

Richard J. Aldrich, Gary D. Rawnsley, and Ming-Yeh T. Rawnsley. *The Clandestine Cold War in Asia, 1945–1965: Western Intelligence*. London, 2000.

Louis Allen. *Burma: The Longest War, 1941–45*. London, 1984.

Anna Allott. *Inked Over, Ripped Out: Burmese Storytellers and the Censors*. Chiang Mai, 1994.

Aung Aung Taik. *Visions of Shwedagon*. Bangkok, 1988.

Aung San Suu Kyi. *Freedom from Fear*. London, 1995.

———. *Letters from Burma*. London, 1977.

Terence R. Blackburn. *The British Humiliation of Burma*. Bangkok, 2000.

Mary Callahan. *Making Enemies: War and State Building in Burma*. Ithaca, NY, 2004.

Maurice Collis. *The Burmese Scene*. London, 1943.

E. D. Cuming. *In the Shadow of the Pagoda: Sketches of Burmese Life and Character*. London, 1897.

Robert F. Dorr. *7th Bombardment Group/Wing, 1918–1995*. Paducah, KY, 1996.

Max and Bertha Ferrars. *Burma*. London, 1901.

Christina Fink. *Living Silence: Burma under Military Rule*. Bangkok, 2001.

Amitav Ghosh. *The Glass Palace*. London, 2001.

Gustaaf Houtman. *Mental Culture in Burmese Crisis Politics*. Tokyo, 1999.

Htin Aung. *The Stricken Peacock: Anglo-Burmese Relations, 1752–1948*. The Hague, 1965.

Ingrid Jordt. *Burma's Mass Lay Meditation Movement: Buddhism and the Cultural Construction of Power*. Columbus, OH, 2007.

Khin Myo Chit. *Colourful Myanmar*. Rangoon, 1995.

Kyemon U Thaung. *A Journalist, a General and an Army in Burma*. Bangkok, 1995.

Emma Larkin. *Finding George Orwell in Burma*. New York, 2005.

Norman Lewis. *Golden Earth: Travels in Burma*. London, 1952.

Zunetta Lidell et al. *Strengthening Civil Society in Burma*. Chiang Mai, 1999.

Bertil Lintner. *Burma in Revolt: Opium and Insurgency since 1948*. Chiang Mai, 1999.

———. *Outrage: Burma's Struggle for Democracy*. Bangkok, 1990.

Ma Thanegi. *The Native Tourist: A Holiday Pilgrimage in Myanmar*. Chiang Mai, 2004.

Andrew Marshall. *The Trouser People: A Story of Burma in the Shadow of the Empire*. Washington, DC, 2002.

Daniel Mason. *The Piano Tuner*. New York, 2003.

Maung Maung, Dr. *Burma and General Ne Win*. New York, 1969.

———. *The 1988 Uprising in Burma*. New Haven, 1999.

Maung Maung, U. *Burmese Nationalist Movements, 1940–1948*. Honolulu, 1990.

Elizabeth Moore, Hansjorg Mayer, and U Win Pe. *Shwedagon: Golden Pagoda of Myanmar*. London, 1999.

Mya Maung. *The Burma Road to Poverty*. New York, 1991.

George Orwell. *Burmese Days*. London, 1934.

Christina Pantoja-Hidalgo. *Five Years in a Forgotten Land: A Burmese Notebook*. Quezon City, 1996.

Alan Rabinowitz. *Beyond the Last Village: A Journey of Discovery in Asia's Forbidden Wilderness*. Washington, DC, 2003.

Robert I. Rotberg, ed. *Burma: Prospects for a Democratic Future*. Washington, DC, 1998.

Inge Sargent. *Twilight over Burma: My Life as a Shan Princess*. Honolulu, 1994.

Sir James George Scott. *The Burman: His Life and Notions*. London, 1910.

Donald M. Seekins. *Burma and Japan since 1940: From "Co-prosperity" to "Quiet Dialogue."* Copenhagen, 2007.

Julie Sell. *Whispers at the Pagoda: Portraits of Modern Burma*. Bangkok, 1999.

Josef Silverstein. *Burma: Military Rule and the Politics of Stagnation*. Ithaca, NY, 1977.

———. *Burmese Politics: The Dilemma of National Unity*. New Brunswick, NJ, 1980.

———, ed. *The Political Legacy of Aung San*. Ithaca, NY, 1993.

Monique Skidmore, ed. *Burma at the Turn of the Twenty-first Century*. Honolulu, 2005.

———. *Karaoke Fascism: Burma and the Politics of Fear*. Philadelphia, 2004.

Martin Smith. *Burma: Insurgency and the Politics of Ethnicity*. Bangkok, 1999.

David I. Steinberg. *Burma: The State of Myanmar*. Washington, DC, 2001.

———. *Strengthening Civil Society in Burma*. Chiang Mai, 1999.

Eric Stover et al. *The Gathering Storm: Infectious Diseases and Human Rights in Burma*. Berkeley, CA, 2007.

Amy Tan. *Saving Fish from Drowning*. New York, 2005.

Robert H. Taylor. *Burma: Political Economy under Military Rule*. New York, 2001.

Thant Myint-U. *The River of Lost Footsteps: Histories of Burma*. New York, 2006.

Pascal Khoo Thwe. *From the Land of Green Ghosts: A Burmese Odyssey*. New York, 2002.

Hugh Tinker. *Burma: The Struggle for Independence, 1944–1948*. London, 1984.

Helen G. Trager, ed. *We the Burmese: Voices from Burma*. New York, 1969.

Shelby Tucker. *Among Insurgents: Walking through Burma*. London, 2000.

———. *Burma: The Curse of Independence*. London, 2001.

Barbara Victor. *The Lady: Aung San Suu Kyi, Nobel Laureate and Burma's Prisoner*. Boston, 1998.

Moshe Yegar. *The Muslims of Burma: A Study of a Minority Group*. Wiesbaden, 1972.

Index

addiction, drug, 38–39, 67–68. *See also*
    drug abuse
The Adventures of Tom Sawyer (Twain),
    9, 37, 86
advertisements, newspaper, 83, 172–73
AFPFL. *See* Anti-Fascist People's
    Freedom League
agriculture, xviii, 22, 41, 43, 46, 50,
    100, 108, 171
aid, foreign, xvii, 164. *See also*
    humanitarian relief; NGOs
AIDS, 164, 172. *See also* HIV
alcohol, 66–67, 88, 109, 163
All Burma Federation of Student
    Unions, 132, 146
Amarapura, 6, 9, 47–48
amnesty, 12, 21, 130, 144, 165, 170
Amoy, 5
anarchy, 5, 130–33. *See also* riots
Anglo-Burmese wars, 4
animal husbandry, 171
Anti-Fascist People's Freedom League
    (AFPFL), 3, 7, 37
antiforeign sentiment, xix, 5, 26, 31,
    119, 128, 147, 157, 168

antigovernment protests, xvii–xix, xxi,
    63–66, 70, 154–55, 174–75. *See also*
    student protests
antigovernment protests of 1988, xviii,
    115–35; anarchy in, 130–33;
    anniversaries of, 147, 154–55; arrests
    of participants in, 134, 140, 143;
    August 8 (8-8-88) in, 121–22;
    curfews during, 117–18, 120,
    137–38; deaths in, xviii, 116, 117,
    122–23, 138; domestic media
    coverage of, 115, 116, 121, 125,
    129–31, 137; end of, 137–39;
    government personnel participating
    in, 127, 129; international media
    coverage of, 119, 121–23, 126, 127,
    139; reprisals against participants in,
    138–41; students in, 115–17, 122,
    132, 139
Arakan State, 3, 4, 5, 56, 118, 146, 171,
    177
Aris, Michael, 128
army. *See* military regime; soldiers
arrests and imprisonment: of Aung San
    Suu Kyi, xviii, 146, 159–60, 167–68;

77–78; rice production during, 22;
struggle against, 3–7, 17, 38 (*see also*
independence struggle); during
World War II, 4–7, 118
Communist Party of Burma (CPB), 2, 3,
7, 56, 97, 141, 147
Community People's Council, 66
"The Conspiracy of Treasonous
Minions" (booklet), 147
constitutions: drafting of (after 1988),
154, 165; of 1947, 48; of 1974,
48–49, 60–61, 123, 139, 165
construction boom, 149–50, 170, 171
contraception, 9, 45. *See also* birth
spacing
Convention on Children's Rights, UN,
167
Convocation Hall, 35–36, 45–46, 65
Cooperative Credit Society, 71, 106,
161
cooperative shops, 23–24, 101
corruption, 20, 169–78
court system, 81, 142–44. *See also* trials
CPB. *See* Communist Party of Burma
crackdowns, government, xviii, xxi, 64,
70, 135, 137–41, 145–46
Cultural Revolution (China), 31, 97
culture, Burmese, 10–11, 29, 47, 56–57,
59, 65
curfews, 31, 117–18, 120, 137–38
currency, 101–3
cyclone, 31; of 2008, xvii, xxi

Dagon township, 130–32, 142, 154
Dala (town), 36, 96
debt, foreign, 100
Defense Ministry, 169
Defense Services Academy, 55, 175
deforestation, 46, 80, 95
democracy, 127, 129, 133
demonetization, 101–2, 103, 105
demonstrations: during colonial rule,
17; in 1976, 78; in 1988, 115, 117,

119, 120, 126, 127, 132, 134, 140,
141, 146, 151; in 1991, 160
Deng Xiaoping, 97
destiny, 15, 60, 177
diaries, 70, 138
discrimination, 31, 59, 70, 99
divorce, 23, 152
drug abuse, 38–39, 67–68. *See also*
addiction, drug; heroin; opium
drug trafficking, 159, 170

ear-piercing ceremony, 13, 14, 151
The Echo (magazine), 45–46, 47, 52, 62
Economic Affairs (magazine), 62
economic survey, in countryside, 49–51
economy, Burmese: corruption in, 169;
crises caused by policies, 31–32;
decline in 1960s, 55; decline in
1970s, 63; decline in 1980s, 93, 99,
100–103, 115; establishment of
socialism in, 16, 20; foreign
investment in, 151, 157; growth in
1980s, 149–51; modification of
centralized, 119; planning for, 49–51,
58, 119; private businesses in, 21–23;
in rural areas, survey of, 49–51. *See
also* Least Developed Country
education: art, 75, 78; decline of,
16–17, 26, 28, 31; establishment of
socialism in, 17, 25–26; health care,
166; legal, 81, 82, 107; medical, 164;
under SLORC, 148. *See also* exams;
schools; teachers; universities
Education Ministry, 33, 117
8-8-88 Uprising. *See* antigovernment
protests of 1988
Election Commission, 141
elections: of 1960, 12, 154; of 1990,
xviii, 145, 153–55, 159, 165;
SLORC plans for, 133, 139, 141
electricity, rural, 44, 46
Encyclopedia Britannica, 62
English language, 9, 16, 58, 60, 83

North Okkalapa, 78, 123, 138
NPC. *See* News and Periodicals
    Corporation
NPE. *See* News and Periodicals
    Enterprise
Nu, U: in antigovernment protests, 17,
    132, 133; and Ba Tin, 6; in elections
    of 1960, 12, 154; after establishment
    of military regime, 16; under house
    arrest, 151; in League for Democracy
    and Peace, 141; as prime minister, 3;
    superstition of, 29
NUP. *See* National Unity Party

Ogata, Sadako, 151
Ohn Kyaw Myint, 73, 74
oil, 20, 38, 151, 169
opium, 67, 159, 170
"Our Belief," 108

Padaung ethnic group, 166
Paddy Birds, 25–26
paintings, 101, 103, 157
Pali language, 13, 18
parliamentary government, 2, 16
Party Affairs (magazine), 62
Party Congress, 74, 75, 119
passports, 39, 55, 97
peace negotiations of 1963, 21
Pegu, 118, 147
People's Assembly, 61–62, 126, 153
People's Daily (China), 97
Pe Pe. *See* Ba Tin
Pepsi Cola, 151, 169
Phaunggyi, 105, 108, 161, 163. *See also*
    political training course
Phone Maw, 116, 121, 126, 146, 174
poetry: antigovernment, 64, 151, 160;
    censorship of, 150, 155, 160; by Kyi
    Aye, 91; by San San Tin, xix–xx, 15,
    27, 46, 52, 68, 77, 81, 90, 91, 95,
    111, 113, 145, 153, 155, 177; by Tin
    Moe, 160

police: in antigovernment protests,
    xviii, 17, 39, 66, 115–18, 123, 129;
    colonial, 22; enforcement by, 59, 78,
    79–80, 96, 173
political parties, 25, 120, 127, 141. *See
    also specific parties*
political prisoners, 2, 16, 21, 159, 165
political training course, at Phaunggyi,
    xix, 105–17, 160; military training
    in, 108, 109, 113; preparations for,
    105–6; rules and regulations at, 107,
    109, 113; student protests during,
    115–17
poverty, 45, 78, 115, 121, 180. *See also*
    economy, Burmese; food; Least
    Developed Country
prejudice, 22, 23, 31–32, 118–19
Press Scrutiny Board, 62, 72, 94, 150, 160
prison: abuses in, 116, 121, 144, 146;
    under caretaker government, 10–11;
    colonial era, 5, 10, 22; detention
    centers, 106, 117; during Japanese
    occupation, 6, 20; release from, 13,
    130, 165 (*see also* amnesty);
    sentences in, 40, 66, 73, 143, 144,
    146, 160, 167. *See also* Insein Prison;
    Rangoon Central Jail; Thayet Prison;
    Ye' Bet Labor Camp
private businesses. *See* businesses
private organizations, closure of, 25, 83
private schools, nationalization of, 26
profiteers, 93, 100
Prome (city), 100, 119
propaganda, xx–xxi; in booklets for
    SLORC, 143–45, 147–48; in BSPP
    magazines, 62; during economic
    decline, 63; and Human Rights
    Commission, 151; literacy campaign
    as, 48; in protests of 1988, 125
prostitution, 59
protests. *See* antigovernment protests;
    student protests; workers'
    demonstrations

nationalization of, 26; under
SLORC, 148; standardized exams in,
28, 31; textbooks in, 17; uniforms in,
xix, 17, 26
Scott Market, 14, 157. *See also* Bogyoke
Market
Sein Lwin, 120, 123, 128, 137
sexually transmitted diseases, 59
Shan language, 166
Shan State, 46, 58, 67, 170, 172
short stories, 25, 72, 94, 98, 150
Shwe Ba, 37, 46, 48, 106
Shwedagon Pagoda, 27, 36, 66, 128–29
Singapore, 167, 170–71
"Skyful of Lies" (booklet), 147–48
SLORC. *See* State Law and Order
Restoration Council
Snow, Edgar, 98
socialism: in China, 98; in constitution
of 1974, 49, 60–61; in economic
policies, 16, 20; in education, 17,
25–26; peace negotiations and, 21;
spread of, 25–33
Socialist Republic of the Union of
Burma, 61
Soe Naing, 116
soldiers: in antigovernment protests,
xviii, 17, 66, 70, 122, 155, 174–75;
in antigovernment protests of 1988,
xviii, 118–19, 122–23, 130–35,
138–39; corruption among, 171; at
NPE compound, 143, 144
"Solitary Flight" (San San Tin), 145
Southeast Asian Peninsular Games,
39–40, 64
SPDC. *See* State Peace and
Development Council
squatters, 23, 78, 134, 149, 150
Stable Party, 12
State Law and Order Restoration
Council (SLORC), 137–76; civil
service under, 139–41, 157; colonial
place names changed by, 146–47;

corruption in, 169–76; economic
growth under, 149–51; elections
under, xviii, 139, 141, 153–55, 159;
establishment of, xviii, 137;
humanitarian relief under, 164;
human rights abuses by, 151, 159;
international pressure on, 151, 159;
name change to SPDC, 176;
propaganda booklets for, 143–45,
147–48; reprisals against protesters
by, 138–41; under Saw Maung, 137,
165; under Than Shwe, 165; torture
by, 144, 146; trials under, 142–44
State Peace and Development Council
(SPDC), xxi, 176, 177
St. John's Diocesan Boys' School, 36,
39, 84, 89, 166
St. John's Convent Girls' School, 57
St. Philomena's Convent Girls' School,
xix, 16–17, 26, 31
strikes: during colonial period, 4, 17, 22,
38; hunger, in 1988, 132, 134–35; in
1974, 63–64; in 1988, 121, 122,
126–27, 128, 129, 130, 131, 132,
133, 139, 140, 149; in 1996, 174
student protests: of 1962, 17, 33, 120,
167; of 1969 and 1970, 39–40; of
1974 and 1975, 65–66, 70; of 1988,
115–17, 122–23, 132, 139; of 1989,
159–60; of 1996, 174–75. *See also*
antigovernment protests
student union, Rangoon University, 17,
33, 35, 65–66
Sule Pagoda, 77, 121, 122, 134–35
superstition, 10–11, 18, 29. *See also*
astrology; folk traditions; *nat* spirits

Tamwe township, 28, 53, 61, 72, 76
Taunggyi, 101, 118–19
tea, 58, 112
teachers, 26, 28, 53, 160
teashops, 58, 87, 126, 167, 171, 177
Telecommunications Office, 127

~

About the Authors

Carolyn Wakeman received her Ph.D. in English literature at Washington University. She taught at the Beijing Foreign Studies University in the 1980s before joining the faculty of U.C. Berkeley's Graduate School of Journalism. There she directed its Asia Pacific Project and taught international reporting for nineteen years. She is coeditor of *Assignment Shanghai: Photographs on the Eve of Revolution* and coauthor of *Bitter Winds: A Memoir of My Years in China's Gulag* and *To the Storm: The Odyssey of a Revolutionary Chinese Woman*, which won the Bay Area Book Award and was nominated for the National Book Award. She divides her time between New York City and Connecticut.

San San Tin received her B.Sc. in Mathematics at the Rangoon Arts and Science University and the RL (Registered at Law) degree from Burma's Ministry of Education. She has written many short stories, essays, reviews, and poems for Burmese magazines and is the author of *A Greener World: Introduction to the Environment* (in Burmese) and the translator—for UNICEF/Rangoon—of *Where There Is No Doctor*. From 1980 to 1991 she worked as reporter and editor for the News and Periodicals Enterprise, Ministry of Information, Burma. Now an international broadcaster at Radio Free Asia, she lives in Washington, D.C.

Emma Larkin is the pseudonym for an American journalist based in Bangkok. Born and raised in Asia, she is the author of *Finding George Orwell in Burma*. She studied Burmese at the School of Oriental and African Studies in London and has been visiting Burma since the mid-1990s.

ML   4/09